Alexander L. Wade

A Graduating System for Country Schools

Alexander L. Wade

A Graduating System for Country Schools

ISBN/EAN: 9783337228071

Printed in Europe, USA, Canada, Australia, Japan

Cover: Foto ©Paul-Georg Meister /pixelio.de

More available books at **www.hansebooks.com**

A
GRADUATING SYSTEM
FOR
COUNTRY SCHOOLS.

BY

ALEXANDER L. WADE,

TWENTY YEARS A TEACHER AND SUPERINTENDENT OF PUBLIC SCHOOLS.

WITH

An Introduction

BY

REV. J. R. THOMPSON, A. M.,

PRESIDENT OF WEST VIRGINIA UNIVERSITY.

"The Common School, oh! let its light
Shine through our country's story;
Here lies her wealth, her strength, her might;
Here rests her future glory."

BOSTON:
NEW ENGLAND PUBLISHING COMPANY,
No. 16 HAWLEY STREET.
1881.

PREFACE.

MANY excellent books have been written in the interests of popular education, and the author of this book has no desire to push aside any of them, but an earnest aim to fill a space occupied by none of them. A glance at the plan and scope of this work may, perhaps, give the reader a glimpse of some prominent points in which it differs from all other educational works.

The common branches are taken as a course of study, and all the plans and appliances of higher schools — annual examinations of graduating classes, granting diplomas, forming alumni associations, and · publishing catalogues — are applied to country schools. This is simply the application of an old plan to a new purpose.

The common branches are considered as the tools of thought, and the teacher is encouraged to give his pupils constant practice in the use of these tools. He is encouraged to take the lead in the establishment of libraries, and in the circulation of newspapers and educational journals. He is encouraged to widen his work, and to elevate the school by giving the people outside of the school-room an intellectual uplift.

The school is considered a joint company, in which the tax-payers are stockholders; and it is maintained that the most sensible method of promoting economy in school expenses is to insist on constant progress in the qualification and skill of teachers and superintendents, and to pay them in proportion to their preparation and skill.

The pupil's health is reckoned an element of supreme importance, alike essential to success in the school-room and in the business of later life; and the teacher is urged to secure, as far as possible, the healthfulness of the pupil's home, as well as the healthfulness of the school-room.

Motives are esteemed more valuable than methods, education is made pleasurable rather than painful, and it is clearly intimated that the teacher who uses the rod as an incentive to study is on the wrong track.

Woman's superior culture, and the refining influences of ornamentation and music, are regarded as elements of inestimable worth in the educational work.

The Bible is accepted as the only standard of morals, and the fact that it is recognized as the seal of the citizen's oath before the court, is, of itself, considered sufficient reason why its sacredness should be impressed upon the child in the school.

The subject of industrial education is introduced, and the teacher is urged to inspire his pupils with a love for the several callings which they are likely to pursue in later life.

The schools of the United States and the schools of Europe are carefully compared, and the light in which both are viewed by leading Asiatic nations is considered.

It is maintained that a uniform system of money, weights, and measures for all nations should be adopted, in order to lessen the labor of school life in all lands, and to bring the business of the whole world into harmony.

Illustrations and diagrams are used in this work wherever they are necessary to make the matter plain.

The author has, all through the work, introduced the testimony of living educators to prove the positions he has taken. In four of the chapters of this book, he has been directly aided by educators especially able in the subjects they have considered; and although due credit in each case is given, he may be permitted, here, to acknowledge his indebtedness to Rev. J. R. Thompson, president of West Virginia University; Prof. D. T. Ames, editor "Penman's Art Journal," New York; and Hon. E. A. Apgar, late United States Commissioner of Education to Europe.

Outside of the author's own work, this book is an embodiment of the best and freshest educational thought of the broadest and foremost educational thinkers, — thought that is alike valuable to teachers and people. This book, therefore, hopes to find a welcome in the family library as well as upon the desk of the superintendent and teacher.

Without any expectation that it will rise above criticism, but in the hope that it may carry sunshine into country school-houses and country homes, this book is submitted to the public by

THE AUTHOR.

MORGANTOWN, WEST VIRGINIA,
November 22, 1880.

CONTENTS.

	PAGE
INTRODUCTION	xiii

LECTURE I.
NEEDS OF OUR COUNTRY SCHOOLS, AND AIMS OF THE GRADUATING SYSTEM 1

LECTURE II.
THE GRADUATING SYSTEM FOR COUNTRY SCHOOLS DEFINED, AND THE MODE OF ITS APPLICATION CONSIDERED . 9

LECTURE III.
THE GRADUATING SYSTEM FOR COUNTRY SCHOOLS DEFINED, AND THE MODE OF ITS APPLICATION CONSIDERED (CONCLUDED) 23

LECTURE IV.
ORIGIN OF THE GRADUATING SYSTEM FOR COUNTRY SCHOOLS 43

LECTURE V.
TRIALS AND TRIUMPHS OF THE GRADUATING SYSTEM . 59

LECTURE VI.
GROWTH OF THE GRADUATING SYSTEM, AND OFFICIAL TESTIMONY OF THOSE WHO HAVE TRIED IT . . . 84

LECTURE VII.
EDITORIAL REVIEWS OF THE GRADUATING SYSTEM BY LEADING EDUCATIONAL JOURNALS 111

CONTENTS.

LECTURE VIII.
WHAT LEADING EDUCATORS SAY OF THE GRADUATING
SYSTEM 121

LECTURE IX.
THE GRADUATING SYSTEM SUITED TO THE PRIMARY
SCHOOLS OF CITIES AND TOWNS 131

LECTURE X.
THE GRADUATING SYSTEM CONSIDERED AND COMMENDED
BY THE NATIONAL EDUCATIONAL ASSOCIATION . . 135

LECTURE XI.
OBJECTIONS TO THE GRADUATING SYSTEM CONSIDERED
AND ANSWERED 138

LECTURE XII.
COUNTRY SCHOOL-HOUSES. — NEED OF A NATIONAL ARCHITECT 144

LECTURE XIII.
FURNISHMENTS OF THE SCHOOL-ROOM 157

LECTURE XIV.
ORNAMENTATION OF THE SCHOOL-ROOM 161

LECTURE XV.
SCHOOL-GROUNDS AND SHADE-TREES 165

LECTURE XVI.
MUSIC IN COUNTRY SCHOOLS 182

LECTURE XVII.
THE DICTIONARY IN THE SCHOOL-ROOM 199

LECTURE XVIII.
How to have a Library in every School-room . . 220

LECTURE XIX.
Newspapers in the School-room and Family . . . 231

LECTURE XX.
Teacher's Salary, Library, and Educational Journals, 242

LECTURE XXI.
Teachers' Training-schools and Institutes . . . 254

LECTURE XXII.
Teachers' Examinations and Course of Study . . 272

LECTURE XXIII.
Teacher's Salary, and Tenure of Office . . . 280

LECTURE XXIV.
Free Text-books in Free Schools 291

LECTURE XXV.
Methods for securing Attendance 296

LECTURE XXVI.
First Lessons in the Common Branches 313

LECTURE XXVII.
Hints upon Teaching Writing 335

LECTURE XXVIII.
Hints upon Teaching Map-drawing 355

LECTURE XXIX.
Hints upon Teaching Letter-writing and Book-keeping 366

LECTURE XXX.
Hints upon Grading Country Schools . . . 385

LECTURE XXXI.
School Government, Manners, and Morals . . . 395

LECTURE XXXII.
Industrial Education in Country Schools . . . 404

LECTURE XXXIII.
Necessity for School Supervision 408

LECTURE XXXIV.
Women as Teachers and School Officers . . . 411

LECTURE XXXV.
A Glance at Education Abroad 421

LECTURE XXXVI.
Uniform Money, Weights, and Measures for the World 431

LIST OF ILLUSTRATIONS, DIAGRAMS, FORMS, AND TABLES.

	PAGE
COMMON SCHOOL DIPLOMA	37
CARD NOTICE OF ANNUAL EXAMINATIONS	56
FORM OF TEACHER'S REPORT FOR ANNUAL CATALOGUE	66
CARD NOTICE OF ALUMNI MEETINGS	71
CARD NOTICE OF SUPERINTENDENT'S VISITS	78
THE CAPITOL AT WASHINGTON	167
NORMAL SCHOOLS IN THE UNITED STATES	256
TEACHERS' TRAINING SCHOOLS IN GERMANY	265
MONTHLY PAY OF TEACHERS IN THE SEVERAL STATES	288, 289
DIPLOMA OF HONOR	301
COUNTY SCHOOL BANNER	304
AVERAGE ATTENDANCE IN THE SEVERAL STATES	310, 311
TIME GLOBE	328
POSITIONS AT THE WRITING TABLE	341, 342, 343
PEN-HOLDING	343
MONOGRAM OF SMALL LETTERS	348
MONOGRAMS OF CAPITAL LETTERS	348
THE SEVEN PRINCIPLES USED IN WRITING	350
DIAGRAM OF NORTH AMERICA	357
ENVELOPES	369, 370
MODELS OF HEADING	373

MODELS OF INTRODUCTION 375, 376, 377
MODELS OF CONCLUSION 379, 380
NUMBER OF TEACHERS EMPLOYED AND SALARIES PAID IN
  THE SEVERAL STATES 412, 413
METRIC TABLE 438
PROGRESS OF METRIC SYSTEM IN VARIOUS COUNTRIES . 441

INTRODUCTION.

IT is idle to talk of the public health when THE PEOPLE are eating tainted meat. Public morality means, not that a few men are sober and trustworthy, but that the people are neither dishonest nor impure. There is no such thing as national religiousness if the people are infidels. Public intelligence is impossible if the great mass of the people are ignorant, or indifferent to education. The nation's health, morality, piety, and intelligence must mean the health, the morality, the piety, and the intelligence of the people. A nation is strong and prosperous only when its citizens are possessed of these qualities.

Mr. Wade has written a book entitled "A Graduating System for Country Schools." The value and significance of this work require emphasis on the word "country." It is written with the avowed object of improving our *country* schools. It is not in opposition to town or city schools. It does not seek to depreciate their work or lessen their influence. It recognizes the place and incalculable importance of the college and the university. This book, however, has a single and most laudable end in view, viz., the improvement of the country school. The whole nation is interested in the character of our country schools, for they are the schools of the people, and the people, in the end, constitute the nation. If the nation is to be pure, strong, just, intelligent, free, the people living in the country must be pure, strong, just, intelligent, free. We are to welcome every honest effort to render more efficient the country school, for in so doing we are directly contributing to the intelligence, the virtue, the health, and the wealth of the whole nation. I can conceive of no greater danger to free institutions than an ignorant country population; and, I think, no doubt can be entertained of the proposition that an intelligent and thoughtful agricultural class must always constitute the strongest defence of a free people. Whoever, then, is interested in the welfare of the nation and the perpetuity of republican government, will regard with favor every effort, like this of Mr. Wade's, to improve the quality of the instruction given in country schools.

I have personal knowledge of the working of the Graduating System in the schools of Monongalia County, West Virginia, and I have no hesitation in pronouncing that work to be " very good." It enlists the parents, it quickens the teacher, it stimulates the pupil, it stirs country communities to almost a fever heat on the subject of education. Whenever a man of Mr. Wade's skill, enthusiasm, and good sense introduces this Graduating System, an educational revival may be confidently expected. The system will not work itself; but in the hands of a county superintendent who loves and honors his work, and is possessed of a reasonable amount of tact and knowledge of human nature, its success is certain. To all such I commend it. In the following pages Mr. Wade gives the history of the Graduating System, recounts its early struggles and triumphs, shows its adaptedness to its work, considers and answers objections to the system, and discusses a variety of important matters in connection with the country school.

INTRODUCTION. XV

It is written in a clear and readable style. Some of its chapters have the charm of fiction. The book ought to have, and, when its merits are known, will have, an immense sale.

This question of the education of the whole people is every day becoming a more serious and important one. We are scarcely past the period when the national vanity was swelling at the respectable figure we had made in the world during the first century of our history. Taken as a whole, the past history of this Republic justifies a sincere and hearty congratulation and rejoicing on the part of its patriotic and liberty-loving citizens. Neither among the republics and empires of antiquity, nor the existing nationalities of the present, can there be found a parallel instance of such unprecedented growth and development in all that makes a nation great and powerful. In the light of the unquestionable facts of our history, a little boasting would seem pardonable.

The real problem of our destiny, however, lies in the future. No amount of glorification over the achievements of the past can blind the eyes of the thoughtful patriot to the duties and dangers of the next century of American history. In thirty years from to-day, according to the present rate of increase in our population, there will be dwelling between the shores of the Atlantic and Pacific Oceans over one hundred millions of souls. This will equal the present aggregate population of England, France, Spain, Switzerland, Portugal, Sweden, and Denmark. What a mighty empire these states would form if they were commingled into one mass, governed by the same laws, ruled by the same potentate! Such a nation will be found on the shores of America in the opening years of the twentieth century. Sixty years from this time, if our population continue to increase in the same ratio hereafter as it has heretofore, there will be dwelling within our boundaries two hundred and forty-six millions of people, equalling the present population of all Europe.

Possibly the child is living to-day who shall witness the period when the population of the United States shall equal the present population of all the republics, empires, and kingdoms of the European continent.

This great mass of commingled peoples, gathered from all quarters of the globe, and representing every possible phase of social and political and religious development, are to govern themselves. No one man is to legislate and execute for the whole. Every man is to hold in his hand the elective franchise; every man is to be a sovereign. The laws are to be made, interpreted, and executed by representatives of the people. *The people* are to hold in their own hands the reins of government, and control, by their action, the ultimate destiny of the mightiest nationality on the globe.

Never before, in all the history of the world, did a single political society hold in its hands such a magnificent prize. They will either demonstrate to the world that man is capable of self-government, and thus put to the rout all the defenders of monarchies and aristocracies, or, by incapacity, faction, intrigue, sordid selfishness, ignorance, immorality, and official peculation, they will blast forever the dearest hopes of oppressed humanity, and turn back the dial of progress for a thousand years. The most opulent imagination can scarcely conceive the possibilities of glory and honorable renown that will open out before this Republic if these millions are true to their high and sacred trust. The most sanguine prophet, in casting the horoscope of our future, would scarcely dare predict the might and power and grandeur of this nation when it shall celebrate its second centennial jubilee.

The problem of the future is, how these coming millions of American citizens shall be fitted for the discharge of their momentous duties. The future of this country is assured only when its destinies are in the hands of a free, intelligent, and virtuous people. The great paramount question of the hour is, how the future generations of American freemen shall be prepared to preserve and perpetuate the Republic. An intelligent and virtuous people always will be a free and happy people. An ignorant and vicious people cannot but be slaves, for ignorance and vice are the conditions of slavery. The *sine qua non* of a republic is the virtue and intelligence of its people. Without these prime characteristics, a transient, dazzling splendor may be attained, but it is only as the hectic flush of the consumptive, betokening the decay within.

Our future is free from peril so long as the masses are reached by the educational and religious forces of the country. Education must not only be so free that all *can* have it, but the state must see to it, on the peril of its life, that all *do* have it. Every citizen must secure that mental culture and discipline which frees its possessor from passion, bigotry, and prejudice. Religion must be more than a history, a creed, a ceremony, a form, a church. Religion must become synonymous with righteousness, and it must be clothed in such an attractive garb that it will irresistibly draw to itself the lowest classes in society, just as the perfectly righteous One drew around him the publicans and sinners of Galilee. At all cost, religion and education must adorn, beautify, and ennoble the homes of the Republic. These are the bulwarks of free institutions. Enshrined in these, as within an impregnable citadel, the hopes and liberty of man are assured forever. Who, then, are the saviors of the Republic? They who are teaching its citizens, either by precept or example, to be virtuous and intelligent. Who are attempting its destruction? They who foster vice, and put a premium on ignorance. The former are gaining on the latter. They are increasing in numbers, devotion, influence.

We are to hold fast to the belief that this land, consecrated to liberty and religion by a baptism of blood, shall forever be the asylum of the oppressed and the hope of mankind. The glad song of freedom shall be wafted by our breezes, shall be murmured by our rivers, shall be caught up by our valleys, shall be echoed by our hills, and shall be borne aloft by our mountains, until its strains of melody shall circle the globe and the long slavery of man shall be ended.

J. R. THOMPSON.

WEST VIRGINIA UNIVERSITY,
November 9, 1880.

A GRADUATING SYSTEM

FOR

COUNTRY SCHOOLS.

LECTURE I.

NEEDS OF OUR COUNTRY SCHOOLS, AND AIMS OF THE GRADUATING SYSTEM.

I HAVE accepted an invitation to deliver a course of familiar lectures on the subject of A GRADUATING SYSTEM FOR COUNTRY SCHOOLS. I am pleased to see before me a multitude of interested persons, embracing parents and pupils, teachers and school officers. These lectures are intended, in the broadest and best sense, to represent the blended interests of all parties, and to invite all who desire better schools to unite in the work of lifting the entire school system to higher and healthier grounds.

While many features of the graduating system are new and original, the cream of what has been written and spoken upon living questions by the freshest writers and the foremost thinkers connected with the cause of popular education, in this country and in Europe, will be made tributary to these lectures.

The graduating system for country schools is not a fabric of theories woven in the loom of fancy; it is a complete system of common-sense plans, which have been tested by practice. Although this system is of recent origin, although it is still in its infancy, it has been officially recommended by State and county officers where its work has been fully tested; it has been favorably reviewed by most of the leading educational journals of the land; it has been heartily indorsed by some of the pioneer thinkers in the common-school cause; and a resolution of the National Educational Association calls the attention of State superintendents throughout the United States to the propriety of its adoption.

It is not my purpose in this introductory talk to give a minute account of the operations of this system, but rather to present its aims, and to give a glimpse of what will be brought to light in future lectures. But before attempting to present these aims, let us glance at the present condition of our public schools and at the results of their work.

It is generally conceded by intelligent people that the common schools of the country are the pride of the present age; and yet no one claims that they have reached anything like perfection. There is, indeed, a growing conviction that they ought to do more, — to produce a higher and purer civilization. The last annual report of the National Commissioner of Education shows a daily attendance of but little more than one third of the school population of the

States and Territories. From this fact alone it is evident that we cannot reasonably expect the most satisfactory results until the attendance upon our public schools be made more general and regular. Calls for compulsory attendance, which come from various quarters, certainly indicate that there is want of harmony between the public schools and the people. Vast multitudes of men and women unable to read and write, found in every State of the Union, all bear testimony to the belief that there must be a missing link in our system of popular instruction.

While the amount of work accomplished by our public schools by no means meets our highest expectations, the quality of the work is even less satisfactory. Many of our young people form in the schoolroom an actual dislike for study; and few of them, upon leaving school, carry with them a love of study which will last throughout life.

Viewing the work of popular education from our present stand-point, we certainly cannot call it a complete and harmonious system. But want of success in the work of our schools is not proof that our teachers have been unskilful in the use of our school methods. The fact that failure has been, in a degree, almost universal, points to the conclusion that the defect is not, mainly, in the manner in which our school methods have been employed, but that it is in the methods themselves.

No one will claim that we have been wanting in the number and variety of our educational methods.

We have had innumerable methods in endless variety. Our school machinery has been too much complicated. Nature points to but few educational methods, and these are all simple and pleasurable. If in our plans for securing attendance, and in our modes of teaching, we will but follow the hints which Nature has given us, she will help us far more than half-way with our work.

It is true that many of our teachers have been guided by Nature's methods in their modes of teaching, and have wielded a mighty influence in lifting whole communities to a higher plane. Close observers have noted the fact that, under such instruction, young people not only complete the common-school branches, but they form, in school, such a taste for study that education does not cease when school days are ended.

The further fact has been noted, that under another class of teachers (so called), pupils take up but few branches and gain but little knowledge of these, and they look forward to the end of their school days as the end of all education.

The former method leaves the pupil with a fair knowledge of all the common branches and with a love of learning; the latter leaves him with but little knowledge of these branches and with an aversion to study. The former method is as far superior to the latter as railroads are in advance of foot-paths.

We have heretofore had no plan for presenting to the public the results of the individual work of each teacher and of each pupil in the public schools of a county. The people of the country, having no opportunity to compare intelligently the work of the several teachers of their own county, sometimes conclude that one teacher is about as good as another, and they therefore prefer to employ the one who will work the cheapest. They do not, as a rule, seek for cheap legal counsellors, or for low-priced physicians. They prefer to employ the lawyer who gains his cases and the doctor who cures his patients, and they cheerfully pay liberal fees for such services.

If the people of the country could see clearly the results of the work of each teacher in their county, they would employ successful teachers, at liberal prices, in preference to unsuccessful teachers at low wages.

The several needs which I have named are met by the graduating system for country schools. It presents in every family of each county, in simple and suitable form, the recorded results of the work done in each school, so that every one may judge of the comparative success of each school and of each teacher in the county.

But this system aims to do more than merely *present* results; it aims to *produce* them. In order to produce the best results, it selects methods which Nature points out as suitable, and adopts plans which experience has proven to be practical.

Close observation will convince that, in gaining

knowledge, the method used by the child before the school period begins, and the method adopted by the man after the school period ends, are the same, — that is, *self-instruction.* If the process of mental growth and of acquiring knowledge is alike in the infant and in the man, we are certainly justified in claiming that the same process should be followed during the period between infancy and manhood.

It is generally conceded by thinking people that the amount of knowledge which the child gains before the school period begins, is greater than in any subsequent period of like duration. This knowledge it gains, too, by the voluntary use of its faculties. It is not forced to learn. It is self-educated. The pleasure it derives from what it learns is sufficient to prompt it constantly to push its inquiries into new and unexplored fields. It is not contented with a single teacher, but it persists in making the knowledge of every member of the family tributary to its education. No scientist of the present day is more busily engaged with his experiments and observations than the child five years of age. We have but to open our eyes to see that this is a universal law of early childhood. It is evident that if we can continue throughout the period of youth this pleasurable method of self-instruction, we have some assurance that study will not cease when school days are ended.

If, however, when the school period begins, we change from the method by which the child has gained its stock of knowledge, and adopt a method of force, education at once becomes a stuffing process, and the child soon loses its keen appetite for knowledge. When the school period is ended, and the restraints of teachers and parents are removed, the man instinctively returns to the methods of infancy. Thenceforth his improvement, as in infancy, must depend mainly upon his own efforts.

It is evident that one uniform method, running through the whole length of life, is great gain in time and labor. The most successful teachers of the present day are pursuing this plan; and the tendency of all modern methods of education is in the direction of this *through line* of Nature's own choosing.

Observation teaches us that there is wonderful uniformity in the intelligence of children before the school period begins; but this line of uniformity diminishes at every step as we pass from childhood to youth, and from youth to manhood. The aim of the graduating system is to lift this line of uniformity until it shall include a knowledge of all the common-school branches.

It has been said that "no system of public education is worthy of the name unless it creates a great educational ladder, with one end in the gutter and the other in the university." The graduating system aims to lift all the youth of the country to the first round of this educational ladder. This it seeks to accomplish, not by regarding the school as a *brain factory*, where the teacher is attempting to get up intellects to order, but by the adoption of a uniform system of common-sense motives tending to bring the aims of all country schools into harmony, and by creating in the minds of the masses a noble passion for having all the young people complete all the common branches before leaving school.

We certainly need some great and harmonious system, which shall be to the educational work of the country what the mowing machine is to the farm, the sewing machine to the family, the power loom to the factory, the locomotive to travel, and the magnetic telegraph to the transmission of news; and I believe that the nearest approach to this which has yet been made is the movement to introduce in all the States of the Union the graduating system for country schools.

LECTURE II.

THE GRADUATING SYSTEM FOR COUNTRY SCHOOLS DEFINED, AND THE MODE OF ITS APPLICATION CONSIDERED.

The graduating system for country schools is simply taking the primary branches as a course of study for graduation, and making application of all the plans and appliances of the best academies and colleges to the common schools of the country.

The time in which each advanced pupil agrees to complete this course of study is announced.

Public examinations of graduating classes are held annually, at points agreed upon, in each county, and diplomas are granted to those who satisfactorily complete the course of study.

An alumni association, holding annual meetings for the mutual improvement of those who have graduated, is organized in every township or magisterial district.

A catalogue, containing a clear statement of the work of each school, is published annually in every county. In this catalogue each school occupies sufficient space to give—

1. The name of the school.
2. The name of the teacher.
3. The number of youths entitled to attend.
4. The number of youths in actual attendance.
5. The number of youths entitled to attend, but not in attendance.
6. The daily average attendance.
7. The daily per cent of attendance, based upon the number in attendance, and the number entitled to attend, but not in attendance.
8. The branches taught and the number studying each branch.
9. The names of pupils who have graduated, and the dates of their graduation.
10. The names of pupils who have undertaken to complete the course of study in one, two, three, or four years, making clear the class to which each belongs. Pupils who cannot complete the course of study in four years or less compose the PREPARATORY DEPARTMENT, but their names do not appear in the catalogue.

This catalogue contains also the annual report of the county superintendent or commissioner, presenting the result of the work of the past year and his recommendations for the future, a synopsis of the proceedings of the several alumni associations, the names of officers and the time and place of the next annual meeting of each association, and also brief obituary notices of teachers and graduates and undergraduates who have died within the year.

THE GRADUATING SYSTEM DEFINED. 11

This system may be introduced into the schools of a State or a county, and it can be tested even in a township or district, or in a single school.

COURSE OF STUDY FOR COUNTRY SCHOOLS.

Orthography, Reading, Writing, Arithmetic, Geography, English Grammar, and *History* are the branches required by most of the States to be taught in the common schools of the country. Some of the States require additional branches, while in others history is not included.

The propriety of readjusting the common-school course of studies and making the course uniform in all the States is worthy of the consideration of the nation's best educators. Until this be done, it is the duty of teachers and school officers to see that pupils pursue the course of study prescribed by the law of the State in which they live.

Every pupil should be early impressed with the importance of COMPLETING this course of study. Many of them may do much more; none of them should think of doing less. The provisions which are now made for the education of the youth of most of the States are more than sufficient to enable each pupil, if well worked, to gain a fair knowledge of all the primary branches; and yet few of them take up all these branches, and still fewer *complete* them.

This may be readily accounted for, from the fact that in many places the educational work in the country has been entirely aimless. We have been depending for success upon methods, rather than upon motives. Methods are essential, but they can no more rise to the dignity of motives than the road leading to a large city, which we are anxious to visit, can rise to the importance of the city itself. No one who begins the world poor will ever, by the work of his hands or his head, have a home of his own, unless he be led by motives to work for this end; and no one will become a scholar, unless he shall first make up his mind to be a scholar.

The graduating system is simply applying to the educational work certain rules or laws of business, which are founded on common-sense. An agreement to complete a certain amount of work in a given time for a specified sum is a rule regulating labor in the best business establishments on the globe, and is found to work equally well in the employment of men, women, or children.

In order to ascertain whether we need such a system in our schools, let us look at the manner in which the courses of study are carried out in the common schools of the country. The branches required by law to be taught in the common schools of the several States compose a course of study far more uniform than any which could be formed by uniting the branches taught in the colleges of this country or of Europe. So little effort has been made, however, to carry out this uniformity, and to *complete* this course of study in our country schools, that the French Commissioners of Education, at our

Centennial Exhibition, after studying carefully our system of public instruction, as presented by the several States of the Union, in their report to the people on the other side of the sea, make this declaration: "The courses of study in ungraded schools are still in the tentative period, not to say in a state of chaos."

So far as I am aware, this declaration of the French Commissioners of Education has not been contradicted by an intelligent journalist. Indeed, the leading journals of education throughout the land have been laboring to impress this same fact upon the minds of educators everywhere, and to enforce the necessity for some great system to harmonize these chaotic elements.

As an index to the sentiment of the public press upon this subject, I make a brief extract from one of our ablest journals, *Barnes' Educational Monthly*. In a leading editorial on "Our Common-School System," found in the February number, 1879, the editor says, "In a multitude of cases, what a child studies depends upon the blind judgment of parents or the momentary convenience or caprice of teachers. The so-called common-school course is no course at all. We most earnestly commend any superintendent or teacher who can suggest any way by which order can be obtained and the confusion now existing avoided."

The unanimous verdict of all who have studied our system of popular instruction is, that the want of uniformity in the course of studies, or rather the want of any uniform plan for inducing pupils to take up and *complete* a course, is the lame limb in our educational work, which has caused so much limping all over the land. This universal lameness in our educational body is the legitimate result of our school management.

I have carefully studied this subject, and I am fully convinced that we should bring our common-sense to the front, and adopt for our country schools plans which have been approved by the best business minds of the age. The methods by which most of our schools are managed would soon bankrupt any extensive farmer, business firm, or factory. If the teacher of a school of fifty pupils should be made the foreman of a factory requiring fifty operatives, and should adopt the loose methods of many of our school-rooms, he would lose his position in less than a fortnight. Under such management he would be unable to hold for a length of time any position of like character where the result of the work is examined at the end of the week.

I would not have you lose sight of the fact, heretofore presented, that the defective work of our country schools is not in the main the fault of our teachers, but that it is the legitimate result of the absence of a uniform system of incentives and aims. The graduating system for country schools carries with it wherever it goes this uniform system of incentives and aims, and embraces all the leading features of the laws of business.

THE GRADUATING SYSTEM DEFINED.

God has wisely implanted in all of us a desire to see our names and the names of our kindred and friends mentioned in connection with honorable positions. This desire is not peculiar to any particular period in life, but is as clearly seen in childhood and youth as in maturity. Neither is it peculiar to any particular rank or station. The common people of the country are delighted at seeing their names favorably spoken of in the local newspapers of their county; and scholarly statesmen enjoy a high degree of pleasure when they see that their acts are approved by the ablest journals of the nation.

The graduating system for country schools seizes upon this universal law of human nature and turns it to account. Under this system, as soon as the child is able to read, and strong enough to study, and old enough to understand something of the character of the common-school branches, it is told by the teacher that as soon as it progresses far enough to be able to complete this course of study in four years, its name will be printed in the catalogue.

Let us take a case for the sake of illustration. A child goes home in great glee with a copy of the catalogue in hand, and tells its mother that as soon as it learns a *little* more its name will be printed in a book like *this;* and it points to the place where its own name will appear. Do you suppose the mother will not be in sympathy with this movement to have her child's name appear in a little volume which will be found in every family in the county? Do you suppose she will feel no interest in letting people know how her child is progressing? Why, it exactly meets the wants of her womanly nature. This book with her child's name in it will tell wherever it goes just what she has been telling in the circle in which she moves, and what she within wishes all her acquaintances, relatives, and friends, at home and abroad, to know; namely, that she has a promising child, and that it is progressing rapidly with its studies. It requires no argument to prove to that mother the propriety of this plan, for she sees at a glance the wisdom of the arrangement, and promises the child all the help in her power. In the tender tones of a mother's voice she says, "Now that will be *so nice:* and mother will try to save money enough to get some extra copies of the catalogue; and we will send them to our uncles and cousins who live far away, to let *them* know what a good student mother's child is."

Encouraged by the mother's counsel, the tender mind of the child is turned into the proper channel, and it then and there *dedicates* itself to the work of its own education. Thenceforth it has an *object* in view, and study is as natural and pleasurable as eating and sleeping.

And do you suppose that the mother will fail to tell these things to the husband and father when he comes from the field? Indeed, she can hardly wait until the time of his return, so anxious is she to tell him all about the teacher's plan, and what *she* pro-

THE GRADUATING SYSTEM DEFINED. 17

poses to do. And do you suppose that the father will be less interested in this matter than the mother? He may, perhaps, appear less excited over it, but he is no less interested in it. He had not supposed that the child was progressing so rapidly. He would like to know just how long it will be before the child can enter the class made up of pupils whose names appear in the catalogue. He resolves to embrace an early opportunity to ask the teacher about this matter. The mother is as anxious to know as the father is. She suggests that as there are several children in the community who are just about the age of hers, she will inquire of their mothers, as opportunity is afforded, how these children are progressing with their studies; and she will compare the progress of each one with that of her own child. She finds these mothers as deeply interested in this matter as herself; and a spirit of emulation, which already exists among the children, is soon created among the parents.

Meanwhile the father has an interview with the teacher, and learns from him the probable time in which his child can complete the preparatory course. He tells the teacher to give him notice of any books that may be needed, and assures him that his child shall not be delayed in its studies for want of proper encouragement from its parents. He informs his wife of this interview, and answers numerous questions which she is ready to ask him.

They scarcely know why it is, but somehow they

believe that this is the best teacher they have ever had in their school; and they are anxious that he may be retained from year to year, until their child's education shall be completed. They believe in him, and are willing and anxious to aid him in any and every possible way. The secret of all this is found in the fact that the teacher has touched, in the hearts of these parents, a chord which vibrates; and human nature is so full of such chords, that if we will but study them, until we know when and how to touch them, we may readily produce the highest harmony in our educational work throughout the whole country.

We now come to that point in the pupil's history when he is so far advanced that he may with propriety agree to complete in a given time the common-school course of study. In our common schools we want no iron-bound system which will destroy the pupil's individuality. The individual will-power of the pupil and his faith in his own ability are elements of power in our educational work which we should not attempt to subdue, much less to destroy. His success in his studies during the school period depends largely upon these elements, and he will certainly need both of them when he reaches maturity. The secret of success in education is not the destruction of these elements of power, but the turning of them into proper channels. When this is accomplished, the more the pupil possesses of these elements of power, the more certain will be his success in any cause which he may espouse.

A sensible and intelligent pupil, who *believes* he can accomplish a course of study in a given time, *can* accomplish it. The declaration of Scripture, that "all things are possible to him that *believeth*," is applicable to mental undertakings as well as to spiritual matters. I find in the *Educational News Gleaner* this gem of thought: "A child can learn *infinitely* faster when *interested* than when *indifferent*." If this be true, and it certainly is, then the thing necessary to increase the pupil's power to learn is to increase his interest.

In order, however, to secure a high degree of interest, the pupil must have an object toward which he is moving, and he must believe that he will be able to *reach* that object. There is no danger of damage from overwork if the pupil is interested, and has a variety of studies and plenty of pure air and exercise. Interest is the lubricating material which prevents mental wear and tear. We seldom become tired when interested, but we are always tired when uninterested. The evenings which a young man spends with his sweetheart seem to him but moments, and the seven years which Jacob served Laban for Rachel, the Bible says, "seemed unto him but a few days." Think, on the other hand, of the dulness of an evening when there is nothing to interest us, and imagine a seven years' servitude without an object before us. How many pupils in our public schools put in their time without any particular aim, and look upon the school period as a tiresome servitude?

The graduating system aims, by incentives, to render the school period as pleasurable to pupils as were the years to Jacob in which he served for Rachel.

No point in the pupil's history is more important and critical, so far as his education is concerned, than the time when his age and attainments are such that he may, with propriety, agree to complete, in a given time, the common-school course of study. If he has been well trained up to the present time, and has determined to complete the course, he will be willing and anxious to give his name and to agree upon a time for his graduation. If, however, he is undecided, the highest skill in the art of teaching is here demanded. His name should not be entered in the catalogue without his hearty consent; and this he cannot give unless he has made up his mind to complete the course. *Decision* is as essential to his becoming a scholar as *conversion* is to his becoming a Christian.

In attempting to lead the pupil to a proper conclusion, let the teacher carefully avoid everything that looks like compulsion. There is a universal law running through human nature which resents any attempt to *drive* us, even in the direction of desirable objects. Let a young gentleman find that his lady-love *demands* his attention, and he soon loses his fondness for her society; or let her become convinced that he is inclined to *exact* her favor, and she will be ready to accept the hand of another,

THE GRADUATING SYSTEM DEFINED. 21

This law of Nature, which common-sense dictates in courtship, should never be violated by the teacher in his efforts to induce the pupil to make the decision that he will complete a course of study. In this work, however, the teacher may, with propriety, summon to his aid all the helps within his reach; and if he is really a *teacher*, he can, through parents and intimate friends of the pupil, wield an influence which is almost irresistible. He should feel that success here makes his pupil a willing student, and that failure here may prove fatal to his education.

We can scarcely estimate the advantages of having the voluntary consent of the pupil to take his education into his own hands. Forcing mental growth is as unnatural as forcing physical growth; and we can no more cause the pupil's mind to grow by compelling him to study against his will, than we can cause his body to grow by forcing food upon his stomach for which he has no appetite.

In early childhood a desire to gain knowledge is as universal as a desire to take food; and with proper management in the home and in the school, this mental appetite will continue undiminished throughout youth and maturity. During all the years of infancy, childhood, and youth, the sensible mother places suitable food before her child; and if at any time it is indisposed to eat, she aims to prepare something more palatable. Sooner than force it to eat she allows it to fast. If the pupil has so far lost his appetite for knowledge that he has little taste for the subjects contained in the course of study, it is the work of the true teacher, by methods and motives, to sweeten these subjects, and thereby render them palatable to the pupil

LECTURE III.

THE GRADUATING SYSTEM FOR COUNTRY SCHOOLS DEFINED, AND THE MODE OF ITS APPLICATION CONSIDERED (CONCLUDED).

WHEN a pupil ten or twelve years of age, under the graduating system, after due consideration of the subject, agrees to take up and complete the common-school course of study in a given time, he feels that his education is his own work. He then has an object in view, a point which he is resolved to reach; and the full force of his will-power carries him onward like a vessel moving with the current. He looks forward with interest to the time when, with his cousins and acquaintances of like grade from other schools of the township, his work will be tested in the annual examination of the graduating classes.

He begins to calculate how much work he must accomplish each quarter, in order to be ready for his graduation. He tries to ascertain from his acquaintances the progress of each pupil who is preparing for examination, and he carefully compares the work of each with his own. The pleasing prospect of obtaining a handsome diploma helps to render his studies agreeable and easy. Fear of failure in the coming examination is readily removed, by assuring him that faithful study will certainly secure success. The more fully he is impressed with the fact that his undertaking has been made public, the more earnest will be his efforts to complete the course of study in the time prescribed.

As the time for his graduation begins to draw near, he finds that there is yet a great deal of work to be done; and he goes at it with a will. He devours history and geography with a greediness that he heretofore knew nothing of; and he solves problems and analyzes sentences with an ease which surprises himself. He now begins to feel conscious of his own strength. The branches upon which he is to be examined form his chief topic of thought and conversation, both in school and out of school. He can hardly lay down his books long enough to do the evening and morning chores about the house.

He observes in the local paper of the county, at the house of a friend (for his father takes no paper), a notice of the examination which will take place the following week. He reads with interest a list of names of those who are expected to graduate, and he finds *his* name among them. Several of his acquaintances are named in the list, and he feels confident that if *they* can pass the examination, he can also. His earnest efforts to complete a course of study have already kindled an interest in the minds of his acquaintances, and they are preparing to be present to witness his examination.

THE GRADUATING SYSTEM DEFINED. 25

It is now evident to the committee of arrangements, that no ordinary school-house can accommodate the multitude that will be present to witness the exercises; and the largest church in the community is secured for the occasion. A popular and practical speaker is engaged to deliver an appropriate address to the graduating class and to the people, on the evening of the day of examination. Arrangements are made to have the best music, vocal and instrumental, both day and night, which the community can produce.

The morning of the long-looked-for day arrives, and our young hero, for that is what we will call him, is present at the appointed time. He is directed to take his place in the class, and he finds himself in the midst of more than a score of girls and boys who have been as busy in preparing for this examination as he himself has been. The church is crowded to overflowing, and he can almost feel in the atmosphere around him that the multitude is in sympathy with this movement. The county superintendent, who is present to take charge of the exercises, in a few encouraging words addressed to the members of the graduating class says, "We will commence this work so gently that you will scarcely know that you are in an examination." The teachers of the territory represented are present, and constitute a committee to consider the merits of each member of the class, as shown in the examination. The secretary takes the name of each member of the class and the name of the school to which each belongs, and calls this roll; and each one, in answering to his name, rises in his place and remains standing for a moment, so that he may be recognized by the audience.

An appropriate song is sung, a short prayer is offered, and the examination begins. In order to avoid embarrassment in the beginning, the first exercise will be in orthography, and will be written. Each member of the class is provided with paper and pencil. The superintendent pronounces distinctly, and each member of the class writes down rapidly a score or more of test words which are of common use in conversation or in public prints. He asks such questions upon the principles of orthography as seem to him proper and appropriate, and each member of the class writes his own answer. These manuscripts are then carefully folded and appropriately indorsed by the members of the class, and delivered to the committee of examination.

The superintendent here informs the class that after music their next exercise will be select readings, and he suggests that during the singing they may take occasion to become better acquainted with each other. They do not wait for a formal introduction, but boys and girls begin at once to inquire of each other how certain words which the superintendent pronounced should be spelled, and they come to the conclusion that most of them, and perhaps all of them, have made mistakes. Finding themselves about on a level with each other, a bond of sympathy is formed, and they begin to feel at home. Many members of the audience have also written the words pronounced by the superintendent, and are comparing papers and discussing differences; while others are so interested in the music that they are unconscious of the conversation which is carried on all around them.

The music ceases, and the superintendent announces that the exercise in select reading will begin. He takes occasion, however, to state that no member of the class will be called upon to read; but that each one will rise when he is ready, and will remain silent until his teacher recognizes him and announces his name and the name of the school to which he belongs, so that all present, while listening to him, may know who he is, where he is from, and who has been his instructor. The superintendent further states that while no disgrace will be attached to the one who reads last, there is an honor in being *first* in the class, and he calls for volunteers.

"Our young hero" here resolves that, for the sake of his parents and friends who are present, and for the honor of himself and his school, he will try to take the front rank in this examination; so, in less time than it takes me to tell it, he rises to read. His teacher, having heretofore selected his piece, and having, as he thinks, thoroughly drilled him in reading it, feels an inward pride in announcing his name and the name of the school to which he belongs.

The selection is from his school reader, for he had no other source from which to select, and his teacher had nothing else. He is perfectly familiar with his subject, and most of the people present are no less familiar with it than himself. He reads deliberately, pronounces correctly, and emphasizes carefully such words as his teacher taught him to render emphatic. He takes his seat, and all are ready to confess that his reading was faultless.

Another member of the class rises to read. He holds a magazine in his hand. He states that his subject is entitled, "Heating Country School-Houses by Hot-Water Pipes at the Feet of each Pupil." The bare announcement of his subject causes people to open their eyes and ears. The article, though short, shows that this method of distributing heat at the floor all over the room is like Nature's method of warming the body by the circulation of the blood; that, although it costs a little more in the beginning, it is a great saving in the end, using much less fuel than the former plan, and that this method of warming country school-houses and churches is likely to become universal. The article closes with a statement that the next number of the magazine will contain a complete description of this heating apparatus, together with the cost of its construction. As he takes his seat, it is evident to everybody that his reading has won; that it will be remembered; that he has given people something to take home with them. It is equally evident that "our young hero" has been placed at a disadvantage, not for want of preparation, but for want of material from which to make his selection.

A young lady rises to read. She has neither a book nor a magazine in her hand, but a printed slip of paper clipped from a column of some journal. She announces as her subject, "Newspapers a Necessity in the Education of a Family." She reads with effect, and her hearers are almost ready to conclude that the newspapers of the present will soon supersede the books of the past; but her subject is quite balanced by another, who reads an article on "The Advantages of having a Family Library."

The oldest member of the class now rises to read. He is preparing to become a teacher, and all are anxious to hear him. His selection is entitled "Educational Journals Indispensable to the Teacher." In a clear tone and earnest manner he declares that, among the great multitude of teachers who read no educational journals, not a single first-class teacher can be found. He proceeds to prove that the teacher's skill cannot be at its best, unless he can command the latest thoughts of the best thinkers; that this he can accomplish only by bringing his mind into contact with the minds of the most skilful educators of the present day, and that educational journals are the most economical means for accomplishing this end.

A young lady rises with a Bible in her hand, and reads a few verses from St. John's Gospel, commencing, "Search the Scriptures, for in them ye think ye have eternal life."

She is followed by another, whose subject is, "The Necessity for an Unabridged Dictionary in every School-House and Family."

One after another, in quick succession, pointed and practical pieces are read by members of the class. Some of the people present are about to come to the conclusion that, from the number of books and newspapers which appear to be needed, there is danger that work and business, and our duty toward each other, may be lost sight of and neglected. Just at this point a young lady reads from the Scriptures the following verses: —

"Not slothful in business; fervent in spirit; serving the Lord;

"Rejoicing in hope; patient in tribulation; continuing instant in prayer;

"Distributing to the necessity of saints; given to hospitality.

"Bless them which persecute you: bless, and curse not.

"Rejoice with them that do rejoice, and weep with them that weep.

"Be of the same mind one toward another. Mind not high things, but condescend to men of low estate. Be not wise in your own conceits.

"Recompense to no man evil for evil. Provide things honest in the sight of all men.

"If it be possible, as much as lieth in you, live peaceably with all men.

"Dearly beloved, avenge not yourselves, but rather give place unto wrath : for it is written, Vengeance is mine ; I will repay, saith the Lord.

"Therefore if thine enemy hunger, feed him; if he thirst, give him drink : for in so doing thou shalt heap coals of fire on his head.

"Be not overcome of evil, but overcome evil with good."

All have now read, and the superintendent announces a recess of a few minutes. Nothing is more natural than the fact that, during recess, the work of the several members of the class forms the chief, and indeed the only topic of conversation. People present could scarcely think of anything else to talk about, even if they would try.

In the conversation which is now going on, it is generally conceded that some members of the class have made selections more appropriate and have read with better effect than others ; but it is equally clear to most persons present that the chief cause of this difference may be traced to the fact that some have had periodicals and libraries from which to make selections, while others have had no such helps.

Recess is ended, and the superintendent announces that, in order to make the exercises especially interesting to the audience, most of the work of the examination will be oral. He states that he has carefully prepared quite a number of topics on each branch upon which the class is to be examined,— topics sufficient to cover, in a general sense, the entire field of each subject. These topics are written on slips of paper, and each member of the class will be permitted, at the proper time, to draw and render one topic on each subject. At the conclusion of each rendering, opportunity will be given to other members of the class for brief additional remarks upon the topic, and for criticisms upon the manner in which it has been rendered. If any member of the class should draw a topic which he is unable to master, he may publicly surrender it and draw another; but such surrender will indicate his want of knowledge on that particular point. This defect he may, however, in a considerable degree, make up by additional remarks or criticisms upon others.

The superintendent here exhibits a number of topics on the subject of geography, and he proceeds to mix and intermingle these topics in the presence of the class and of the audience. He states that in rendering these geographical topics, more attention should be given to the principles of the science, and to the facts pertaining to the face of the country, and to the character of the people, than to the names of unimportant places. He suggests that in rendering any geographical topic which pertains to a country or a place, the person rendering it should, first of all, locate said country or place, by stating in what direction it is, and about how far from the point where he is standing, and by what mode of travelling he would be able to reach it. He should not confine himself to his text-book. A knowledge of any matter of especial interest to the public which may be transpiring in any country is certainly as important as a knowledge of the boundary lines of that country, and if omitted by the one who renders the topic, should be mentioned by some other member of the class.

Each one now draws from the superintendent's hand one topic; and, notwithstanding the choir discourses excellent music while the members of the class are preparing to render these topics, so deep is the interest that they are unconscious of its melody.

Music ceases, and the superintendent calls for some one to rise, voluntarily, and render his topic. One after another, topics are read aloud and rendered, and interesting additional remarks and criticisms follow in almost every case. So deeply interested are the people who are present, that at certain points in the discussion of these topics some persons can scarcely refrain from speaking out publicly. The advantages gained by members of the class who have had access to periodicals and libraries, over members who have had no such help, are even more clearly seen in the examination in geography than in the exercises in select reading.

The hour for dinner is now at hand, and the superintendent announces the order of the examination for the afternoon, as follows: —

"*Arithmetic,* — An examination which will not be difficult to the class nor uninteresting to the audience.

"*History,* — An examination running back into the past and coming down to the present.

"*Penmanship,* — A specimen of the handwriting of each member of the class, giving illustrations of the leading principles of the art of writing."

I desire to say that all these subjects may be rendered interesting to an audience by the touch of a skilful hand; and the superintendent has studied these subjects, in connection with human nature, until he knows how to interest patrons and pupils.

The choir sings a closing piece, and the audience is dismissed for dinner.

Most persons who are present have provided themselves with basket-dinners, and with a sufficient supply for supper also, as they expect to remain during the day and the evening. It is unnecessary to say that the noon hour is spent in earnest discussions about the work of the examination. Every man and every woman present has an opinion to offer, and each one is ready to give a reason for his opinion.

The members of the graduating class have now lost most of that timidity which is so natural to young people in the opening exercises of any public performance, and each one is quite as much at home as he would be in his own school. It is true that each one has discovered that in every branch upon which he has been examined, there are many

THE GRADUATING SYSTEM DEFINED. 35

points which he has not yet mastered; but it is gratifying to each one to know, also, that most members of the class are in a similar condition.

The hour for resuming the work of the examination has arrived, the several members of the class are in their respective places, the audience is seated, and the choir sings an appropriate song. It is scarcely necessary for me to follow the course of these exercises throughout the afternoon. I will simply say that, as the work of the examination progresses, the interest increases, until it reaches a degree almost equal to white heat.

We have now reached the closing point in the work of the examination. The superintendent announces that the evening exercises will consist of an address to the graduating class and to the people, by an invited speaker, to be followed by the conferring of diplomas by the superintendent, and that all the exercises will be interspersed with excellent music.

The audience is dismissed and the teachers retire to a private room, arranged for the purpose, to consult about the merits of each member of the class. Oliver Wendell Holmes, in his wonderful work of wit and humor, entitled "The Autocrat," says, " Little-minded people's thoughts move in such small circles that five minutes' conversation gives you an arc long enough to determine their whole curve." This quaint saying of Dr. Holmes is not applicable to the members of this class, for they are not little-minded people; and yet the work of this day will certainly give to the committee of examination, and indeed to all close observers, a fair index to the knowledge which each one possesses of the several branches upon which the class has been examined.

The first point to be settled by the committee of examination is whether or not the members of the class are all worthy of graduation. Some are, without doubt, superior to others; but it is decided that none stand so low that they deserve to be rejected. This decision is quietly communicated to the members of the class, so that they may feel, in a degree, easy with regard to the result. This information is quite a relief to them, and they have a special relish for their suppers, as they now feel certain that their day's work has not been a failure.

The committee of examination has now completed its work of grading, and all the diplomas are signed, ready for delivery. I present you here a miniature diploma or honorary certificate, which shows that the work of each pupil is graded upon a scale from one to ten, — five being medium and ten excellent.

THE GRADUATING SYSTEM DEFINED. 37

Department of Public Schools
OF THE

State of................................, County of................................

➤➤✳HONORARY CERTIFICATE.✳⬅⬅

GRADE NO. ....

It is hereby certified, That..
a pupil in the Public School in..............................School-House
No..............., District (or Township) of................................,
County of......................and State of..................., has
accomplished a Course of Study in branches prescribed by law, viz.:

*Orthography, Reading, Penmanship, Arithmetic, Geography,
English Grammar and History,*

as evidenced by the signature of..,
Teacher of said School.
Said....................has also this day, at........................,
in the presence of..............of the Teachers of said District (or Township), passed an examination in the branches above named, all of whom direct the County Superintendent of this County to grant........................this

HONORARY CERTIFICATE,
WITH THE ACCOMPANYING GRADE.

The President of the School Board of said District (or Township), also, by his signature hereto attached, certifies that said
..............................is a person of good moral character.

Done at........................, in the County of........................,
State of........................, this............ day of..............., A. D. 1880.

....
County Supt. of..........................County.

........................Teacher of School No............

........................President of the School Board.

Scale of Grade.—No. 10 signifies excellent; No. 5, medium.

You will observe that the teacher of each pupil who is entitled to the same, certifies that the holder of this certificate has accomplished the course of study therein named. This is required as a matter of good faith on the part of the teacher, and it shows that, in his judgment, the holder is worthy. Each certificate is signed by the president of the school board, who certifies that the holder is a person of good moral character. This is required as an incentive to good morals; and no one should be graduated who is unworthy of such certificate. Each certificate is signed also by the county superintendent, who certifies that the holder has been by him examined in the presence of the teachers of the township or district, and that these teachers direct him to grant this certificate with the accompanying grade. No certificate should, in my opinion, be granted where the grade is below seven, on a scale from one to ten.

It is now time to begin the exercises of the evening, and the house is crowded to its utmost capacity. The members of the graduating class are seated together, and it is evident to all present that they have become pretty well acquainted with each other. They have done a hard day's work, but they have rather enjoyed it; and they are almost sorry that the time for separation is so near at hand. As soldiers from different States standing side by side, braving together the dangers of battle, become, in a single day's action, warmly attached to each other, so the members of this class have in this examination formed a friendship for each other which neither distance nor time can sever.

After the opening exercises are concluded, the orator of the evening is introduced to the audience. He is a plain, practical speaker, and he understands the wants of the country people. He announces the title of his evening talk: "Education *pays;* Ignorance *costs.*" By argument, and from statistics, he proves clearly to all present that money paid by the State for the enlightenment of the people becomes an investment at compound interest. He proves that property must educate and so enable the people to take care of themselves and earn something more, by which the State is enriched; or property must be taxed to support the paupers and punish the criminals, which grow up and curse and burden the State with costs, for lack of education.

He proves to parents that, next to providing food and raiment for their families, the best investment they can make is to take stock in the education of their children. He asserts, and proves by persons present who have travelled, that prosperity is invariably seen in States where the people take a lively interest in the education of the masses. He proves that this prosperity is seen in the fertility of the farms, in the comfort, convenience, and beauty of the homes, and in the health, wealth, virtue, and happiness of the people.

He makes it a point to prove that the reverse is true wherever the masses are groping in ignorance.

He shows that the branches upon which the class has this day been examined are but keys to unlock the storehouses of knowledge, — the printed pages of volumes and of periodicals. He insists that parents should see to it that their children are provided with a sufficient supply of suitable books and papers to enable them to occupy pleasantly and profitably all their otherwise idle hours.

Turning to the members of the graduating class, he tells them that this day's examination gives them an index to their weak points, — points which they must fortify in the future. This they can best accomplish by remaining for some time in school; but when the school period is ended, they should by no means cease to study. They should not merely perfect themselves in these branches, but in every possible way enlarge the boundaries of their knowledge.

In conclusion, he indulges the hope that the members of the class will so fit themselves for future work, that they may become better farmers and mechanics than their fathers, better housekeepers and cooks than their mothers, and that they may all be intelligent and enterprising citizens, and earnest and useful Christians.

The choir now sings, while the audience rises to become rested. The thoughtful expression of all who are present indicates that the speaker has set the people to thinking on a higher plane.

"Our young hero" here resolves that he will, by a

THE GRADUATING SYSTEM DEFINED. 41

course of reading, make himself more than a match for those with whom he has this day measured arms, and this seems to be the personal sentiment of each member of the class.

Parents are pondering the propriety of purchasing books and subscribing for papers. New light has been let in upon their minds, and they see things as they never before saw them.

Singing is ended, the audience is seated, the secretary calls the roll, and the members of the graduating class take their places, standing in front of the platform or pulpit. In the presence of the people, amidst unbroken silence, the superintendent presents each member of the class a handsome diploma. In a few pointed and appropriate remarks he urges them to make themselves strong in hand and head and heart. He tells them that this is their first public victory, and he hopes it will be followed by a succession of greater victories won by each in the battle of life.

He tells them that they should regard themselves from this hour as an Alumni Association, and that he proposes, some time within the year, to call them together for permanent organization and for a public performance, consisting of original and select orations, essays, and select readings.

He announces that the First Annual Catalogue of the common schools of the county will be published as soon as the necessary information can be collected.

He thanks the class for earnest work, the choir for

excellent music, and the people for faithful attention. The choir sings, the audience is dismissed, and the people disperse.

We have now witnessed the beginning of a great educational revival in this community. Time will not permit us at present to trace its influences. This revival is not the result of an unnatural stimulus, nor was it produced by appealing to laws which are local. It is simply the response obtained by an appeal to nature's universal law, and under this law we would receive a like response from any civilized people on the face of the earth. Other methods of conducting examinations of graduating classes and holding commencements — methods which by many are regarded superior to the foregoing plan — will be presented briefly at some future time.

LECTURE IV.

ORIGIN OF THE GRADUATING SYSTEM FOR COUNTRY SCHOOLS.

The graduating system for country schools had its origin in Monongalia County, West Virginia. The first classes under this system were organized in the autumn of 1874, and the first examinations were held in the spring of 1876. The first country-school catalogue was issued in the summer of 1876, and the first alumni associations were organized in the following winter. I make these statements after consulting the best sources of information upon the subject, and I shall hereafter present some of the testimony upon which these statements are founded. A brief account of the location and educational facilities of the county which gave birth to this system will not be inappropriate.

Monongalia County is situated in the valley of the beautiful Monongahela. On the east it reaches the slopes of Laurel Hill, a spur of the Alleghanies; from thence it stretches westward, bordering on Mason and Dixon's line, a distance of nearly forty miles. It is triangular in form, and its greatest width is a little more than twenty miles. It has a population of about 15,000, embracing over 5,000 youths who are entitled to attend its public schools. The seven country-school districts of this county contain eighty-five neat frame school-houses, nearly uniform in size and architectural style. Morgantown, the county seat, beautifully located on the east bank of the Monongahela River, has long enjoyed a reputation as a literary town. Monongalia Academy, Woodburn Seminary, and Morgantown Female Collegiate Institute were for many years flourishing institutions in this "Athens of West Virginia." It is at present the seat of West Virginia University, Morgantown Female Seminary, and a free graded school.

In order to present a satisfactory account of the origin of the graduating system for country schools, it is necessary to narrate some of the circumstances which led to its discovery.

In the autumn of 1873 I was employed by County Superintendent H. L. Cox, to visit the schools of Monongalia County, West Virginia. Most of my work as an educator previous to that time had been confined to the school-room. I had long entertained the belief that there is somewhere a *missing link* in our educational work, and that its place, when found, would most likely be in our system of common schools. I resolved that while visiting the schools of the county I would study the secret springs of action in school life, and try to devise a plan to facilitate primary school work as broad in its application as the system which seeks to educate and to elevate the race. To this end I began to study the principles which prompt pupils to action, and the motives which move men and women to make sacrifices for the education of their children.

I found in Sect. 55 of the school law of the State my duties set forth as follows: —

"The county superintendent shall visit the schools within his county at least once, at such times as he may deem necessary and proper, and note the course and method of instruction and the branches taught, and give such directions in the art of teaching and the method thereof in each school as to him shall seem necessary or expedient, so that *uniformity in the course of studies* and method of instruction employed shall be secured."

A careful study of this section of the law convinced me that my time in each school must not be devoted mainly to speech-making. I made up my mind that I would visit two schools each day, and spend a morning or an afternoon in each; that I would examine carefully the work of each school, try to ascertain its wants, and see if I could suggest some way of relief. I soon found that there was a painful want of uniformity in the course of studies of the several schools. Some schools had taken up twice as many branches as others, and arithmetic seemed to be the stopping-point in a majority of cases. Many parents reserved the right to dictate the branches which their children should study, and many teachers regarded their work well done when they had given instruction in those branches which happened to suit the convenience or caprice of either parents or pupils.

In looking to the school law for the settlement of the question as to what branches should be studied in the public schools of the State, I found the course as clearly defined as the course in any college or university, and that it was by no means an *optional* course of study. In order to make this matter plain, I here present Sect. 11 of the school law of the State:—

"In the primary schools there shall be taught Orthography, Reading, Penmanship, Arithmetic, English Grammar, History, Geography, and such other branches as the Board of Education may direct."

I presented this section of the law in every school which I visited, and insisted that the entire course of study should be taken up by all the older and more advanced pupils. Many teachers suggested that there were insurmountable difficulties in the way of such an undertaking, among which they named a want of necessary books and an indisposition on the part of pupils to take up additional branches. The more skilful teachers, however, testified that they had no difficulty in inducing pupils to take up additional studies, no trouble to procure from parents the books they needed, and that pupils who had taken up all the branches contained in the course of study were making better progress in *each* than were pupils who had taken up but *half* the branches contained in the course. I observed that the testimony of these teachers had great weight with parents and pupils, so I presented such testimony wherever I went. I found that if I expected to secure uniformity in the course of studies in all the schools of the county, as the law required, I would have no time to hear recitations; so I devoted myself mainly to the work of ascertaining what branches each pupil was pursuing, and to the task of aiding teachers in the organization of additional classes, and procuring such books as were needed.

I kept a journal in which I aimed to enter all items of general interest connected with the work of each school. I observed that teachers and pupils were all anxious to know whether any person beside myself would have access to this journal, and whether these items would in any way be made public. I soon became satisfied that the easiest way to induce pupils to take up additional branches, and to influence parents to purchase necessary books, would be in some way to make public the work of each school. I began first by announcing in each school that I would report its work in the school which I would next visit. I observed from that time forth that whenever I entered a school-room I found pupils present from the school which I had last visited, and I learned that they were there by permission of their teacher to hear their school reported, and to compare their own work with the work of their neighbors.

The desire of teachers and pupils and parents to hear the reports, and to compare the work of the several schools, became so strong that, in order to gratify this desire, I held each evening an educational meeting in one of the school-houses visited during the day. These evening educational meetings became a matter of public interest in every part of the county. People were not long contented with a knowledge of the condition of the schools of their own community, but frequently called for reports of schools in other sections of the county in which they chanced to have acquaintances. I made it a point in each meeting to state the number of schools I had up to that time visited, and the number in which classes had been formed in all the branches; and in many places I was called upon to name the schools in which such classes had been formed, and the teacher in charge of each. Teachers, pupils, and patrons of schools having classes in all the branches came from every direction to attend our meetings and hear their schools reported. Classes in many of the schools were organized in advance of my visits, and I was notified of the fact and requested to report them. Thinking that I had touched the true key to success by making public the work of each school, I published at the end of the school term in our local paper, the *Morgantown Post*, a list of schools in which classes had been formed in all the branches, and the name of the teacher in charge of each. This county contained at that time seventy-eight country schools, and thirty-two of these were reported in the published list, the "*roll of honor!*" Quite a number of teachers whose names had *not* been published, informed me, soon after the publication of the list, that they did not intend to be left off the roll of honor next year. I observed that teachers felt more interest in having their *names* published than pupils and patrons felt in having their *schools* published. This convinced me that the most effectual way to reach pupils and patrons of our public schools is, in some way, to make public the *individual work* of those pupils who are most deserving of praise. Believing that it would aid teachers in organizing classes and obtaining books, I announced in the county newspaper that in the evening educational meetings which I proposed to hold while visiting the schools of the county the next winter, I would make public the *names of all pupils* who would take up the entire course of study.

In the autumn of 1874, soon after the schools were opened, I received word from various directions that classes embracing all the branches had been organized in nearly every school. I was highly delighted with the progress made in this matter, and I came to the conclusion that my plan was already a success. Soon after this I commenced visiting schools, and began to inquire for pupils who had taken up the full course of study, intending to enter their names in my journal for the purpose of reporting them in our educational meetings, when, to my surprise and mortification, I found that scarcely any of them had taken up more than two studies. One had taken up arithmetic and geography, another had taken up arithmetic and English grammar, and still another arithmetic and history, according as they had "likes and dislikes" for these branches. Feeling that I had not yet accomplished my purpose, I next undertook to organize in each school a class of advanced pupils who would agree to take up *all* the branches. This was thought to be, as one who entered the class expressed it, "no fool of a job"; and yet, by the aid of the teachers, I succeeded from day to day in most of the schools. In our educational meetings, which were held each evening, I reported the names of pupils who had entered the classes in each of the schools visited during the day, and in other schools near by. The relatives and friends of pupils composing these classes were much pleased with these reports, and in most of our meetings the greater part of the audience was made up of relatives and friends.

Some of our best teachers entertained fears that at the close of the school term the special interest would cease, and most of the members of these classes would backslide, and thus render it necessary for us, the next term, to "do our first works." I soon became satisfied that these fears were well founded. Pupils had entered these classes, supposing that the end of the present school term would release them from all obligations. Very few of them had made up their minds to *complete* the course of study. In order to obviate this difficulty I undertook to organize in each school a class of volunteers who would agree not only to *take up* the free-school course, but to *complete it.*

Pupils very naturally inquired, before giving their names as volunteers, "How soon is this work to be completed, and who is to judge whether or not it is well done?" I told them we would have to trust to each class to do this work well, and to do it in a reasonable time. I organized two classes upon this principle, and in our evening educational meeting I reported my plan. I observed, however, that my statement of the plan produced no special interest on the part of any who were present. Several short speeches were made, but none of the speakers referred to my plan. It was evident that they could see nothing in it. I myself felt that it was a failure.

After the meeting adjourned I retired at the house of a friend, but I found no rest. I was full of tossings to and fro. For the first time in my life I regretted that my lot as an educator had been cast in the common schools. I said, "Oh, that I were a president of a university, a professor in a college, or a principal of a high school, where the work of each pupil is annually tested by a thorough examination." I remembered noticing, not long before, upon the wall of a parlor in West Virginia, a diploma belonging to a young lady, a graduate of the high school of Fort Wayne, Indiana, my native State. Then the inquiry came into my mind, — if *they* graduated pupils in *high* schools, why not graduate them in *low* schools? In a moment the darkness fled from my mind; the light flashed, and I almost fancied it was day. I felt sure I had made the discovery. I said, "We will bring all the plans and appliances from the higher schools and apply them to the primary schools; we will have annual examinations and commencement exercises, and we will grant diplomas and form alumni associations."

Early next morning I entered upon my duties with renewed energies, and undertook to organize, by the aid of the teacher, in each school a class of volunteers, who would agree not only to take up the entire course of study, but to *complete it in a given time and to pass a public examination in the same*. I found very few pupils who were advanced far enough to enable them to complete the course during that term; so I proposed that a public examination be held by the county superintendent in each district (not sub-district) in the county at the end of the school term of the *next* year, and that each pupil who should pass such examination creditably would receive a handsome diploma or honorary certificate, signed by the county superintendent and the teacher of the school in which he had completed the course. This class was termed the graduating class of 1876. I found, however, that pupils who were willing to enter this class were not numerous. Many parents expressed their doubts about the propriety of their children making such pledges. The teachers, almost without exception, and the more intelligent people gave the plan their hearty co-operation.

At the ensuing election, held Aug. 13, 1875, I was, without opposition, elected county superintendent. This I regarded not only a compliment to myself, but an indorsement of the graduating system which I had inaugurated.

In the autumn of 1875, as soon as the schools were fully in operation, I commenced my visitations, taking with me a sample free-school diploma, — a handsome certificate, nine by fourteen inches, neatly framed, which I exhibited in each school. I found that the graduating system was rapidly growing in popular favor, so I undertook to organize in each school, where there was material for doing so, not only a class for 1876, but also a class for 1877. Our educational meetings, which were held each evening, had, in the mean time, so increased in interest that school-houses were insufficient for the accommodation of our vast audiences, and trustees of churches opened their houses of worship for our accommodation. I held, while visiting that winter, forty-three of these meetings, twenty-seven in churches. Numerous topics connected with popular education were discussed at these meetings, and addresses were delivered by professors in the University, ministers of the gospel, teachers, farmers, and mechanics.

No cne element added more to the interest and pleasure of these meetings than the music furnished by the young ladies and gentlemen of the several communities in the county. I availed myself each evening of the opportunity to report the names of those who had entered the classes of 1876 and 1877. I proposed to publish these names in the county newspaper; and a spirit of emulation arose between the schools of each district, and an equal rivalry between the several districts, as to which school in each district or which district in the county should excel in the number and quality of its graduates. Teachers, pupils, and patrons of the schools became recruiting agents to obtain volunteers. The ranks were frequently increased by pupils publicly entering the classes at our educational meetings, and almost every mail brought me letters giving names to be added to the classes.

In addition to the classes of 1876 and 1877, I suggested that each teacher form two other classes, so that each school would have four classes; and most of them did so. Pupils unprepared to enter either of these classes composed the preparatory department. One grand result of this classification was the effect produced upon pupils who entered the graduating classes. They had voluntarily consented to do a certain amount of work in a given time, and their work would be publicly tested. Every student of human nature could anticipate the result. Pupils began to count the months and weeks and days in which this work was to be accomplished. They were found numbering the pages in their history, geography, and English grammar, and counting the problems in arithmetic, in order to ascertain how many pages should be studied, and how many problems solved each day, in order to complete these studies, and review, before examination day. One boy said to his comrade, after they had both given their names for graduation, "Now, Tom, we have no more time for shooting paper wads at the ceiling or flipping beans at the girls." But the effect of this classification was by no means confined to the members of the graduating class. Most of the younger pupils caught the example and inspiration of the older ones, and they too began to think and talk of the time when they would also complete the course of study. Government in the school-room seemed to take care of itself, giving the teacher full time for his legitimate work, teaching.

The time for the examination of graduating classes began to draw near, and croakers were busy, prophesying that the whole system would prove a failure. "Such a thing," they said, "as graduating in country schools never has been done and never will." I watched anxiously the effect of these predictions, and I was highly gratified to find that teachers and pupils were already beyond the region of uncertainty, and were only strengthened in their determination to make the plan a success. So far were they from fearing failure, that they requested me to make the examinations thorough and public, and as far as possible oral, so that the people could see and hear for themselves.

In order to make public the time and place of each examination, I sent to each teacher, school officer, and minister of the gospel in the county, the following printed postal-card notice of examinations: —

OFFICE SUP'T OF FREE SCHOOLS OF MONONGALIA COUNTY,
MORGANTOWN, W. VA., Feb. 16, 1876.

To Teachers and Friends of Free Schools:

The First Annual Examination of the Graduating Classes, for the several districts of this county, will be held at the places and dates named below: —

For GRANT DISTRICT,	Zoar,	Friday, Feb. 25, 1876.
For UNION	"	Pierpoint's, Saturday, Feb. 26.
For MORGAN	"	Pleasant Hill, Friday, March 3.
For CASS	"	Bethel, Saturday, March 4.
For CLAY	"	Mooresville, Tuesday, March 7.
For BATTELLE	"	West Warren, Thursday, March 9.
For CLINTON	"	Goshen, Saturday, March 11.

Each examination will commence promptly at 10 A. M., and continue during the day.

Every pupil should have a pencil and several sheets of foolscap paper.

At night the Graduating Class from each school will be represented by an Oration, Essay, Declamation, or Select Reading from one of its members. The granting of DIPLOMAS, and an Address to the Graduating Classes, by some *experienced educator*, will close the exercises.

Friends of Popular Education are invited to be present. We expect the best music, vocal and instrumental, both day and night, which each district can produce.

Basket dinners, and suppers too, will be in order.

Very truly yours,

A. L. WADE, *County Supt.*

I also sent copies of these card-notices to many of the public papers, and to all the county superintendents of the State. The coming examinations were, therefore, published in all the schools of the county, announced from the pulpit, and noticed by the press. Great was the desire of the public to know the names of those who were expected to graduate at each place named in the notice; and when I published in the local paper of the county, the week previous to the first examination, a list of names of the graduating classes for the following week, and announced that I would continue this each week, until all the classes would be published, copies of the paper containing these lists were looked for with unusual interest, by parents and pupils, teachers and school officers, and by all who were interested in the educational work.

Unwilling to assume the responsibility of conducting these examinations without aid, I secured the services of Prof. H. L. Cox, principal of Morgantown Graded School; Prof. W. R. White, late State Superintendent of Free Schools of West Virginia; and Profs. Lyon, Purinton, and Owen, of West Virginia University. I gave notice through the press, that one or more of these professors would be present to aid me in each examination, and to deliver an appropriate address in the evening.

Although most parents were well pleased with the thought of having their children graduate, I observed, as the time for examination drew near, an increasing anxiety on the part of these parents about the final result. I received numerous letters, was occasionally called upon, and sometimes sent for, by parents who had children in the graduating classes. One fortunate feature connected with this anxiety was, that these parents, almost without exception, were unwilling to let their children know that they had any fears as to their final success in the examination.

An incident which took place a short time previous to the first examination will serve, in some degree, to illustrate the depth of parental feeling in this matter. Riding on horseback along a country road, I was passing a farm-house, when the proprietor, a man whom I knew very well, gave me a signal which indicated that he wished me to come to the house. On entering the door, I saw, in the manner of the man and his wife, unmistakable signs of great anxiety. Without any of the usual formalities, the man began: "The children are all at school; wife and I have been wanting to see you for some time. You have got our daughter into this graduating class, and *she* seems to think that it is all very nice. Some people say that the object is to disgrace the children in the presence of a lot of college professors; and wife and I have hardly slept any for a week. Our daughter knows nothing about how anxious we are." Rising from his seat and approaching me, as I sat in his own house, without any sign of anger, but with deep feeling, pointing his forefinger at me, he said, "My daughter is a good girl, and she studies hard: I will go with her to the examination, and I intend to see that she is not abused."

LECTURE V.

TRIALS AND TRIUMPHS OF THE GRADUATING SYSTEM

The 25th of February, 1876, — the day which was to decide whether graduation in country schools should be a success or a failure, — dawned beautiful and bright. I was well aware that if the first examination should be a failure, it would be impossible, in this county, to rally a class at any subsequent time ; and I had felt a deep anxiety for this day to be fair. When the sun rose, the sky was clear, the air balmy and mild as a May morning. Full of hope, I was on my way to the appointed place, when I met a messenger who hurriedly handed me a letter. I saw, on opening it, that it was from one of the foremost teachers of the district in which the examination would be held. It was a short note, and I here present it in full : —

Laurel Point, Feb. 25, 1876.

A. L. Wade,
   County Superintendent of Schools.

My Dear Sir, — A report is in circulation that you will demand a fee of five dollars for each diploma granted, and that twenty-five cents will be charged each person as admission to Prof. White's evening lecture. I fear that this report will affect the attendance, and I hope you will at once correct it, through the papers Yours in haste,

GEORGE BARB.

While I had all confidence in the sincerity of the writer, I could not believe that intelligent people would credit the report; and yet my anxiety was, I think, little less than that felt by Cyrus W. Field when the "Great Eastern" left the shore to lay the Atlantic cable. On nearing the church in which the examination was to be held, great was my gratification when I saw both sides of the road literally lined with horses and carriages, and the enclosure about the church almost filled with people. On entering the door I found the house already full; and as I passed down the aisle toward the pulpit, an excellent choir, accompanied by a good organ, began to sing an appropriate song. Every teacher of the district was present, and a graduating class of fifty was seated in a suitable place. Professor Cox, my predecessor in office, a man of large experience and superior skill in public examinations, who had promised to aid me upon this occasion, was present, ready to perform his part. Professor Purinton, of West Virginia University, was elected secretary, and was furnished with a blank book, for the purpose of making a permanent record of the proceedings.

To give a detailed account of the work of this day and of the evening would be but a repetition of the spirit of the examination described in my last lecture. In order, however, to show the principal points of interest in this and the subsequent examinations which had been announced, I here present an account copied from my official report for that year. The report says: —

"These district examinations of graduating classes were held in churches in the following order: —

"*Grant District*, at Zoar Baptist Church, on Friday, Feb. 25, 1876. This district has thirteen schools, and all the teachers were present. The printed roll (of volunteers for graduation), numbering sixty-one, was called, and fifty members responded. The residue, having failed to complete the course, were transferred to the class of 1877. The examination was conducted by the county superintendent, assisted by Professor H. L. Cox, principal of Morgantown Graded School. In the evening addresses were made by Professor W. R. White, ex-State Superintendent of Free Schools of West Virginia, and Professor D. B. Purinton, of West Virginia University.

"*Union District*, at Peirpoint's Methodist Episcopal Church, Saturday, Feb. 26, 1876. This district has eight schools, and all the teachers were present. The roll, numbering fifty, was called, and thirty-eight responded. The examination was conducted by the county superintendent, assisted by Professor F. S. Lyon, of West Virginia University, and Professor H. L. Cox. Addresses were delivered in the evening by Professors White, Lyon, and Purinton.

"*Morgan District*, at Pleasant Hill Baptist Church,

Friday, March 3, 1876. This district has eight schools, and all the teachers were present. The roll, numbering twenty-one, was called, and nineteen responded. Professor White assisted the county superintendent in conducting the examination. Addresses in the evening by Professors Cox, White, Purinton, and Owen.

"*Cass District*, at Bethel Methodist Episcopal Church, on Saturday, March 4, 1876. This district contains eight schools, and all the teachers were present except two, and these two were non-residents. The roll, numbering thirty, was called, and twenty-one responded. Professor White assisted the county superintendent in conducting the examination, and in the evening delivered an address.

" *Clay District*, at Valley Chapel Christian Church, on Tuesday, March 7, 1876. This district contains thirteen schools, and all the teachers were present except one, — a resident of this county. The roll of twenty-three was called, and seventeen answered. Professor Lyon assisted the county superintendent in the examination. In the evening addresses were made by Professor Lyon and Hon. William Price.

"*Battelle District*, at West Warren Baptist Church, on Thursday, March 9, 1876. This district has thirteen schools, and all the teachers were present except two, — one a resident of this county and the other a non-resident. The roll, numbering thirty-four, was called, and twenty-four responded; but four of these withdrew from the class, not being fully prepared in all the branches of the course. One teacher who was present — a non-resident — declined to take any part in the work of deciding who were entitled to diplomas. Professor Lyon assisted the superintendent in conducting the examination, and in the evening addressed the audience.

"*Clinton District*, at Goshen Baptist Church, on Saturday, March 11, 1876. This district contains fourteen schools, and all the teachers were present. The roll, numbering forty-two, was called, and thirty-one answered. Professor Lyon assisted the county superintendent in conducting the examination. In the evening addresses were made by Professors Lyon, Owen, and Purinton.

"The county superintendent, each evening, after the addresses were ended, in the presence of the audience, delivered to each member of the class who was by the teachers of the district adjudged worthy of the same, a Diploma or Honorary Certificate, 9 x 14 inches, duly signed as heretofore set forth; which, when framed, is an ornament to a parlor and an honor to the holder.

"Two hundred and sixty-one pupils entered the class of 1876, and of this number, one hundred and ninety-six completed the course and obtained diplomas."

So far as I could learn, not a single pupil who had undertaken to complete the course of study for graduation stayed away from the examination from fear of failure. With the exception of a few who were unable to attend, all who were prepared were present. Those who were unable to graduate in 1876 were transferred to the class of 1877.

As an indication of the interest which the teachers took in these examinations, I may refer to the fact which appears in the report I have given; viz., only five teachers were marked absent.

In order that I may, in some degree, give an idea of the interest which the masses manifested in these examinations, I quote further from my report of that year: —

"With a single exception, the largest churches in the several districts were insufficient to accommodate, even during the day, the vast numbers who came to witness the examinations. And these were not disinterested spectators; they were our most intelligent people, — the cream of society, — men and women who had sons or daughters or grandchildren or friends in the class, in whom they were deeply interested."

In order to show the thoroughness of these examinations, the success of pupils in passing through them, and the aims of those who graduated, I quote once more from my report: —

"These examinations were no 'child's play'; they were intended to test the knowledge of each pupil in the free-school branches; and yet, with a very few exceptions, the members of the several classes displayed a coolness, a courage, and a knowledge of the common branches which many of our teachers do not possess.

But they do not expect to cease to study because they have graduated in the primary branches. They expect to work to obtain a more thorough knowledge of these branches, and many of them intend to take up a higher course of study."

You will please bear in mind that the quotations which I have made form a part of an official report, prepared when the facts were fresh in memory, — prepared for circulation among the very people who were familiar with these facts.

As soon as the last examination of graduating classes was ended, parents and pupils, teachers and school officers, began to inquire how soon the catalogue of the schools of the county would be published. Reports of these examinations had been published from time to time in the local paper of the county, and they had been read with interest, but they were scattered through several editions of the paper, — difficult to find for reference; and the information which they gave, though good as far as it went, was incomplete, and by no means met the want that was felt in every family. A complete report, in cheap and convenient form, by the aid of which each family could compare intelligently the work of the several schools of the county, seemed to be essential. With a view of publishing such a pamphlet, I had, on the day of each examination, placed in the hands of each teacher who was present the following: —

FORM OF REPORT FOR CATALOGUE.

REPORT OF.. *School,*

Sub-District No.,............*District of*............................,

For the Term ending...........*day of*....................*1878.*

.... *Teacher.*

Number of youths entitled to attend . . . .
Number of youths in attendance . . . .
Number of youths entitled to attend, but not in attendance . . ..
Daily average attendance . . . .
Daily per cent of attendance of all entitled to attend . . . .

Branches taught and number of pupils studying each branch, as follows:—

History	Penmanship . . . .
English Grammar	Reading . . . .
Geography	Orthography . . . .
Written Arithmetic	
Mental Arithmetic	

☞ (Name any other classes, if any.)

The following pupils graduated in 1876:—

CLASS FOR 1877.

....
....
....

CLASS FOR 1878.

....
....
....

CLASS FOR 1879.

....
....

I agree to pay .... member of the Publishing Committee of .... District, ...Dollar and............Cents for........................Copies of the First Annual Catalogue of the Free Schools of Monongalia County — being ten cents per copy — at the time they are delivered to me.

.... *Teacher.*

The teachers of each district, on the day of examination of graduating classes, had chosen from their own body one member of the Committee on Publication of the Catalogue.

This committee met at the Court House on the twenty-sixth day of June, 1876, having reports from most of the schools, and awarded the contract for publishing the First Annual Catalogue to the editors of the Morgantown "Post"; six hundred copies for $60. A little over $50 had been subscribed, and the residue was paid by the county superintendent. A few teachers had failed to fill up and return their reports, and in such cases abstracts were taken from the superintendent's journal.

About the first of September, 1876, we published the First Annual Catalogue of the Free Schools of Monongalia County, which embraced the annual report of the county superintendent, and a report from every school in the county. This catalogue, which was a 32mo pamphlet of ninety-six pages, was purchased of teachers by parents and pupils, and read and studied by both young and old, until almost every one became familiar with the educational work of the whole county. No other single book, except the Bible, seemed to present so many points of interest to the people of every community in the county. The per cent of attendance, which is clearly presented on every page, was carefully studied by teachers and school officers. Parents and pupils having relatives and acquaintances residing in remote parts of the county looked carefully in the catalogue to see whether the names of their cousins and friends were to be found in any of the classes. The individual work of each teacher, as presented in the catalogue, indicated, in a good degree, his worth, and was carefully considered by those who wished to employ public instructors. Many other points of interest connected with this catalogue I must pass unnoticed.

While the masses were generally well pleased with the work of the graduating system, there were some persons who had not ceased to prophesy that the plan would yet be a failure. "These examinations," they said, "were successful because the system was then new; but the excitement will die away within the year, and it will be impossible to repeat them. These graduates," they said, "are sure in the end to be worsted, because they will certainly cease to study, as it is generally understood that graduation means that they have learned all."

In the autumn of 1876, as soon as the schools were fully at work, I commenced my annual visits. I was gratified to find the predictions that those who had graduated would cease to study were false. I found about ninety per cent of these alumni in school, either as teachers or pupils, many of them pursuing studies beyond the primary branches.

Desiring to give the young people of the county the highest mental training that our common schools can possibly afford, I introduced a plan which gave a large number of the graduates the privilege of writing for the press. Another newspaper, called the "New Dominion," had lately been started at the county seat. We now had papers representing the interests of the two leading political parties, and both papers were warmly interested in the educational work. At each of our educational mass meetings, held each evening, a correspondent for each of our county papers was chosen. These correspondents were usually selected from the alumni of the schools visited during the day, and generally consisted of a lady and a gentleman. Each correspondent was expected to furnish the paper which he represented a condensed account of the proceedings of the meeting, and a sketch of the educational work of the community in which it was held. Each issue of our county papers was anxiously looked for, especially by friends of these correspondents and by the schools which they represented. Thus, in a single school term, nearly one hundred of our young people commenced the high work of writing for the public papers.

I had, at the several examinations of graduating classes held at the end of the previous term, announced that some time within the next school year an alumni association would be organized, and an entertainment would be given, in each district, by those who had graduated. I had stated that the exercises at these alumni meetings would consist of original and select orations, essays, and select readings; and I had requested the young people to make preparation for these public performances. I had further announced that the officers of each association would be chosen by ballot, from and by the members of its own body, and that each would also elect from among its members a gentleman to deliver an oration and a lady to read an essay at the next annual examination of graduating classes in the district.

The average age of those who had graduated in the county was a little less than sixteen years; and it was suggested by some that alumni associations could not be made a success if managed by officers so young in years, and that it would probably be better to choose these officers from the ranks of citizens. Other persons prophesied that, when the time for holding these alumni meetings should come, there would be no difference of opinion about the election of officers; for, as they believed, such meetings would never be held, — nobody would make preparation for them, and nobody would attend them. I was well aware, however, that the young people were making thorough preparation, and that many of the young men were making themselves familiar with rules of order for the government of deliberative bodies.

In order to make public the time and place of each meeting, I sent to each teacher and school officer of the county, and to many of the older members of the alumni, the following printed postal-card notice of alumni meetings: —

OFFICE SUP'T FREE SCHOOLS OF MONONGALIA CO.,
MORGANTOWN, W. VA., Jan. 8, 1877.

To Teachers and Friends of Free Schools:

The First Annual Meeting of the Alumni of the Free Schools of the several districts of this County will be held in the following churches and at the dates named below: —

For GRANT DISTRICT, Saturday, Jan. 13, at Cold Spring.
For MORGAN DISTRICT, Friday, Jan. 19, at Drummond Chapel.
For CASS DISTRICT, Saturday, Jan. 20, at Cassville.
For BATTELLE DISTRICT, Friday, Jan. 26, at Union.
For CLAY DISTRICT, Saturday, Jan. 27, at Mt. Hermon.
For UNION DISTRICT, Friday, Feb. 2, at Peirpoint's.
For CLINTON DISTRICT, Saturday, Feb. 3, at Goshen.

The exercises will commence at half past six o'clock, and will consist of Original and Select Orations, Essays, and, Select Readings.

Teachers will please meet as early as 5 P. M., to prepare a programme for the evening We expect the best music — vocal and instrumental — which each district can produce Each member of the Class of 1876 will be entitled to take part in the exercises in the district in which he graduated.

Friends of Free Schools are invited to be present.

A. L. WADE,
County Sup't.

In order to show the result of this attempt to organize these associations, I quote from my official report of that year: —

"An alumni association was organized in each district in the county. Each association elected by ballot, from its own body, president, vice-president, and secretary. A gentleman to deliver an oration, and a lady to read an essay at the next annual district examination and commencement exercises, were also chosen by each association.

"No public meetings pertaining to our free-school work have elicited more interest or attracted larger crowds. More than eighty members of the class of 1876 embraced the opportunity to speak and read in the presence of large audiences.

"The self-possession shown by the members of the various classes in their performances, and in the election of officers, elicited universal commendation. The privilege of addressing popular assemblages, and reading to full houses, is not often given to the youth who attend our free schools. It is claimed by some that the ability to speak and read in public is possessed in a high degree by but few persons. If this be true, it is the more important that the schools in which the *masses* are educated, give opportunity for the development of this gift wherever it exists.

"The graduating class of 1877 has been added to the alumni, and will take part in the several annual meetings, which will be held at the call of the officers of each district. Due notice of the time and place of each will be given."

The time for holding our second annual examinations of graduating classes was now at hand. These were held, as in the preceding year, in seven churches; the first on the 24th of February and the last on the 17th of March, 1877. In order to show the result of these examinations and of the work of the year, I quote from my official report: —

"It will be seen from the reports of district examinations that *one hundred and ten pupils completed the course*, and obtained diplomas. These were granted by the teachers present, on a scale from one to ten, — five being medium and ten excellent. No pupil graduated whose average grade was not above seven. It was not expected that the class in the county this year would be as large as it was last year, as we had last year the *cream* produced by several years' work. Many persons at the close of the examinations in 1876 were of the opinion, that in order to have graduates in 1877, it would be necessary to use *skimmed milk*. Many of these, however, after witnessing the examinations of the classes of 1877, agree that the graduates of this year are *richer* than last.

"The attendance upon these examinations, both day and night, and the interest manifested by the masses in them, were quite equal to last year. The same may be said of our educational meetings, which were held each evening while I was visiting schools. I held in the year, including district alumni meetings and examinations, fifty-two educational mass meetings in the county, forty-two in churches, and ten in school-houses."

Rev. J. R. Thompson, who had lately been elected president of West Virginia University, heartily indorsed the graduating system, made the tour of the county, was present at most of our second annual examinations of graduating classes, and delivered evening addresses. Several other educators took part in these exercises, prominent among whom I may name Prof. F. H. Crago, principal of Moundsville Graded and Normal Schools. Mr. N. N. Hoffman, one of the editors of the Morgantown "Post," accompanied President Thompson on his trip through the county. The presence of a journalist increased, in no small degree, the inspiration, upon each occasion. His editorial reports of examinations and evening exercises were read with interest by the people, and were copied by the leading papers of the State.

The Second Annual Catalogue of the Free Schools of Monongalia County was published about the 1st of September, 1877. Copies of this catalogue were sent to county superintendents throughout the State, and to many of the public papers.

In the autumn of 1877, when I began my annual visits, I found that close observers believed the severest trials of the graduating system were ended, and that its triumph, throughout the county, was generally conceded. I found, from the discussions in our evening educational mass meetings, that teachers and patrons were thinking on a higher plane than heretofore. The need of teachers thoroughly trained for their work, the necessity for securing a full attendance upon the schools, and the importance of giving the masses a better education and a broader culture, were subjects which seemed to occupy uppermost places in the public mind.

The second annual meetings of the alumni were favored with audiences quite equal to those of last year, and the exercises indicated a good degree of reading and of research on the part of the performers.

We were now nearing the time for holding our third annual examinations of the graduating classes, and President Thompson again agreed to make the tour of the county. Mr. J. E. Fleming, one of the editors of the Morgantown "New Dominion," gave notice that he would accompany President Thompson; and Mr. N. N. Hoffman, of the Morgantown "Post," who had attended most of the exercises of the preceding year, again arranged to be present at a part of the examinations.

George W. Atkinson, Esq., editor of the Wheeling "Standard" (daily and weekly), who had himself been a teacher, and who was already a warm advocate of the graduating system, announced his intention to be present at several of our examinations, in order that he might carefully study the character and work of the system for the purpose of presenting it to the public.

The "Standard" of March 4, 1878, contains a leading editorial, in which Mr. Atkinson makes his report and presents his conclusions. As his article is too long to be presented in full, I make the following extracts: —

"At the instance of County Superintendent Wade, of Monongalia, we made a tour last week of a portion of that county, attending what Mr. Wade calls his annual public examinations; and such crowds of people we have never seen assembled, even at barbecues during political campaigns. Mr. Wade has thoroughly systematized the schools of his county, and his plan is simply this: The pupils of every school in the county are arranged in classes after the fashion of colleges and universities, and every year a greater or less number of students graduate from every school in the county. The commencement, or graduating exercises, are held in each district, and all the schools from the sub-districts have their graduating pupils present at some central point in the district where the examination takes place; and those who pass creditable public examinations receive diplomas which certify that the holders have taken the course of study laid down in the school law of the State, and have passed a public examination upon the studies thus laid down in the law. The parents and immediate relatives of the members of the graduating class never fail to be present during the entire examination, and every parent is anxious for his or her child to be most successful.

"The examinations begin at 10 A. M. and usually continue until 5 P. M., giving one hour for dinner. Then, in the evening, addresses upon some educational topic are delivered by gentlemen whom Mr. Wade never fails to have on hand to interest and to instruct the people.

"We cannot commend Mr. Wade's plan too highly. It is just the thing to bring our public schools up to the standard of usefulness and respectability which they were intended by the authors of the law to be. It is a common-sense plan, and wherever it has been introduced it has worked like a charm. The fact that it awakens an interest on the part of the people is of itself sufficient to commend it to the Superintendent of Public Instruction, if it possessed no other advantages. But it does possess other advantages:—

"*First*, it classifies the studies laid down in the law to be taught in our public schools.

"*Second*, it induces pupils to go through the entire course of study, which a great many would otherwise not do.

"*Third*, it arouses the ambition of the student to excel. It is really surprising to see how determined each boy and girl is to be the flower of the class, or the *cream* of the class, as Mr. Wade terms it.

"*Fourth*, it has a tendency to increase the attendance at school; for it is only reasonable to conclude that the more people are interested in education, the more they will be stimulated to send their children to school.

"After having witnessed the entire workings of the system inaugurated by Mr. Wade, we are now more than ever in favor of it, and sincerely hope that our State Superintendent will make it a part of his next report to the Legislature, asking its adoption."

The Third Annual Catalogue of the Free Schools of

Monongalia County, which was published about the first of September, 1878, showed that eighty-eight pupils had graduated, and that fifty evening educational meetings — thirty-six in churches and fourteen in school-houses — had been held within the year.

In the fall of 1878, about the time I was ready to begin visiting schools, I received numerous notes from citizens residing in sundry parts of the county, stating that the patrons of each school wished to be present at the time of my regular visit, and that they would be pleased if I could notify the parents as well as the teacher of the time when I would visit each school. They wished to be present to see for themselves the work of their school, and to aid in collecting facts for the superintendent's evening report. In order to gratify these requests with the least possible labor on my part, I concluded to notify the patrons of each school through the teacher. I gave each teacher timely notice of my coming, by a printed postal card which required but little labor to fill the blanks. I here present a card notice of superintendent's visit: —

Office of Sup't of Free Schools of Monongalia County,
Morgantown, W. Va.

COUNTY SUPERINTENDENT'S WORK.

I expect to visit the school at ....
school-house, on .... the .... day of
.... at about .... o'clock, ... M.,
to remain until .... M.

Please have a full attendance of pupils, and try to have the trustees and patrons of your school present.

Please make a list of names of pupils entitled to attend, but not in attendance, and state, so far as you can, the cause of the non-attendance of each. State also the daily average attendance, and the daily per cent of attendance.

Will you please organize the graduating classes for at least four years, if they are not already organized?

I will hold an Educational Meeting at ─────────── at night.

Please allow me to depend upon you and ─────────── to announce it and to make necessary arrangements for the meeting. Let us have the best music your community can produce.

A L. WADE,
County Superintendent.

I generally found, upon reaching each school, a house well filled, embracing not only pupils, but patrons; not only fathers but mothers, each parent anxious to see how the work of his child would compare with the work of other children of like age and opportunities. I found, almost without exception, that parents who were present were ready either to give a reason for the absence of children who were not in attendance, or they were willing to aid the teacher in his efforts to bring in these delinquents. Almost every school-room was made home-like by the presence of beautiful pictures and pure mottoes, and by the sweet strains of music. Most of the teachers regarded themselves, in a degree, responsible for the health and happiness of their pupils, and were conforming to the laws of life, by giving close attention to warming and ventilating their school-rooms. Before dismissing for the noon exercises, in many schools, dinner was eaten with order and decorum, as in a well-regulated family. The testimony of our best teachers proved that the time which was given to culture greatly increased the pupil's power to learn, and made him more thorough in all the branches which he studied.

The third annual meetings of the alumni, which were held during the winter, were to the first and second annual meetings, what the super'ative degree in English grammar is to the positive and comparative degrees.

The time for holding our fourth annual examinations of graduating classes was now near at hand. In accordance with my purposes, announced the preceding winter, this year would end my official work in the schools of Monongalia County, and I desired to see the graduating system thoroughly tested under circumstances which would surround it in a county where there was neither a college nor a university.

After consulting President Thompson, I secured speakers, for our commencement exercises, entirely outside of the university, most of them from a class that may be found in any county, — the Christian ministry; and the result proved that under these speakers the public interest was undiminished. Eighty-two pupils graduated in the year ending Aug. 31, 1879, making in all, since the system of graduation was introduced in 1876, four hundred and seventy-one pupils who have graduated in the common-school branches in this county.

As an indication of the culture and intelligence of the teachers of this county, I may be permitted to refer to the fact, that my last annual report shows that of ninety-two teachers employed, eighty-three were subscribers to some educational journal. The editor of the "National Journal of Education," Boston, in referring to this fact says, " We fear that no county in New England could make so good a showing." This in itself is proof that the graduating system is a success in the training of teachers.

As a proof that the people were not weary, after four years' trial, of the work of the graduating system, I may refer to the fact, that my last annual report shows that we held during the year fifty-three evening educational mass meetings, — thirty-seven of them in churches, and sixteen in school-houses.

In presenting the "trials and triumphs of the graduating system," I have intentionally confined myself to the county which gave birth to the system. In my next lecture, I propose to speak of the success of this system in several counties, and in different States.

In conclusion, I can present no better proof of the triumphs of this system, than the following extract from an editorial written by Rev. J. R. Thompson, president of West Virginia University, and editor of " West Virginia (Weekly) Journal of Education." In the issue of Dec. 4, 1878, of that journal, in speaking of the graduating system, the editor says : —

"It has indeed produced in Monongalia County, and is destined to produce all over the State of West Virginia, an educational revival. It is safe to say that no subject so interests the people of Monongalia County to-day as the education of their sons and daughters. They talk about that more than anything else. No subject presents such charms as that of education, and larger crowds can be gathered to witness the annual examinations in the several districts than can be called together by the most eloquent preacher or the most popular political orators. The writer of this article has accompanied Superintendent Wade twice through the county on the occasion of these examinations, and he has marvelled again and again at the deep and abiding interest of the people in the school work. They come early to the house in which the examination is being held, they come in all kinds of disagreeable weather, they come from three, four, or five, and sometimes ten miles. Their interest never flags through the entire day; they remain until eleven and sometimes twelve o'clock at night, and they go away as from half-finished feasts, with appetites keen as ever for mind-food, affectionately and enthusiastically devoted to the schools of the people.

"We are among those who believe that it is possible for this State to have a prosperous, honorable, influential future, but we are quite confident of the truth of the statement that this future is possible only by the general education of the people; and we are sure that no better plan has thus far been devised to secure this very desirable end than the introduction into the public schools, by efficient county superintendents, of this system of graduation. Let it be tried."

LECTURE VI.

GROWTH OF THE GRADUATING SYSTEM, AND OFFICIAL TESTIMONY OF THOSE WHO HAVE TRIED IT.

The graduating system for country schools is still in its infancy; its work has been tested in but few counties; and official reports of its operations are not numerous. I shall therefore, in this lecture, present all the official testimony which I have been able to collect upon this subject. This testimony is taken from the published reports of the general superintendents of public instruction of three several States, into which the system has been introduced, viz., West Virginia, Pennsylvania, and New Jersey. I am aware that it has very recently been introduced into sundry counties of several States where no official reports have since been published. I learn from reliable sources that its work in these counties is quite satisfactory, but I propose at present to confine myself to such counties as have published official reports of its operations.

It is more than likely that I have overlooked some reports which have been published; but this, if true, will in no way weaken the testimony which I have collected. Some of these official reports were made by men who, although working on a kindred system, knew nothing of each other. It will be found that these official reports, coming from officers separated from each other, run in the same channel; which fact of itself would give weight to their testimony, before either judge or jury, in any court of justice. But before introducing any testimony, I desire to say something of the causes which led to the introduction of this system into several counties of West Virginia.

The great educational revival produced by the introduction of the graduating system into the primary free schools of Monongalia County, West Virginia, was not long confined to that county. The success which attended the system was, from time to time, noticed by the local papers of the several counties and by the leading journals of the State. The propriety of its universal adoption in the free schools of West Virginia was freely and fully discussed by the public press and by the leading educators of the State. As an indication of the unanimity of sentiment upon this subject, I present an official copy of the

ACTION OF THE STATE TEACHERS' ASSOCIATION OF WEST VIRGINIA.

At the State Teachers' Association held at Martinsburg, W. Va., August 28, 29, and 30, 1877, a resolution was presented by Professor E. Bonar, of the Moundsville Graded School, and amended by Professor J. McMurran, of the Shepherdstown Normal School, which amendment was adopted by the Association, and reads as follows: —

"*Resolved*, That the system introduced into the free schools of Monongalia County by Superintendent A. L. Wade, providing for grading schools, holding district examinations, and granting diplomas to pupils who complete the free-school branches, be recommended to county superintendents throughout West Virginia for their adoption.

"Attest: T. MARCELLUS MARSHALL,
"*Sec. State Teachers' Ass'n.*"

Some time after the adoption of the above resolution, Hon. W. K. Pendleton, State Superintendent of Schools, wrote me from Wheeling, West Virginia, under date of June 8, 1878, as follows: —

"The next meeting of the State Teachers' Association will be held at Parkersburg, Aug. 27 to 29. Would like you to prepare a paper setting forth, in practical detail, the methods of grading common schools. This matter is attracting interest in many parts of the State, and many counties are in condition to introduce the system."

While this subject was attracting attention throughout the State, a few of the foremost counties had already adopted the system and were now testing its merits. The first county that fell into line in West Virginia, under this system, was Marshall, situated on the Ohio River.

At a county institute which I conducted at Moundsville, Marshall County, West Virginia, during the holidays in 1876, the graduating system, after being freely discussed, was unanimously adopted.

The system was at once put into operation by Mr. W. M. Wirt, county superintendent, who wrote me under date of Feb. 19, 1877, " We are having a revival of education in our county. We have been holding educational meetings for some time, and the people are very much interested in education. Please send me a blank diploma, as we want to get some printed."

In his annual report to the State Superintendent, for the year ending Aug. 31, 1877, Superintendent Wirt says : —

" With the help of the teachers, I introduced Superintendent Wade's plan of holding district examinations and granting diplomas to those who could pass a creditable examination in the current common-school branches. This, I think, had a good effect, as many pupils studied with an object, and endeavored to acquire a more practical knowledge of what they were studying than before. Diplomas were granted to two pupils in Liberty, to two in Union, and to three in Clay Districts, and to seventeen in the Independent District of Moundsville, while more than one hundred entered the graduating class of the present year. I think the system a good one, and would recommend it to the superintendents and teachers of other counties, as it has worked well so far as tried in this county.

"Our schools have made decided improvements;

have had better teachers and have taken deeper root in the hearts of the people than ever before."

In his annual report for the year ending Aug. 31, 1878, having tested the system another year, he says: —

"Our schools have been more efficient during the past year than during the preceding one, and much more so, in my judgment, than in any year since their introduction in our county.

"I attribute the great success of our schools to two principal causes: first, better teachers; second, the 'graduating system.' But to the 'graduating system,' more than to any other cause, do we owe the revival of our educational interests. The introduction of this system has met the hearty concurrence of the great majority of the people, and where I have had the co-operation of the teachers in its introduction, it has been a success; but it has, like all new things, having for its object the advancement of society, met with some opposition.

"In the spring months I held examinations in the different districts, which were very interesting occasions, as the graduates delivered speeches in the evenings. In a few instances their commencement exercises would compare favorably with similar exercises in colleges and seminaries. There were seventy-six graduates during the year, most of whom showed a thorough knowledge of the common-school curriculum. There will be more than one hundred graduates in the incoming year. I will simply say to superintendents of other counties, Try it with a determination to make it a success, and you will soon be convinced of its adaptability to the work to be done."

Mr. T. N. Parks, county superintendent of Tyler County, West Virginia, in his annual report to the State Superintendent for the year ending Aug. 31, 1878, says: —

"Much of this increased attendance, with the superior work done in the schools last winter, we attribute to the teachers' institutes that were held in the county; especially the one held in Middlebourne in November, 1877, conducted by the county superintendent and Mr. Wade, county superintendent of Monongalia County, assisted by President Thompson, of the State University, and Mr. G. W. Atkinson, editor of the Wheeling "Standard." Many questions of vital importance to the public schools were discussed in the institute, prominent among which was the graduating system, as originated and introduced by Mr. Wade into the free schools of Monongalia County, and as adopted and practised in other counties of the State. The teachers of the county voted unanimously to adopt it in Tyler County.

"In carrying out the graduating system, and in order to test the thoroughness of those who wished to graduate in the free-school course, we held district examinations about the time the schools were closing in the spring. As the classes in some districts were small from want of material, we thought best to combine as far as convenient. Four examinations were held in the county: one at Zion schoolhouse in Union District; one at Sistersville, in Lincoln District; one in Middlebourne, for Elsworth and Meade Districts; and one in Centreville, for Centreville and McElroy Districts. At these several examinations persons were examined in the seven branches directed to be taught in the free schools of the State, viz., orthography, reading, penmanship, arithmetic, English grammar, geography, and history; and many of them in several higher branches, such as physical geography, algebra, etc. All but five who entered the graduating class for 1878 were examined, unless prevented by sickness. Nearly all who were not examined requested to be continued another year. Several who were examined will teach the coming winter, and all are among the most promising young men and women of the county. The number in the graduating class for 1879 will be more than double the number in the class for 1878. The real usefulness and benefits of such a system will be known only as its effects are seen in the future.

"To each one who sustained or passed a good and creditable examination, we granted a diploma neat'y printed in colors on fine paper, and signed by the county superintendent, the president of the Board of Education, and the teacher of the school to which the pupil belonged. It was deemed best not to grade these diplomas as in other counties, but fix a standard to which all should attain or not pass, which standard was fixed at seventy-five per cent of all the questions asked; also to give pupils the chance to pass on higher branches, and have them inserted on the face of their diplomas, which was thought to be a greater encouragement to scholarship than grading diplomas."

In his annual report for the year ending Aug. 31, 1879, having tried the plan another year, he says: —

"The graduating system as applied to public schools has done much to improve their general character in this county. At the graduating exercises held at the close of the schools this year, fifty-seven presented themselves for examination and graduation in the full free-school course of study. It is a source of regret to all lovers of our schools, that the law is so amended that the county superintendent hereafter cannot visit the schools, and thus assist in this work. It will be very hard to carry out this system under the present law."

Mr. J. M. Satterfield, county superintendent of Marion County, West Virginia, wrote me under date of Dec. 31, 1877: —

"Allow me to congratulate you upon the great success with which your graduating system is meeting. The system has certainly worked wonders in the short time during which it has been in operation. One by one the counties are introducing and trying it. Marion County is laying the plan to this end. Quite a number of graduating classes have been formed, some to complete the course this year. So far as I have acted in this direction, the greatest encouragement has attended me, and I am led to believe that the system has something grand in way of results for our county."

In his annual report to the State Superintendent for the year ending Aug. 31, 1878, he says: —

"This report, compared with last year's, indicates a gain or improvement in many important particulars, while I believe there is no marked falling off in any direction to be taken as unfavorable or detrimental; and while the language of figures speaks for us an advancement in the cause of education, our progress, I think I am safe in saying, is readable more in the *spirit* that is seen to pervade the different departments of the work.

"Another great auxiliary in the work with us, as it is recognized by almost every one, is our system of gradation and examination for scholars, introduced during the year. Though the extra labor demanded of me to introduce this feature, and carry on its operations during the term, was very considerable, I feel, on viewing the results, well satisfied with the project, and know that my labor has not been in vain. As I forwarded you a copy of our catalogue, reporting this work in full for the year, I will not consume space in detailing the particulars *here*, and will remark no further concerning it, save to express the earnest desire that all our county superintendents may introduce and give this system a trial."

In his annual report to the State Superintendent for the year ending Aug. 31, 1879, having tried the system two successive years, he says: —

"The graduating system introduced by me the previous year was kept in operation through the term. Ninety-seven pupils passed the examination and received certificates. One hundred and twenty-eight passed the year before; so that in all two hundred and twenty-five of our scholars have graduated, so to speak, since the plan was introduced.

"Classes have been formed for future years, and my successor informs me that he will continue the work."

Mr. G. W. Lowther, county superintendent of Ritchie County, West Virginia, in his annual report to the State Superintendent for the year ending Aug. 31, 1879, says:—

"The teachers of our county assembled in institute adopted the graduating system, as explained by Mr. Wade. It had a marked effect upon the schools."

Hon. W. K. Pendleton, State Superintendent of Free Schools of West Virginia, after watching carefully the work of the graduating system for two successive years, in his biennial report to the governor for the two years ending Aug. 31, 1878, recommends its universal adoption by law. In his report, above named, under the head of "GRADED PRIMARY INSTRUCTION," he says:—

"All education should be conducted with method; a rational progress towards a definite end is the secret of success in every undertaking. But in our primary schools, while we have a prescribed set of subjects and text-books, there is no prescribed order in which the subjects shall be studied, nor arrangement of the pupils in classes, nor designation of the time to be given to them respectively. There ought to be a beginning, a regular order of progress, and end, to the primary course of instruction. This has been felt by some of our best county superintendents; and Superintendent Wade, of Monongalia County, has succeeded in introducing a method, in the schools of his county, that has worked with admirable success. But so long as it is left to each teacher to do as he lists, with respect to the organization and conduct of school work, we can have but little system or uniformity in it. I suggest that authority be given to prescribe a regular course of primary instruction, to be generally followed in the schools, with provision for the examination and graduation of all pupils who satisfactorily complete it."

The following letter, which I received soon after the adjournment of the Legislature, shows the action of that body in this matter, and presents more fully the superintendents' proposed plan for carrying out the graduating system. The letter contains suggestions which should be carefully considered by those who think of testing this system.

DEPARTMENT OF FREE SCHOOLS STATE OF WEST VIRGINIA,
WHEELING, W. VA., April 24, 1879.

MR. A. L. WADE,
County Superintendent.

Dear Sir, — I was greatly disappointed at the action of the Legislature on the subject of grading our common schools. I prepared the following bill on the subject : —

"The State Superintendent shall prescribe a regular course of primary instruction to be followed in the schools throughout the State, arranging the order in which the several subjects shall be taken up and studied, and the time to be devoted to them respectively, with provision for advancement from class to class; also for the examination and graduation of all pupils who satisfactorily complete the prescribed course.

"He shall in like manner prescribe courses of study to be adopted and followed in graded and high schools."

This bill was adopted by the Senate, but was stricken out in the House. Had the Legislature adopted this bill, my plan was to call a meeting of the best educators in our State and agree upon a course with such flexibility as to make it adjustable to special cases, and then attempt, as far as practicable, through the institutes, to so explain and introduce it to the teachers as that in a short time all could work by it, and it could be made generally efficient.

I had cherished this amendment to our school management with especial interest, because I believe it would have done more to give efficiency and fruitfulness to our system than any other one thing that we could devise.

But our Legislature thought otherwise, or perhaps did not think about it at all, and so we must wait another two years. You will readily see, however, that the plan cannot be made to work satisfactorily without restoring the visiting feature of county superintendency (repealed by the Legislature), and at the same time securing, in many counties, superintendents of higher grade of qualification. There has, I think, been a marked improvement in our county superintendents during the last few years; and I believe it is entirely practicable, with the former salary, to raise up in due time — through the force of public sentiment, the quality of work demanded by the central management, and the advantages of experience — men as county superintendents, who would prove to be a most efficient and satisfactory arm of the school system.

Respectfully yours,

W. K. PENDLETON.

I desire now to call your attention to some official testimony which I find published in connection with the report of the State Superintendent of Public Instruction of Pennsylvania.

Mr. A. F. Silvius, county superintendent of Greene County, Pennsylvania, in his report for the year 1878, says: —

"The subject of making a classification of the schools, and of introducing a system of gradation and promotion, was submitted to a committee of teachers at the county institute, and the following is the report: —

"*Resolved*, 1. That we believe that the best interests of education demand a thorough classification of all the schools of the county; and to this end we favor the adoption of a graded course of studies that shall provide for instruction in proper order in all the common-school branches, and that we will use our influence and efforts to secure such a course of studies and classification of all the schools of this county at the earliest practicable day.

"2. That the county superintendent, with the aid and co-operation of the school directors and teachers, hold examinations in each township, for the purpose of giving those pupils found worthy of the same a certificate signed by the county superintendent, the board of directors, and the teachers constituting the examining committee, stating that the holder is a person of good moral character, and has completed the common-school course of study.

"ARGUMENTS IN FAVOR OF THE SYSTEM.

"1. It will enable our teachers to accomplish much more than they can by the present arrangement, by which the studies pursued are determined largely by the judgment of the parents or the pupils.

"2. It will enable pupils to accomplish much more than by the irregular, ill-proportioned course pursued at present.

"3. It will secure more interest and closer inspection on the part of directors and parents.

"4. It will be an incentive to pupils.

"5. It will secure more regular attendance.

"6. It will give an impulse to education.

"7. It will save money in buying books.

"8. It will direct the efforts of the county superintendent, so that he can accomplish more good than by the present mode of visitation."

"In accordance with this report," says the superintendent, "I suggested a course of study, and near the close of schools, held examinations at Garard's Fort, Taylortown, Mt. Morris, Newtown, Rogersville, Bridgeport, Carmichael's, Kinsley school-house, and Jolleytown, at which eighty-three pupils passed satisfactory examinations, and were granted diplomas. Literary exercises were connected with the examinations, and the meetings gave universal satisfaction. I know of no better means to arouse emulation among pupils, schools, and districts, and to give an impulse to education, than perfecting the system now introduced."

I wish now to present the official testimony of several county superintendents, which I find published in connection with the annual reports of the State Superintendent of Public Instruction of New Jersey. Several points worthy of the consideration of all who are interested in the graduating system, appear in this testimony. I desire to call special attention to the extended course of study for country schools, and to the several plans for examining graduating classes and holding commencement exercises. None of them, it seems, publish catalogues.

Mr. F. R. Brace, county superintendent of Camden County, New Jersey, in his annual report for the year ending Aug. 31, 1877, says:—

"It is gratifying to be able to report that the past year has been one of progress. The course of study marked out in my last report was completed in nine of our schools, and nearly reached by several others. Questions in the various branches for examination were prepared and sent to the different schools; the examination was conducted on the same day in each school, and the papers brought to me in Camden on Saturday of the same week. All the papers were examined and marked by myself. Twenty-four pupils obtained the necessary average. On June 22, in presence of the State Superintendent, the county superintendents of Burlington and Gloucester Counties, the city superintendent of Atlantic City, teachers and other friends of education, diplomas were given to the successful pupils.

"In conference with trustees and teachers, it has been thought best to extend the course of study so as to give a knowledge of the principles of mechanics, chemistry, and industrial drawing. This, we think, will give a more even development to all of our pupils, and enable them to enter, with greater facility, into any department of work. I am satisfied that our public schools can accomplish much more than has been attempted in past years, and all that can be accomplished we are in duty bound to undertake. Nearly all our teachers are in heartiest sympathy with this upward and onward movement, and I think I can say nearly every Board of Trustees is also. All that is needed is to have the course of study, the best plans, the best methods pointed out, and with intelligent work and intelligent supervision the result can be reached.

"It would be well for every teacher to know how much can be reasonably expected of him in his year's work. A regular course of study should be marked out, and every teacher expected to carry it out. There is no reason why the same results attained in the districts mentioned above should not be attained in every district in the county. There is not a difficulty in those remaining districts that does not exist in others. Many are rapidly approaching the standard. A few have only primary schools. Taking into account all hindrances and difficulties that arise from the ignorance and prejudices of trustees or parents in these few districts, I am constrained to believe that the condition of these schools is owing to the incompetence of the teachers. The work of the county can be systematized, and as much accomplished as in the large towns and cities"

In his annual report for 1878, he says:—

"The past year has been one of fair progress. The regular course of study marked out for the schools has been steadily pursued. The number passing the final examination was less than the previous year. The questions sent to the schools were more difficult. The branches in which the pupils were examined were reading, spelling, writing, geography, practical arithmetic, English grammar, history of the United States, Constitution of the United States, book-keeping, algebra, drawing, physiology, and natural philosophy. In the circular prepared for the guidance of teachers and pupils, at the examination, it was stated that the pupils who should pass in the first six branches would be deemed meritorious; in the first nine, honorable; and those who should pass in all would receive a diploma."

In his annual report for the year 1879, having tested the system three successive years, he says:—

"The regular course of study has been faithfully pursued in nearly all the schools. The number of pupils that passed the final examination in the thirteen branches of our course was twenty-six. Some districts that had pupils to pass the final examination in former years had none the last year; not because the schools have retrograded, but because pupils in the advanced classes have left the schools and gone into business, and it will take from two to three years to bring the next class up to the required grade. The grade of each school is determined mainly by the result of the examination.

"Eleven districts are now marked first-grade; nine, second-grade; ten, third-grade; eleven being below third-grade. These eleven have not had the same advantages as the other districts, either in the well-qualified, earnest, live teachers, or in deeply interested trustees. Teachers that are content to hold third-grade certificates for six or eight years, or that have not the ability to get higher-grade certificates, are not able to do the work required of them; that is, cannot do work commensurate with their pay. I am expecting a marked change in some of these districts the coming year."

Mr. Edgar Haas, county superintendent of Burlington County, New Jersey, in his annual report for the year ending Aug. 31, 1877, says:—

"Finding the schools so various in their studies, and believing that much more could be effected by having them uniform, a course of study has been prescribed for all the schools in the county, consisting of five divisions. It embraces reading, spelling, writing, arithmetic, geography, etymology, grammar, composition, United States history, mensuration, algebra, geometry, book-keeping, physiology, and natural philosophy.

"The books to be used in it are those recommended to the trustees by the county superintendent.

"It is proposed that at the end of each school year, there shall be held an examination of such pupils of the public schools of the county as have completed the course prescribed. This examination will be conducted by the County Board of Examiners, and all those who pass it will receive a county diploma, setting forth the same."

In his annual report for the year 1878, having tested the graduating system, he says:—

"The year through which we have just passed has been one of unusual gain to the schools of the county; resulting, doubtless, from the great interest taken in the prescribed course of study for the county, the County Teachers' Association, and the County Teachers' Institute.

"It is a noticeable fact that wherever we find schools that have not been classified, and that have not followed the prescribed course of study for the county (and I am glad to say that their number is becoming less and less day by day), we also find that they have, in a great measure, failed to make that progress and give that satisfaction rightfully demanded by an interested community; while on the other hand, those that have been classified and that have closely followed the prescribed course of study show highly meritorious and satisfactory work. The most marked results are those attained by thirteen schools in completing the course of study, and attested by a general examination by the county superintendent upon questions prepared by him."

"Out of the forty-eight pupils examined, there were but three that failed to reach the necessary average, seventy per cent. The other forty-five successful ones were graduated as the 'Class of 1878,' the first of the public schools of Burlington County, on the twenty-ninth day of June, in the Concert Hall at Mount Holly, in the presence of about six hundred people.

"After introductory remarks by the county superintendent, the exercises by the graduates, and a stirring address on 'The Relation of the Public Schools to the Cause of Education,' by Professor J. B. Maugham, principal of the Tuckerton schools, all enlivened with music. the county superintendent conferred upon the graduates the very neat Burlington County diploma.

"Although the graduates had not been brought together for preparation, yet they acquitted themselves most nobly and creditably through the whole of the exercises. No one present could fail to see the great interest manifested in the cause. And who, in after years, as interest increases, will be able to measure the inspiring and encouraging influence of these yearly commencements upon our schools?

"Immediately after this examination upon the course of study, eight of the successful ones, who intend to follow teaching as a profession, passed the May examination for teachers' certificates, — all standing high and receiving the third-grade certificates, the highest the law permits them now to hold."

In his annual report for the year ending Aug. 31, 1879, having still more fully tested the plan, he presents clearly the influence of the system upon the schools of his county, as follows: —

"While statistics exhibit in condensed form what has been accomplished as an end, yet they do not always show what has been employed as a means to that end; it therefore becomes my duty, if I wish to be just to myself in enumerating the amount and kind of work done, and explicit to the reader interested in educational matters, to accompany them with a brief statement, pointing out the relation between cause and effect in every important result.

"The year starting off with the great momentum of the remarkable progress of the previous year, it was expected that there would be a corresponding gain in the general results for this year. In summing up, we find that our expectations have been most eminently realized.

"The grand end and aim of our system of public schools is the assurance of a good general education to each and every child in the State; and the extent to which this is carried, is to be determined only by a thorough examination in a high course of study provided by the schools. If from year to year, under similar circumstances, the number of pupils passing such examinations continues to increase, the schools are making real, substantial power for future advancement.

"With the view of knowing the comparative standing of the schools of the county from year to year, I determined to institute just such examinations. The result of last year's examination was seen in having forty-five pupils pass the fiery ordeal. This we then pronounced a grand success. But whether its influence upon the schools would be lasting or spasmodic remained to be seen. This year seventy-two passed the examination, seemingly making a gain of sixty per cent over that of last year.

"In order to know whether this gain is real or seeming, we must take into consideration the circumstances under which it has been obtained. The one circumstance above all others to be considered is that of the age of pupils, for we cannot expect as much of tender age as of more mature years. This year the average age of those passing the examination is much less than that of those passing last year; last year there were but a few too young to graduate upon their successful examination, while this year there are fifteen, — a result showing the real clear gain to be even greater than that which appears in the figures above. Hence the excess must be attributed to other causes, and these can be but three in number: the encouragement by the parent, the enthusiasm of the teacher, and the application of the pupil. It is ever these three harmoniously working together that have produced the grand results of which we feel so proud. And thus continuing the work from year to year, our school system will soon be in a fair way of accomplishing its grand end and aim, that of giving a good general education to each and every child in the State.

"The general examination of the pupils of the schools who completed the course of study for the county was held during the week commencing Monday, the seventh day of April. There were seventy-four pupils examined, seventy-two of whom passed, the remaining two being rejected because of their inferior papers. Five of those that passed were graduates of last year, thus leaving sixty-seven fresh ones for this year; fifteen of these being too young, there remain but fifty-two to be graduated on Saturday, the thirteenth day of September, as the class of 1879, in the Concert Hall, at Mount Holly, when and where we expect to have an interesting time. Fourteen of the said fifteen too young for graduation are of the schools of the city of Burlington, and the other one is from the schools of Mount Holly."

Mr. S. R. Morse, county superintendent of Atlantic County, New Jersey, in his annual report for the year ending Aug. 31, 1878, says: —

"In order to advance the cause of education, and bring the schools to a higher standard, I called all the trustees together, and submitted a plan for a course of instruction similar to that in Camden and Burlington Counties. The trustees all heartily indorsed it. I then called the teachers together, who as heartily indorsed the plan, and a course was adopted. This course embraces reading, spelling, writing, arithmetic, geography, grammar, history, book-keeping, physiology, and algebra, and will consist of four divisions.

"The books to be used in the course are those recommended to the trustees by the county superintendent. A written examination in the last three divisions will be made in April, and all those getting above a certain average will have their names and standing published in the county papers, while all those who pass the examination in all the studies of the highest grade will receive a county certificate, to be presented at a public commencement to be held in some central place in the county. I believe this plan will be of great benefit to our schools in many respects. The teachers and pupils have an incentive to work. It will induce pupils to commence school earlier in the year, attend more regularly, and continue there longer. Parents will take more interest in the education of their children; and if moving from one district to another, the pupils can enter the same grade they have left."

In his annual report for the year ending Aug. 31, 1879, he gives the result of one year's trial of the system. He says:—

"I believe all interested persons will agree with me in the statement that more real work has been done, and greater advancement made in our schools during the year just closed, than in any previous year. Much of this is due to the course of study which has been adopted and carried out in most of the schools.

"Our Teachers' Association, Institute, and other causes have also done much good.

"The examination of all the schools, except those of Egg Harbor City and one school that had been closed, showed the difference, when a comparison was made, between those that had worked under the new plan and those that had worked under the old."

The report from which the foregoing extract is taken, shows also that the county superintendent prepared and sent, under seal, to each teacher, questions for examination of graduating classes, and that examinations were held in the several schools of the county at the same time. For the benefit of those who wish to study one of the most thorough plans for the examination of graduating classes in country schools, I copy from the report the following circular of instruction to teachers: —

"1. The teacher will not open the envelopes containing the questions before the date marked on them, and then in the presence of the school.

"2. The teacher will hold the examination on the days designated by the county superintendent, and in his or her own school-room.

"3. The teacher will open envelope No. 1 the first day, and, taking out one subject at a time, in the order numbered, write as many of the questions on the blackboard as he thinks can be answered before intermission. The second-day envelope No. 2 will be opened in the same manner.

"4. No explanations of *any* kind are to be given by the teacher or other person.

"5. The teacher will seat the pupils in such a manner that no two pupils of the same grade shall be near each other.

"6. All books will be removed from the desks, all maps and charts rolled up, and no pupil allowed to have aid from any source.

"7. The papers must be sent or handed to the county superintendent just as the pupil left them. Any help given, or corrections made, will render the papers null.

"8. Each pupil will write his name and the subject of examination at the head of each page. The pupils need not copy the questions, but number each and leave one space between each answer. If they cannot answer a question, they will number it and write, 'I cannot answer.'

"9. The pupils are requested to take great care of their papers, as they will be preserved. The work may be done on waste paper or a slate, and then copied before handed to the teacher, but not afterward; neither can any mistakes be corrected.

"10. In all mathematical questions the pupils will give the work as well as the result.

"11. No one can leave the room till the set of questions is completed and handed to the teacher, except at intermission; then only those who have completed the set."

I propose to conclude this testimony by submitting the following appreciative letter from Hon. E. A. Apgar, State Superintendent of Public Instruction of the State of New Jersey:—

STATE OF NEW JERSEY,
DEPARTMENT OF PUBLIC INSTRUCTION,
TRENTON, Feb. 4, 1880.

MR. A. L. WADE, *Morgantown, West Virginia.*

My Dear Sir,— I have examined your "Graduating System for Country Schools" with both pleasure and profit. I regard it as eminently practical, and calculated, where introduced, to elevate our country schools to the standard of our best village and city schools.

Wishing you success, I am,
Yours truly,

ELIAS A. APGAR,
State Superintendent of Public Instruction.

I submit, without argument, the foregoing official testimony of those who have tried the graduating system.

LECTURE VII.

EDITORIAL REVIEWS OF THE GRADUATING SYSTEM BY LEADING EDUCATIONAL JOURNALS.

HAVING, for three successive years, tested the merits of the graduating system, I determined, in the autumn of 1878, to make an effort to present it more fully to the public. To this end, I sent copies of the catalogue containing my annual report to a few of the foremost educational journals, widely separated from each other, in sundry sections of the United States. I wrote to each editor, requesting that the system might be reviewed, criticised, condemned, or approved. The unanimity of sentiment expressed by these journals may be seen in the following editorials.

The January number, 1879, of "The Teacher," Philadelphia, concludes its notice of the graduating system for country schools, as set forth in the Third Annual Catalogue of the Free Schools of Monongalia County, West Virginia, in these words: —

"It remained for the latter half of the nineteenth century to originate, develop, and mature such a free-school system as would challenge the admiration of the nations of the earth. Germany, deep in its lore, rich in its universities and academic halls, has invited our system to her shores; and far-off Japan already has planted the nucleus which must soon change still more largely its ancient landmarks. The graduating system, as described in the pamphlet before us, is a grand forward step in the march of education. We hail with satisfaction an appliance of this kind, coming, as it does, from a live teacher, and exhibiting the results of practical experience in the school-room."

The "American Journal of Education," St. Louis, March number, 1879, presents at some length, without comment, the West Virginia graduating system for country schools. In the April number, 1879, of that journal, the editor gives his opinion of the plan, in the following words: —

"We hope the article on 'Schools in West Virginia,' published in our last issue, was very carefully read.

"We see in it many things to admire and to commend.

"As a means of interesting both the pupil and the parent, it proved to be eminently successful. The parents, too, were tax-payers, and it gave the teachers an opportunity to demonstrate to the tax-payers the worth and the measure of their work. We should have more liberal *estimates* made for all our schools in this State, if the tax-payers knew what and how much our teachers are doing.

"Not knowing much about it, they are disposed to

cut down the estimates for teachers' wages and other necessary things to the lowest figure possible.

"For this, our teachers themselves are very much to blame. They do not take care that the tax-payers shall be kept well posted on what the schools are doing, — on what improvements are being made.

"This graduating system, adopted and so successfully carried out by Mr. A. L. Wade, of Monongalia County, West Virginia, would certainly work a much-needed reform in this direction.

"There is so much of real practical value in it, touching as it does this vital question of the *worth* and the work of our teachers, that we are disposed to strongly commend it to the attention of our friends all through the West and South."

The "Educational Weekly," Chicago, of March 28, 1879, contains a critical review of this system. Under the head of "Grading Country Schools," the editor says : —

"Mr. A. L. Wade, of Morgantown, West Virginia, county superintendent of schools, has introduced, and carried forward to gratifying results, a graduating system in the public schools of Monongalia County, which has attracted considerable attention in neighboring counties, and which has been adopted in several other counties in that State and in various places in Western Pennsylvania. The various features of this system have been discussed at most of the teachers' associations throughout the country, although their adoption has not in general been thought advisable. According to Mr. Wade, the plan which he has so successfully carried out for four years past has produced an educational revival in that part of the country. According to his plan, a course of study is adopted for the free-school branches, the more advanced pupils being organized into four separate classes, according to their grades. A time is fixed in which each pupil is expected to complete the course; an annual examination is held, with commencement exercises in each district, and diplomas are granted to those who, upon examination, are found to be worthy of them. Among these graduates alumni associations are formed, and an annual catalogue is published, in which the names of graduates and undergraduates appear in the classes to which they respectively belong. It is simply applying to *primary schoo's* a system which, centuries ago, was adopted in universities and colleges, and more recently in academies and high schools.

"There can be no question but that such a course will very materially quicken the interest of both pupils and parents in the public schools. The same personal ambition is appealed to in the children as that which inspires the academic or college student to apply himself diligently to his studies, and finally graduate from the course with a formal certificate of attainments. And this is also the testimony of Superintendent Wade, after having well tried the plan. He says, 'Wherever it has been properly tested, it has created an interest among pupils and parents never before witnessed in free-school work.' He furnishes abundant testimony of a similar kind from others who have tried the plan, and strongly urges its general adoption throughout the country.

"The tendency toward such a graduating system is apparent in the public schools of the cities and larger villages everywhere. Each year some city school adopts for the first time the practice of giving diplomas or certificates to pupils who are not expecting to remain in school long enough to reach the highest department. And where the rural schools are competently superintended and the patrons are generally constant from year to year, it is not only possible, but certainly desirable, that the course of study should be definite and uniform in the various districts of a county. However, without a competent superintendency, such a system would result in just that which is now everywhere condemned and in too many places practised, especially in the primary grades, — viz., a system of cramming and overwork, which is the result of an ambition to accomplish the most possible in the shortest time. If, with the experience and ability of our city superintendents and teachers, there is still an evident excess of competition, too much high pressure, and too little individual instruction, how can younger and less experienced teachers be expected to avoid these evils? Further, it may be tolerable for the young man or woman in academy or college to be placed on — his, her, their — mettle, and tested to the highest capacity; yet if such strain should be placed upon the delicate and sensitive nature of childhood, the result would be disastrous in the extreme. It is just this fault which is to-day provoking most criticism and threatening most seriously the unity of the system in large cities. The lower grades are suffering from over-taxation. Too much is required of pupils and teachers, as the result of severe grading. The memory is pressed beyond its natural capacity, and the education of the child is lost sight of in the anxiety to accomplish the results indicated by the printed course.

"This question is one of great importance in the administration of our public-school system, and the friends of that system should give it fair and sober consideration. While, therefore, the 'Weekly' would approve and defend every such movement as that of Superintendent Wade in West Virginia, if judiciously and wisely conducted, it would caution all who are devoted to such progressive steps to advance slowly, and carefully guard against abuses which are apt to follow close upon the heels of all true progress. Anything which will elevate the teacher and his work, anything which will deepen the interest of parents in the education of their children and secure for the teachers and the schools better facilities and better compensation, anything which will tend to popularize the public schools of the country, should receive the encouragement of all who have been connected with these schools as teachers or pupils, and thus learned by experience their value and importance to the highest interests of the people and the nation."

It may not be amiss to call attention to the fact that the criticisms contained in the foregoing article are aimed, mainly, at severe grading in the lower departments of the schools of large cities, and not at the system under consideration. The evil complained of is carefully guarded against in the graduating system for country schools, where, as stated in a former lecture, only the older and more advanced pupils are permitted to have their names entered for graduation.

"Barnes's Educational Monthly," New York, February number, 1879, contains an editorial entitled "Our Common-School System," which I present in full. The editor says: —

"The question has frequently been asked of late, What is meant by a common-school course? It has been nothing but a mixture of reading, writing, and arithmetic, with a quantity of geography, history, and science, in quantities to suit the taste; there has been no course in it. In a multitude of cases, what a child studies depends upon the blind judgment of parents or the momentary convenience or caprice of teachers. The so-called common-school course is no course at all. We most earnestly commend any superintendent or teacher who can suggest any way by which order can be obtained and the confusion now existing avoided. Mr. A. L. Wade, county superintendent, Monongalia County, West Virginia, has done more in this direction than any other person of whom we have heard. In his work he has accomplished the following results, which we commend to all similar workers throughout the Union: —

"1. The primary branches are taken up as one course of study for graduation.

"2. The time in which each advanced pupil agrees to complete a certain course is fixed.

"3. Public examinations of graduating classes are held annually, and diplomas are granted to those who complete prescribed courses.

"4. Alumni associations of those who have graduated are formed.

"5. An annual catalogue containing the names of all advanced pupils attending school in the county during the year is published. In this catalogue the names of all pupils are placed in their appropriate classes, showing from year to year what advancement has been made.

"In all this work there is needed careful and intelligent supervision. The plan is admirable; and if it should be universally adopted, it would give our county commissioners and superintendents a definite work to do, and unify our common schools, so that we could point, with some show of truth and reason, to the common-school system of the United States of America."

The "New England Journal of Education," Boston, May 8, 1879, published the foregoing article from "Barnes's Educational Monthly," and adds: "We hope to examine the results of Mr. Wade's efforts more fully, when we shall be better able to judge of their merits."

I might greatly multiply these editorial reviews by including those of later date, as many leading educational journals have recently reviewed the system; but I propose to conclude this subject by presenting a single additional article.

The "Monthly Normal Review," July number, 1879, contains a leading editorial on the graduating system, from which I make the following extract: —

"It is simply the application to primary schools of a well-grounded principle employed in all higher schools. Every student who enters college, for example, has his course mapped out for him. He may do more, but there is a minimum of work which he must do. So here, as soon as a child passes from the preparatory grade to his class, he knows how much work he has to do, and how much time he has for doing it. It insures also a variety of studies; and we do not believe Mr. Wade states it too strongly when he says, 'My opinion is that a pupil from fourteen to sixteen years of age, who has had some advantages in school, will do better in *each branch*, if he takes up the entire free-school course, than he will do if he takes up nothing beyond arithmetic.' It furnishes the pupil an incentive to work. He has publicly pledged himself to accomplish a certain thing, and has associated himself with others striving for the same end; and now it is no longer the teacher who urges him on, but his own self-pride, his emulative feeling, his love for the approval of friends, and added to these, and equally potent with any of them, the desire for the approval and fear of the condemnation of public opinion, at whose bar he is now judged. Our country schools certainly need some attention, and we know of no plan more promising of good than this. It has been tried in some places, and we would gladly see it adopted in more; for though objections may be found to it, nevertheless it is a step in the right direction, and it is certainly freer from faults than many other plans already in vogue. At the very least it merits a fair trial and a full discussion, and we hope it may have both these as soon as possible."

LECTURE VIII.

WHAT LEADING EDUCATORS SAY OF THE GRADUATING SYSTEM.

I HAVE, in the course of these lectures, presented the official testimony of State and county superintendents who have tried the graduating system; I have brought forward editorial reviews from some of the leading educational journals, and I now offer the carefully prepared opinions of other distinguished educators.

I shall first present the opinion of Dr. James G. Blair, principal of the State Normal School at Fairmont, West Virginia, and formerly vice-president of the University of Ohio. In the September number, 1876, of the "West Virginia Educational Monthly," of which he was editor, he discusses, at length, the graduating system for country schools, which had then been tested in but one county in the United States, and draws his conclusions in the following words:—

"The plan is eminently practical, and unifies the schools of the county into one working graded school. It places before the teachers of the county a definite object to be accomplished. That object is feasible.

It requires progress, and avoids spurious efforts with no definite aim. It marks each step in the work of both teacher and pupil, and cannot fail to enlist the ambition of both the schools and communities. Each step in the pupil's progress is noted, and when the work is done the diploma is awarded.

"This plan links in the educational talent of the county, and uses it advantageously in the details of its work. It thus popularizes the educational work, and makes parents equally interested with their children. Superintendents in West Virginia will do a great work if they will adopt this system in their several counties. It would give West Virginia an advantage which no State in the Union, so far as we now know, possesses."

Hon. John D. Philbrick, for many years city superintendent of the schools of Boston, and late Educational Commissioner from the United States to the Paris Exposition, in the following letter gives his opinion of the graduating system: —

36 DARTMOUTH STREET, BOSTON, Feb. 28, 1879.

Dear Sir, — I have the honor to acknowledge the receipt of your letter of the 22d inst., with the accompanying copy of your report as county superintendent of schools.

I have read with interest your account of the "graduating system," and I cheerfully comply with your request to give you my opinion of it. The essential features of the system, as I understand it, consist of three elements, namely: —

1. The classification of the pupils according to their grade of advancement, in *all* the required branches.

2. A final examination each year, to ascertain what pupils

have satisfactorily completed the prescribed course of instruction.

3. The granting of diplomas to such pupils as have completed the course.

To your system, so far as it embraces these features, I give my cordial approval. Wisely administered, it would produce, without doubt, very beneficial results.

I have never before heard of such a system being thoroughly carried out in all its details in the rural districts in the country. In its application to city schools the plan is not novel. The system of classification and graduation has been in operation in the common schools of this city from time immemorial. About ten years ago the diploma feature was added, and it has produced excellent results. It has been the fashion here for nearly a century to have, at each school, annually, at the time of graduation, a public examination or exhibition.

But the system is liable to abuses, which should be carefully looked after.

1. The *high-pressure* abuse, — too much stimulus, especially in the case of girls.

2. The *cramming abuse*, — the loading of the memory in preparation for an examination.

3. The *competition abuse*, — teachers more anxious to *put through* a large number of graduates than to *educate* them in the best manner.

4. The *show abuse*, — the showing off of pupils on the commencement occasion, and especially *young* pupils, which is the general curse of Sunday-school exhibitions and concerts.

From your report I feel convinced that you are doing an admirable work, and I have no doubt that your county ought to be marked as a bright spot on the educational map of the country. Very truly yours,

JOHN D. PHILBRICK.

A. L. WADE, Esq.,
    Superintendent Schools,
        Monongalia County, W. Va.

I desire now to present a letter from a State superintendent in the South, giving his opinion of the graduating system: —

OFFICE OF STATE SUPERINTENDENT OF PUBLIC SCHOOLS,
NASHVILLE, TENN., Feb. 25, 1880.

Mr. A. L. WADE,
Morgantown, W. Va.

Dear Sir, — I have read your report with great pleasure, and am satisfied that under the supervision of a competent, diligent, and active supervisor, your plan for graduating in public schools will greatly improve the schools in any county or State.

Yours very truly,
LEON. TROUSDALE,
State Superintendent.

The following letter from Hon. John W. Simonds, late State Superintendent of New Hampshire, shows the light in which he views this system: —

FRANKLIN, N. H., Dec. 5, 1879.

MR. A. L. WADE,
County Superintendent of Schools,
Morgantown, W. Va.

My Dear Sir, — The pamphlet containing your address on "A Graduating System for Country Schools" was received, read, and carefully considered. I heartily approve of your plan, and have no doubt, if it were generally adopted, it would add great interest to our public schools, and prevent many of the wastes that now impair their efficiency.

A lack of interest and many sources of waste have fastened their pernicious influences upon the public-school system, from the want of an intelligent and well-devised plan for directing teachers and scholars in their work. Your system, as I understand it, proposes to remedy these defects by establishing a well-arranged course of study and providing for suitable examinations, and at the same time secure a general awakening of interest in school-work on the part of teachers, scholars, and parents.

Very respectfully,
JOHN W. SIMONDS,
Late State Superintendent of Public Instruction.

I find the following article in the March number, 1880, of the "Excelsior Quarterly," Farmington, Me. It is from the pen of Professor William Harper, of Farmington Normal School. Under the heading, "Why not graduate Pupils in Country Schools as well as Others?" Professor Harper says:—

"The educational requirements of these days of steam and lightning, when 'many run to and fro, and knowledge is increased,' are not only greater than ever before, but constantly increasing. This is so evident to every observer that proof is unnecessary, and it follows that our schools must be kept constantly improving, in order to meet the demands upon them *as well as formerly.* But we cannot reasonably be satisfied even with that, for the schools of our fathers certainly were not perfect; and indeed, in view of the interests represented in every school-room, it is not too much to say that no school is good enough, nor ever will be.

"Country schools generally labor under various disadvantages which do not affect the village and city schools, such as lack of a regular course of study, so that the work is without beginning or end, and consequently loses greatly in interest, and the same work is sometimes taken over and over with little or no advantage to the pupil. There is also frequently a lack of efficient supervision, and a small and perhaps diminishing attendance. Hence it becomes doubly necessary that whatever is practicable should be done for their improvement.

"Mr. A. L. Wade, of Morgantown, West Virginia, has devised, and in his work as county superintendent of schools carried into successful execution, the common-sense plan of a graduating system, long ago successfully applied in all other grades of schools. He forms four classes in each school, so far as the requisite material exists, to complete the course of study and graduate in successive years. The remainder of the school constitutes the preparatory department. Annual examinations with regular commencement exercises are held, and diplomas are conferred, but only on those who successfully pass the examinations; and the names of the graduates, with considerable other information regarding each school, are published in the annual report. Various other means, such as would naturally suggest themselves to an enthusiastic worker, are also employed to enlist the interest and co-operation of parents, teachers, the press, and the friends of education generally.

"The results have been wonderful; a true educational revival has taken place, and the interest has continued unabated during the four years in which the system has been in operation. Among the definite results are the following: —

"1. Increased interest of the pupils.

"2. Far greater progress; all the advanced studies prescribed by law (in West Virginia they are arithmetic, grammar, history, and geography) being completed in *less* time than *one* previously. Experienced teachers will not think this by any means incredible; and a method which makes the school worth more than four times as much to many of the scholars, to say nothing of the value of the better habits formed, is certainly worthy of a trial everywhere.

"3. The attendance increased twenty per cent in a single year.

"4. School discipline is more easily maintained, on account of the greater interest of pupils in their work.

"Connected with these results there must be many others scarcely less valuable, such as better and improving teachers, better habits formed by pupils, which for very many of them decides the question of their success in life, longer terms of school and less frequent changes of teachers, more interest and co-operation on the part of parents, etc.

"The State Educational Association of Maine, at its recent meeting in Gardiner, after a presentation and discussion of the system, indorsed it by the following resolution: —

"'*Resolved*, That a course of study for all our common schools, such as will admit of a regular graduation therefrom, is of the greatest importance, and we would recommend to all concerned in the management of such schools, an examination of Wade's system of graduation in West Virginia.'

"It has also received wide indorsements elsewhere, and is exciting interest from Maine to California. The next annual report of the National Bureau of Education will contain an account of it."

Professor F H. Crago, principal of the public schools of Moundsville, West Virginia, and lately nominee of the minority party of his State for the office of General Superintendent of Public Instruction, having thorough personal knowledge of the work of this system, in an article published in the "Intelligencer," Wheeling, West Virginia, March 4, 1879, says:—

"I think I am prepared to speak knowingly, as to the workings of Superintendent Wade's system. I regard it a great success. I find less opposition to it now than two years ago, larger audiences at examinations, larger classes, and classes that compare favorably with former classes. One excellent feature, I notice, is that many of those who graduated in former years are still attending school pursuing higher branches, and are in attendance at the examinations, ready and willing to express an opinion whenever called on to do so. I give it as my opinion that Mr. Wade's plan is the plan to revolutionize our free-school system. It is attracting attention all over the land; and if our school system is made thoroughly effective, something of this kind must do it."

I have presented the carefully prepared opinions of eminent educators of several States. I offer, in conclusion, the views of a number of leading educators of a single State.

The "National Journal of Education," Boston, Jan. 8, 1880, contains an account of the thirteenth annual meeting of the State Educational Association of Maine, held at Gardiner, Dec. 30 and 31, 1879, and Jan. 1, 1880. Among the proceedings of this association there is an abstract of a paper on "Wade's Graduating System for Country Schools," read by Wm. Harper, of Farmington. As the article which I have already presented from Mr. Harper's pen embraces the leading features of this paper, I will present only the discussions which followed its reading and the conclusions reached by the association: —

"DISCUSSION.

"G. A. Robertson, of Augusta, opened the discussion, and favored the idea of having graduating exercises in all the country schools. They would tend to hold the pupils in the schools until some regular course of study could be completed. Such exercises would help to quicken the interest in the communities toward the schools and teachers. One of the first things to be accomplished in the improvement of the country school is the establishment of a course of study which should be uniform for this class of schools throughout the State.

"Hon. E. S. Morris, State Superintendent, strongly

favored the plans of Mr. Wade, of West Virginia, as far as he understood them, and was decided in the opinion that a uniform course of study should be adopted. Such action would produce a continuity of teaching. Too much time is expended under present management in getting new teachers to work. Every new term of twelve weeks is half spent in finding out what to do.

"REPORT OF COMMITTEE.

"C. C. Rounds, chairman of the Committee on Resolutions, reported the following, which were adopted : —

"*Resolved*, That some system of examination and certificating teachers, that shall be effective in securing qualified teachers for all grades uniform throughout the State, and shall carry with it an authority recognized throughout the State, is absolutely necessary to any marked advance in public instruction.

"*Resolved*, That a course of study for all our common schools, such as will admit of a regular graduation therefrom, is of the greatest importance, and we would recommend to all concerned in the management of such schools an examination of Wade's system of graduation, in West Virginia."

LECTURE IX.

THE GRADUATING SYSTEM SUITED TO THE PRIMARY SCHOOLS OF CITIES AND TOWNS.

Though the avowed aim of the plan which I have been presenting is the improvement of country schools, the system is admirably adapted to the primary schools of cities and towns. In support of this declaration I offer the testimony of a distinguished educator, who has seen the system thoroughly tested in the primary schools of a great city. Hon. John D. Philbrick, of Boston, in a letter dated Feb. 28, 1879, which I have already presented, in speaking of the graduating system, says: "In its application to city schools the plan is not novel. The system of classification and graduation has been in operation in the common schools of this city from time immemorial. About ten years ago the diploma feature was added, and it has produced excellent results."

While Boston and several other cities and towns have adopted this system in primary schools, the plan is by no means universal.

When we consider the fact that in cities and towns most of the youth leave school before they have finished the higher courses of study, and a majority of them before they have accomplished even the common branches, it is evident that there is need of a popular plan which will induce pupils to remain in school until a course of study of some kind is *completed*. However desirable it may be to have the masses highly cultured, it is not absolutely necessary, neither is it at present possible even in cities, for *all* to obtain a high-school education. A fair knowledge of the common-school branches is a necessity, and it is the duty of educators everywhere to see that all obtain this knowledge. In order to accomplish this desirable purpose, a more popular element — an element that will move the masses — must be introduced into the public schools of cities and towns. The laboring classes, especially, should be enlisted in the cause of popular education. Parents and pupils must be inspired with a zeal in favor of a thorough common-school education; and this can be readily accomplished under the graduating system.

The schools of cities and towns, being graded, and having the advantages of thorough supervision, are already prepared for the introduction of this plan. All that is wanted in such cases is an arrangement to graduate pupils in the common branches, as well as in the higher courses of study. The graduating exercises of the common-school department should be made as popular as possible. An annual catalogue of each ward school should be published and placed in every interested family. The names of graduates and undergraduates in the common-school course should occupy a prominent place in this catalogue. The student of human nature can conceive of the influence which this catalogue will exert in leading pupils to complete a course of study, and in prompting parents to take a deeper interest in the educational work.

But the best work of this system remains to be seen after the school period is ended. The impetus given by habits of study, in this course of training in the common branches, not only causes pupils to remain longer in school than they otherwise would do, but tends to keep up through life better modes of thinking. Alumni associations, for the mutual improvement of those who have graduated in the common branches, should be organized in every ward in the city. In addition to the public performances at the annual meetings, these associations should be organized into reading societies of the common people, where pure literature, taking the place of the sensational newspaper of the baser sort, would form the mental food for the masses, thereby turning the current of popular thought into purer channels.

The pioneer thinkers of the present day are beginning to inquire whether it would not be to the best interests of society to provide, under the public-school system, in all our great cities, for supplying young people, even after they leave school, with suitable reading matter. I am not aware that any public journal has taken ground in favor of such an advanced movement; but the *need* of something of this kind is clearly seen in the following extract from an editorial in the March number, 1880, of the "Atlantic Monthly." In speaking of public schools, the editor says: "Long experience has proved that it is a doubtful blessing to teach a man to read, and then turn him upon the world to pick up such further education as the cheap literature of great cities affords. The immense sale of sensational newspapers of the worst class proves this fact, and is admitted to be one of the most threatening signs of the times."

The best interests of society, when left uncared for by the law-maker, must be provided for by the philanthropist, and this want of reading-matter is met in large cities by public libraries; but public libraries avail nothing unless they reach the people. What we most need in this direction at present, in towns and cities, is a supplement to our public-school system for holding young people together as students, in organized bodies, after they leave school. In order to meet this want, the graduating system should be adopted and carefully carried out in all the common schools of cities and towns.

LECTURE X.

THE GRADUATING SYSTEM CONSIDERED AND COMMENDED BY THE NATIONAL EDUCATIONAL ASSOCIATION.

FINDING in the spring of 1879 that the graduating system was receiving from the press and the people of other States where it had been presented the same popular favor which had attended it in West Virginia, I sent a copy of my official report to Hon. John Hancock, of Dayton, Ohio, who was then president of the National Educational Association, asking his opinion of the system. In his response, bearing date April 8, 1879, he says: —

"I have read your report with much interest, and most heartily commend your graduating system for primary schools as worthy the consideration of educators throughout the country. I make no question that the system will serve a very valuable purpose in stimulating youth to greater exertions in study, and at once prove an incentive to the acquisition of knowledge both effectual and healthy."

President Hancock, after expressing an earnest desire that this system should be presented at the next meeting of the National Educational Association, to be held in Philadelphia the 29th, 30th, and 31st of the following July, further says: —

"Our programme for the general meetings of the National Association was about completed when you wrote me; but it is possible there may be a vacant place on the programme of the Elementary department, which would be a good place for the presentation of this topic. I shall write to the gentleman at the head of that department at once, to ascertain whether such be the case; and in case there is, will recommend him to open a correspondence with you. The head of this department is Professor G. P. Brown, of Toledo, Ohio."

Soon after this I received a letter on this subject from Professor Brown, of Toledo, in which he says, "The subject is an important one, and I will give it a place on the programme if I can."

At a later date I received a letter from the president, asking me if I would accept a place upon the programme for the presentation of this subject. In accordance with this invitation I prepared and read a paper entitled "A Graduating System for Country Schools." On the following day, July 31, 1879, the General Association adopted a resolution, of which the following is an official copy: —

"At the eighteenth annual meeting of the National Educational Association, held in the city of Philadelphia on July 29, 30, and 31, 1879, a resolution presented by Superintendent A. L. Wade, of Morganntown, West Virginia, was, on motion of

President G. P. Hays, of Washington, Pennsylvania, amended, and passed by the Association : —

"*Resolved*, That the attention of State superintendents of public instruction throughout the United States be called to the propriety of adopting a graduating system for country schools. Attest:

"W. D. HENKLE,
Sec. Nat. Ed. Asso."

LECTURE XI.

OBJECTIONS TO THE GRADUATING SYSTEM CONSIDERED AND ANSWERED.

I propose in this lecture to consider and answer such objections as have been urged against the graduating system for country schools. From what I have observed in the foremost educational journals, from what I have seen in the opinions of leading educators, and from what I have learned in my associations with the people, I conclude that the principal objections to this system consist of four elements, namely: —

1. The graduating system may produce too much excitement, and place too heavy a strain upon childhood.

2. The graduating system may encourage cramming, and not furnish true education.

3. The graduating system cannot be successfully carried out without thorough school supervision.

4. Graduation may lead the pupil to conclude that he has learned all, and thereby cause him to cease to study.

In attempting to answer the first objection, I desire to repeat what I have heretofore stated, that under this system none but the older and more advanced pupils are permitted to have their names entered for

OBJECTIONS TO THE GRADUATING SYSTEM. 139

graduation. Close observation leads me to conclude that it is safe to allow a healthful pupil, ten or twelve years of age, who has already made a fair start in study, to undertake to complete the common branches in four years. It is true that under this system the younger pupils look forward with great interest to the time when their names will appear in the catalogue. This interest, however, is entirely pleasurable; and it requires no argument to prove to intelligent people that a considerable degree of pleasurable stimulus is more healthful for pupils than painful confinement in the school-room, without sufficient motives to study. This objection to the graduating system, when applied to country schools, which are kept open in many places less than half the year, where pupils have plenty of pure air and exercise, is but a feeble argument. It may be urged with greater force against the graduating system in colleges, academies, and all schools of high order, which are kept open nine or ten months of the year, and where pupils have but little exercise in the open air.

In attempting to answer the second objection to this system, I wish to call attention to the several modes of conducting examinations of graduating classes in country schools. So far as official reports have thrown light upon this subject, three methods have been adopted, namely: —

1. Examinations and commencement exercises, conducted by the county superintendent, are held at several points in each county.

2. An examination with commencement exercises, conducted by the superintendent, is held at the county seat.

3. Questions on the various branches are prepared by the superintendent, and sent, under seal, to each teacher; a written examination is conducted on the same day in each school throughout the county; examination papers are sent to the county superintendent, who inspects and marks them; and at a commencement exercise subsequently held at the county seat, the superintendent grants diplomas to those who are found worthy of them.

In all three of the modes named, the county superintendent either prepares the questions or conducts the exercises. It is evident to every thoughtful teacher and pupil, that cramming is poor preparation for examination, when it is known that a stranger will prepare the questions and conduct the exercises. In all schools of high order where the instructors themselves examine the graduating classes, the cramming or pouring-in system could be more successfully carried out, without detection, than it could be under a graduating system in country schools.

I come now to consider the third objection to this system; viz., "It cannot be successfully carried out without thorough school supervision." The evidence of educational experts who have testified upon this subject proves the truth of this charge, and I will not attempt to deny it. Instead, however, of this being an objection to the system, it is, in the judgment of many, an argument in its favor. It proves that the system has the ring of business about it. No joint company composed of sensible stockholders could be induced to employ, from year to year, two or three hundred laborers or operatives, without placing over them a skilful superintendent. Skilful supervision is everywhere regarded essential in all matters of business, and is universally acknowledged to be absolutely necessary in schools of high order. Then, if every college must have its president, if every high school must have its principal, if every extensive firm or factory must have its manager, why leave the schools of the masses in the hands of young and inexperienced teachers without thorough supervision? If want of skilful supervision in a cotton factory will produce bankruptcy, what may we expect from the same course in the common schools of a county? The fact that the necessity for supervision in country schools is, in many places, at this time, unsettled, is proof that these schools have not been conducted upon a business basis; and the fact that the graduating system for country schools cannot be successfully carried out without thorough school supervision, is a strong argument in its favor.

In conclusion, I invite your attention to the fourth and last objection to the graduating system; namely, "Graduation may lead the pupil to conclude that he has learned all, and thereby cause him to cease to study." This objection, which is not offered by educators, but by some parents who have not seen the system tested, reminds me of the story of little Johnny Ray. Johnny, it seems, had learned his letters under the old A B C method, without having any intimation from the teacher that these letters are the keys to unlock the storehouses of knowledge. The story is rendered in rhyme, after this fashion: —

"He did n't like to go to school,
　He only wished to play;
A lesson was a dreadful thing
　To little Johnny Ray.

"The letters of the alphabet
　Seemed hard as hard could be;
He toiled and fretted from great A
　Way down to little z.

"But work will win. He conquered all
　At last from A to &;
Then like a victor home he marched,
　The primer in his hand.

"'I shall not have to go to school,'
　Said Johnny, 'any more!'
And, like a colt from harness free,
　He capered on the floor.

"'Why not?' asked kind papa, and held
　The boy with kite and ball;
He answered with an air assured,
　'Because I 've learned it all!'"

Johnny's joy at his success was natural. It was the feeling of one who had completed an undertaking. His pleasure, however, would have been much greater, his dislike for school would have been much less, and his conclusions would have been widely different, if he had been taught under more modern methods. The time was when country people in some places regarded graduation as an end of study; but this view of the subject is now considered by most persons as ludicrous as the conclusions of little Johnny Ray.

Experience has proven that habits of study formed while pursuing a course for graduation are likely to last through life. Alumni associations, holding annual meetings for the mutual improvement of those who have graduated in country schools, are likely to ripen into reading societies, and thereby to greatly increase the general intelligence of the common people.

I have, in the course of these lectures, presented the needs of our country schools and the aims of the graduating system; I have defined the graduating system and shown the mode of its application; I have given a history of its origin, trials, triumphs, and growth; I have taken the official testimony of superintendents in three several States who have tried the system; I have reported the action of the National Educational Association calling the attention of State superintendents to the propriety of its adoption; I have proven that the plan is suited to the primary schools of cities and towns; and I have considered and answered such objections as have been urged against the system. In subsequent lectures I propo e to discuss various subjects of vital importance to the educational work of the country.

LECTURE XII.

COUNTRY SCHOOL-HOUSES. — NEED OF A NATIONAL
ARCHITECT.

THE country school-house is one of the most important elements in our educational work. It is idle to expect the highest progress in public education, even under the most thorough teachers, if school-houses are so arranged as to render pupils unhealthy or unhappy. The most earnest teachers and the most interesting text-books "become as sounding brass or tinkling cymbals" in school-rooms which are imperfectly heated or improperly ventilated. Mental growth, like vegetable growth, is largely dependent upon surrounding circumstances.

Farmers are familiar with the fact that warmth, sunlight, and showers are essential to the growth of grass and grain. They are aware that the greatest industry on the part of the laborer can never make up for the want of these elements, and that the application of the most powerful fertilizers, in the absence of these essentials, is simply waste of time and money, as such soil can produce at best only short-lived, sickly plants.

Millions of money have been expended in efforts

to educate the masses under circumstances not less forbidding than would be an attempt to raise grain in a forest. Careful thinkers and close observers agree that ill-arranged school-houses have, in times past, not only restrained mental growth, but greatly impaired public health.

It is confidently believed, however, that a better day has already dawned. Never in the past history of public education was there so general an effort, as at present, to render school-houses healthful, convenient, and handsome. Men of means are offering liberal rewards to architects for the most suitable plans for public school buildings; and the wisest business men are taking ground that it pays a county, State, or country to construct school-houses with a proper regard to style and finish, as well as to comfort and convenience.

The publishers of the "Sanitary Engineer," New York, recently offered the sum of $500, in four prizes, to be paid to the parties submitting the four best designs for a public school-house. The desire of the publishers offering these prizes was to obtain a plan for a school building which would have an abundance of fresh air and no drafts; plenty of light, without the least glare; and suitable apparatus for warming alike every part of the room early in the morning, and never to get too hot or too cold at any part of the day. Over one hundred and eighty plans were placed on exhibition at the Academy of Design, New York, in response to the competition instituted by the offer of these prizes. These plans were in the highest sense representative, having been contributed by architects from all parts of the Union, and also from Canada, and one from a Japanese architect. These designs were examined by a committee appointed for that purpose, and the several prizes were awarded as follows : The first prize, $250, was awarded to Arthur T. Mathews, of Oakland, California; the second, $125, to Samuel F. Thayer, of Boston; the third, $75, to H. C. Koch & Co., of Milwaukee; and the fourth, $50, to R. G. Kennedy, of Philadelphia.

Accompanying the report of this committee are several vital recommendations, from which I select the following :—

1. "In each school-room not less than fifteen square feet of floor area should be allotted to each pupil.

2. "In each school-room the window space should not be less than one fourth of the floor space, and the distance of the desk most remote from the window should not be more than one and one half times the height of the top of the window from the floor.

3. "The height of a school-room should never exceed fourteen feet.

4. "The provisions for ventilation should be such as to provide for each person in a school-room not less than thirty cubic feet of fresh air per minute, which amount must be introduced and thoroughly distributed without creating unpleasant draughts, or causing any two parts of the room to differ in temperature more than 20° F., or the maximum temperature to exceed

70°. This means that for a school-room to contain fifty-six pupils, twenty-eight cubic feet of air per second should be continuously furnished, distributed, and removed during school sessions. The velocity of the incoming air should not exceed two feet per second at any point where it is liable to strike on the person.

5. "The heating of the fresh air should be effected either by hot water or by low pressure steam.

6. "The fresh air should be introduced near the windows; the foul air should be removed by flues in the opposite wall."

This act of the publishers of the "Sanitary Engineer" is a step in the right direction, and is worthy of great praise. Nearly two hundred architects, embracing various nationalities, have thus been led to use their highest skill in producing plans for a sanitary school-house.

Want of attention to the laws of life, in the education of our young people, is threatening to make us a nation of invalids; and the public health depends more upon the condition of our country school-houses, and upon the instructions given therein, than upon all other causes combined. Nature has laid down a law of life which has no exceptions, namely, *Warm feet and a cool head are essential to good health, and indispensable to mental growth.*

We may just as reasonably expect to raise cotton in a cold climate, as to hope for good health when our hands and feet are constantly cold; and it is quite as reasonable to suppose that an artist can produce a first-class photograph when his chemicals are impure, as to expect the brain to perform high work when the blood is chilled in its course every time it reaches the extremities. Bathing the extremities in tepid water will often ward off an attack of disease; and some of the foremost writers of the present century have done their finest thinking while their feet rested in a vessel of warm water.

When we remember that heated air always rises, we will at once see that it is not an easy matter to avoid violating the law of life, by heating the head at the expense of the feet. An eccentric educator has suggested as a remedy, that pupils be required to stand on their heads. The common-sense plan, however, is, to place the heat near the floor, where it is needed.

The almost universal plan of heating country school-houses by stoves has done much to impair public health. It is generally conceded that heat generated by a stove is not healthful; but even if it were, it is too far from the floor, and is not equally distributed throughout the room. It is like attempting to warm your feet of a cold night, by placing a hot brick at your back. I have visited schools where the atmosphere which the pupils were breathing seemed to me, when I entered, almost as hot as a furnace, and yet I observed, some distance from the stove, ice formed upon the floor. It requires no argument to prove that pupils can neither enjoy good health, nor make fair progress in their studies, if their heads are at fever heat and their feet at the freezing point.

In winter, the time when our country schools are in session, many pupils come with feet damp, and cannot become comfortable if they at once take their places far from the fire. It is certainly undesirable to have pupils crowding about the stove striving to warm themselves, but they must be, in some way, rendered comfortable, or they cannot successfully recite or study their lessons. Some teachers require all pupils to take their places as soon as they enter the school-room, and allow no changing of seats during the day. In order to warm those who are farthest from the fire the stove is made red hot, and those who sit near it are almost roasted. It is not an easy matter to estimate the amount of suffering endured by the young people of the country, in a single session, for want of a common-sense plan for heating our school-rooms.

If we go to Nature, asking how we ought to warm our school-houses, she will point to her plan for warming the body, — the circulation of the blood. The fact that Nature uses circulating fluids for warming the bodies of both men and animals, is a clear intimation that this is her choice method; and it is strange indeed that we have been so slow in taking this hint which she has given us. The stove method of warming school-houses is as if Nature had kindled somewhere in the body a single fire sufficient to warm the extremities. Our present knowledge of Nature's laws leads us to the conclusion that such an arrangement would have rendered the body rather uncomfortable.

The nearest approach to Nature's plan, that has yet been reached, is the method of heating by hot water carried through pipes to all parts of the room. Examples of this method may be seen in first-class cars on any of our leading railroads. Hot-water pipes at the feet of each passenger, even in the coldest weather, render all parts of the car equally comfortable.

Heating large buildings by hot water has been a popular plan for some time past, but its application in a single room is of recent origin, and, so far as I am aware, it has never been introduced into country school-houses. So little has been said on the subject of introducing this method of heating country school-houses, that I propose to give some of the circumstances which led me to conceive and favor its universal adoption.

In the month of January, 1880, with cold extremities, I entered a palace car on the Pennsylvania Railroad. Force of habit led me to draw near to the stove for the purpose of warming myself. An acquaintance tapped me on the shoulder and invited me to take a seat with him in the other end of the car, stating, at the same time, that I could warm my feet by the pipes better than by the stove. Seating myself by the side of my friend, and placing my feet upon the pipe which passed under the seat in front of me, I soon found myself quite comfortable. I had frequently travelled in cars warmed in this way, but never before had I so fully appreciated the comfort and convenience of such an arrangement.

I soon reached the end of my journey, bade adieu to my friend, and left the train, but the recollection of that heating apparatus lingered in my mind. I said to myself, what a blessing it would be to our race if this beneficent arrangement could have a universal application. Quick as thought, the idea of its application in country school-houses and country churches flashed upon my mind.

Determined to carefully consider the feasibility of heating a single room by hot water, I opened a correspondence with a first-class engineer, manager for an extensive establishment, manufacturing "heating and ventilating apparatus," in a great city. Without indicating the cause which led me to make the inquiry, I simply asked the engineer if his establishment could furnish an apparatus for heating, by hot water, a single room twenty-eight by thirty-six and twelve feet high; and if so, what would be the cost of such apparatus. In response to my inquiries, the engineer wrote me, under date of Feb. 3, 1880, as follows:—

"Our regular car-warmer would warm the space you name very nicely, and would be very economical as regards fuel, burning about one peck of hard coal in six hours, and keeping a steady, even heat. Our price for the car-warmer, with everything complete, pipes, fittings, valves, etc., ready to set up, is $325. The above is the cheapest, and in fact only thing we have suitable to warm as small a space as you name. You could heat four rooms for a small advance on that."

Finding that the cost of this heating apparatus would be a hindrance to its introduction, and believing that the price could be greatly reduced, and desiring information on other points connected with this plan, I wrote again to the same party. His response, dated Feb. 20, 1880, was as follows:—

"You are correct as regards price being greatly reduced if it could be introduced simulantcously into a number of buildings. For warming rooms of the size you mention *hot water* is cheaper than any steam apparatus that could be used, and is a positive and even heat, and can be regulated to any degree required. Your best plan for ventilating as well as warming your school-houses would be by indirect radiation, that is, place the apparatus in cellar of building. This system is a little more expensive than direct radiation, but it keeps the air pure and changes the entire air in a room every few minutes. The cheapest way would be to place the car stove in one corner of the school-room, and run pipes horizontally under the windows; *one* coil arranged so fresh air from outside could pass over it, become warmed, and discharge into room through a grating or register, and the foul air exhausted through a chimney-flue, with a register or grating at bottom near the floor. This would serve to ventilate as well as warm."

I will not attempt to give a minute description of this heating apparatus. It may be seen and studied in any first-class car on most of our leading railroads. I will say, however, that it is not a machine, but simply a stove with an arrangement for heating water, and sending it on a circuit to all parts of the room, and returning it to be heated again. It is as simple as an ordinary suction pump, used by our farmers all over the land, and it is so constructed that fire is the only force needed. A careful inspection of this apparatus will, I believe, convince any candid man that it may be manufactured and sold at a price which will make its introduction into country school-houses a matter of *economy* as well as a matter of comfort.

If railroad companies find that it pays them to place hot-water pipes at the feet of each passenger, are we not justified in the conclusion that it would pay the people of the country to place hot-water pipes at the feet of each pupil? The individual, or company, that shall furnish, at fair figures, an apparatus for heating country school-houses by hot water, providing for thoroughly healthful ventilation, and secure its introduction throughout the country, will lessen human suffering and lengthen human life.

The usual plan for depending entirely upon open spaces at the top of the windows for ventilation, is certainly not the common-sense method. A moment's consideration ought to convince any one, that if we wish to provide a crowded school-room with plenty of pure air, we must let the air in low down, where it is needed. This we cannot do, in safety, unless we have some method of warming the air before it strikes the pupils. The plan of heating by hot water furnishes the means of warming the air as it passes into the room.

Another important matter which should be carefully considered in the ventilation of school-rooms is the fact that a considerable portion of the poisonous matter thrown from the lungs in breathing, being heavier than air, settles, and can be best carried away through a chimney flue having an opening near the floor. It would be better still if this opening consisted of a common fireplace, in which to keep live coals constantly burning.

Perhaps the most dangerous impurity connected with a crowded school-room is the effluvia from the skin. This poisonous matter settles upon the furniture and floor, and upon the clothing of pupils. It is not, like the gases, subject to the law of diffusion, and the mere opening of a door or window will not remove it from the room. The most successful manner of removing this matter from the furniture and floor is by *flushing*, that is, by opening the door and the windows in the front and rear, so as to secure, as far as possible, a rush of air through the room. This can be done best at recess and noon, while pupils are at play, and it should never be neglected. In order that this work may be well done, there should be a door in the rear of the room as well as in front, or else the windows should come down almost or quite to the floor.

It is idle to expect of pupils the highest progress, even under the most thorough teachers, if they are not supplied with plenty of pure air. We might as well feed our children on tainted meat and then expect them to enjoy a high degree of health, as to crowd them year after year into badly ventilated schoolrooms, where they are compelled to breathe vitiated air, and then expect them to possess strong bodies and sound brains, — conditions which are essential to success in life.

It would certainly pay the people of any State in the Union to employ a first-class architect, at a fair price, to devote at least a part of his time to the study of school architecture, and the preparations of plans for buildings yet to be erected, and to the introduction of the most approved methods of heating and ventilating houses which have already been built.

The foremost step that could possibly be taken would be the appointment of a national architect, who would devote himself entirely to the study of school architecture. We would not be without a precedent in making such an appointment. Belgium, several years ago, employed one of her best architects, and gave him three years to visit other nations and make the best model of a school-house, with the most healthful arrangements for heating, lighting, and ventilation. Thoughtful educators who visited our International Exhibition in 1876, will long remember the Belgian school-room as the highest model of a healthful school-house on the Centennial grounds.

The propriety of appointing a national architect for this country is certainly worthy the consideration of Congress. It is a matter that ought to attract the attention of our wisest statesmen. If the Federal government feels an interest in the health, happiness, and intelligence of the people, let Federal aid be used for the purpose of doing that which single States cannot so readily accomplish.

But in the absence of an official architect it will pay the people of any county, where houses are to be erected, to procure, at reasonable cost, the best model of a sanitary school-house. Where school officers are unwilling to expend money in procuring plans, they should at least consult the foremost teachers and the most intelligent people upon this subject. Let each new school-house represent the highest architectural skill and the purest taste of the most cultured people of the community in which it stands.

I recommend all who are interested in school architecture to carefully study the suggestions of the committee that awarded the prizes offered by the publishers of the "Sanitary Engineer." These suggestions alone, if carefully carried out, would produce a happy revolution in our school architecture.

LECTURE XIII.

FURNISHMENTS OF THE SCHOOL-ROOM.

The school-room should be furnished with everything that is essential to the health and comfort of teacher and pupils. It should also be supplied with whatever is necessary to a clear understanding of the subjects to be studied.

Perhaps no one thing, in the last half-century, has done more to popularize our public school system than improved school furniture. School officers who, in this age, conclude that it is economy to continue the use of the school furniture of their fathers, may be honest in their intentions, but they are mistaken in their conclusions.

If the seat upon which a child is placed the first day it attends school is uncomfortable, it will form an unfavorable opinion of the school-room; and this opinion is likely to grow with its .growth and strengthen with its strength. It will, as a rule, have but little love for the teacher who placed it in such an uncomfortable situation; for there is a law of life which leads us to love those who give us pleasure, and, if we are not careful, we may be led to hate those who give us pain.

No teacher is likely to be popular unless he can

command the means which will render his pupils comfortable. Let us take a case for the sake of illustration. Suppose a school-house is so seated that the teacher is compelled to place small pupils on tall benches, where their feet cannot touch the floor; nine tenths of them will go home and tell their parents that they don't like the *teacher*, when in truth the *benches* are to blame. Or, suppose the school-house is so seated that the teacher is compelled to place tall pupils upon low benches, where, day after day, they lean forward bending the breast bone, curving the spine, and distorting every part of the body; is it not natural for these pupils, while suffering, to cherish dislike for the teacher who keeps them confined in this manner?

Lessons studied while pupils are suffering leave no lasting impressions upon their intellectual natures; and there is great danger, under such circumstances, that they will form, not only a dislike for the teacher, but a hatred of school and an aversion to books.

While it is true that very few country school-houses of the present day have furniture so antiquated as that used fifty years ago, many of them are provided with seats made by a common house-carpenter. We do not now think of employing a carpenter to manufacture seats even for our dining-rooms. If we wish to promote public health and happiness, and encourage the cause of universal education, we must supply our school-houses with seats and desks bent and shaped to suit the body.

FURNISHMENTS OF THE SCHOOL-ROOM. 159

In addition to seats and desks there are many other things which are essential to the school-room. I will name some of these essentials: —

1. Inside shutters by which light can be let in or shut out, without interfering with ventilation.
2. Black-boards — a plentiful supply — and erasers which will not "raise the dust" every time they are used.
3. A clock, placed where all pupils can see it.
4. Two thermometers, one placed at the warmest and the other at the coldest point occupied by pupils.
5. Blocks for illustrating certain subjects in arithmetic.
6. A good globe, to illustrate the shape and motions of the earth, and to show the position of the several countries upon its surface.
7. A Bible and an unabridged dictionary, placed side by side upon the teacher's desk, as books of reference, to be used whenever needed.
8. A sweet-toned bell to call pupils from their play, and a still sweeter to call them to their class recitations.

Numerous other things will suggest themselves to the live teacher as they are needed. All necessary supplies ought to be provided by school officers, but in some sections of the country many things which are needed must be furnished by the teacher, or they will be wanting.

As a high degree of success in school work cannot

be reached without these essentials, let the teacher use his best efforts to secure from school officers such things as are needed. In case he should not fully succeed, I suggest that he may with propriety pay for his want of skill by purchasing such essentials as he is unable to procure from school officers. If, however, he should, term after term, fail to such an extent that he cannot afford to furnish what is wanting, he should inquire of himself whether this is an intimation that he has not been called to the teacher's work. Some one has said that "a great man is one who causes things to come to pass"; and I may be permitted to add that the clearest proof of a teacher's skill is his success in what he undertakes. Our real worth as teachers depends upon what we do, but not upon what we know; and the world will give us credit for our work, but not for our knowledge.

LECTURE XIV.

ORNAMENTATION OF THE SCHOOL-ROOM.

FINE pictures, in former times, were possessed only by rich people. In this age the parlors, sitting-rooms, and sleeping apartments of many of the poorer people are adorned with better pictures than were the palaces of kings a few centuries ago. The manner in which the home is adorned in this day depends, not upon the wealth, but upon the culture of its inmates.

While nearly all pupils in the country come from homes which are adorned with pictures, very few of them find the school-room ornamented in this manner. It would perhaps be difficult to tell why teachers have been so slow to introduce these tokens of culture into country school-houses. The uncertain tenure of the teacher's office has no doubt had much to do in this matter, but even this is not a sufficient reason for neglecting to render the school-room beautiful and attractive.

Without attempting to argue the necessity of making the school-room as attractive as possible, I propose to give a plan for introducing pictures into country school-houses, with very little cost to those who accomplish the work. The plan which I present is one which I have thoroughly tested.

While superintending the schools of Mongolia County, W. Va., I observed that the few teachers who introduced pictures into their school-houses seemed to have no trouble in the government of pupils. The general appearance of these schools seemed to be so far above those around them, that I resolved to devise a plan for placing pictures in every school-room in the county. The plan is as simple as it was successful, and I commend it to all who may feel an interest in school æsthetics.

I sent to the city for one hundred neat chromos, ten by twelve inches, which cost only a trifle at wholesale prices, and I carried several of these with me wherever I went in my work of visiting schools. In each school I proposed to present one of these pictures, upon condition that the teacher and pupils would promise at least one more for their school-room. The proposal accepted, a committee of pupils, ladies and gentlemen, appointed by the teacher, would make choice of a picture, which I then presented to the school. The interest in pictures flew in all directions, and in many places they anticipated the superintendent's coming by performing their part of the contract in advance. The method adopted to accomplish this was as follows: —

The teacher furnished one picture and gave permission to each family, sometimes to each pupil, to furnish one. In rural districts, where pictures were not plenty, some pupils clipped them from magazines and almanacs. I was pleased to see, even in these cases, ingenuity and taste in framing them, using, as they did, for this purpose, wood, leather, paper, cornstalks, shells, autumn leaves, and fern. In other communities cultivated mothers, yielding to the earnest appeals of their children, selected from the parlors their finest pictures and purest mottoes for the adornment of the school-room. These beautiful pictures and mottoes paid their cost in a single session. They strengthened in the pupils a love of the beautiful, a love of cleanliness, a love of order, and a love for their own school. The walls and windows of these school-rooms were kept clean and clear of cobwebs, and scrapers and mats were placed at many of the doors. Cleanliness of person and neatness of attire became marked characteristics, not only of teachers, but also of pupils throughout the county. The inspiration produced by this æsthetic culture was caught by many of the less fortunate pupils, and is still shedding sunshine into their humble homes. No man can measure the influences of such culture upon the coming generations.

I can name no field in which a teacher of culture can accomplish so much lasting good for the common people by the expenditure of so small an amount of time and money, as in the work of making the school-room more handsome and attractive. From numerous authorities which I could call up in support of this opinion, I quote first the language of Ex-Governor Hendricks, of Indiana, who says: "I do not know of any duty more important for the teacher than that of making the school-room pleasant." Rev. Henry Ward Beecher, while speaking upon this subject in an address before the American Institute of Instruction, said: "No church, no cathedral, or rich man's mansion ought to be so beautiful as the houses provided for the children of the common people."

But the teacher ought not to attempt to ornament the school-room without the help of his pupils. If he can induce all of them to aid him in this matter, he will find that they will all be more than ever interested in the success of the school. If pupils feel that they have helped to make the walls of the school-room beautiful, they will also take an interest in keeping the floor clean. The influence which cleanliness and ornamentation exert upon the conduct of pupils may be clearly seen by all. It is a rare thing to find disorder in a school-room where the furniture and floor are kept neat and clean, and where the walls are adorned by handsome pictures and pure mottoes. Ornamentation of the school-room has also a powerful influence in prompting pupils to regular attendance. Taking it altogether, I can think of no other investment that will pay so large a dividend as that which is expended to ornament the school-room.

LECTURE XV.

SCHOOL-GROUNDS AND SHADE-TREES.

It is unwise economy to select a cheap and unsuitable spot of ground upon which to erect a schoolhouse. It is equally unwise to have school-grounds so small that there is not sufficient room to give the sexes separate places for private walks and playgrounds. There should also be on every school lot considerable space, covered with shade-trees and shrubbery. A school-house is a public building, and it should, in a proper sense, be the pride of the district in which it stands.

The taste of the people of any country may, in a degree, be measured by the location and architectural style of their public buildings; but their true taste is, perhaps, more clearly seen in the extent and condition of the grounds connected with these buildings. No one can visit Washington without being impressed with the fact that the Capitol stands upon the most beautiful elevation found at the "City of Magnificent Distances."

As it is a matter in which every citizen of the United States feels an interest, I will present a brief description of this beautiful building and its surroundings. It is taken from the "Youth's Companion," Boston: —

"No one can go to Washington and gaze upon the great white temple of liberty on Capitol Hill, without feeling the heart beat high with pride and patriotism. Critics may tell us that it will not be a perfect building while the central front recedes, — that is, until that is built out beyond the fronts of the wings, — and until the main dome is supported by lesser domes that are visible. But nobody cares for critics when gazing at the marble pile rising over the velvet turf, and lifting its snowy dome, like a cloud itself, among the clouds.

"Wherever you go, in Washington or its neighborhood, turn about, and there is the dome looking over your shoulder. You see it as you approach the city, you see it when you are far down the river, you see it from Arlington Heights, from the Maryland hills, and out at the Soldiers' Home; not only through the famous vista, where it rises out of the surrounding branches all by itself, like a phantom of old Rome, but as you look over a charming landscape where the Potomac gleams like a silver thread out of the deep blue of the haze on the horizon, and the dim classic outlines of the other splendid public buildings, made almost dreamlike by distance, give you a doubt if you are on this Western continent.

"The Capitol stands almost in the centre of the

plan of the city. The corner-stone was laid in 1793 by Washington. The building was of freestone from Acquia Creek, painted white, and was originally much smaller and more symmetrical. It was burned by the British in the war of 1812, and was only rebuilt after a stormy debate in Congress, which was assembled somewhere else. But with the growth of the country it was found much too small; the extensions were ordered, their corner-stone was laid, with Daniel Webster as the orator of the day, and

THE CAPITOL AT WASHINGTON.

they were completed in 1863. The structure has cost, in all, about $13,000,000.

"One would gather little idea of the size of this building by being told that it is seven hundred and fifty feet long by three hundred and twenty-five feet broad. One might better comprehend it, perhaps, on learning that its ground plan occupies three and a half acres.

"As you stand before it, you see that it consists of the old building in the centre, a beautiful thing in itself, of classic style, connected on each side by a corridor of fluted columns with the vast wings, which are built of white marble from Massachusetts, and are each a temple in itself. The one on the south side is the Senate wing; the other is used by the House of Representatives. The whole stands upon a 'rustic basement' of granite, and beneath that is a sub-basement, hidden by the green turf of the terraces.

"Each of the wings has three porticos of fluted Corinthian columns, every column cut from a single piece of marble. A carriage-way runs under the eastern porticos, by which one enters the basement, the middle entrance opening into the crypt; and on the fronts are the most superb staircases of white marble that can be imagined, supported by immense blocks or buttresses, broad and lofty.

"As you mount the central one of these flights, you observe on the pediment — that is, the pointed, gable-like portion above the columns and entablature — a group carved in high relief, representing the Genius of America replying to flattering Hope by pointing to Justice holding the Constitution; a corresponding group by Crawford occupies the same position on the front of the Senate wing.

"On the flat top of the upper buttress of the main

stairway are two groups of statuary, one representing Columbus holding a globe, with an Indian girl at his feet; and the other representing Civilization, or the settlement of America, by means of a hunter with his dog, saving a woman and her boy from the tomahawk of the Indian.

"The portico itself here is one hundred and sixty feet long, and carries twenty-four columns, each thirty feet high. In niches at either side of the great doors are colossal figures of Peace and War, and over the doors is another bas-relief representing Fame and Peace crowning Washington.

"As you pause now and look back, you have the Capitol surrounded on every side by an ample space of greensward. Directly in front of it stretches a paved space in which is Greenough's huge, semi-nude statue of Washington, and on either side of that, and beyond it, picturesquely enclosed by low copings of colored stone, is a park exquisitely laid out with flowers and urns, fountains and lamps, and many trees.

"Over all this beauty towers the dome, rising, from base to crest, a height of three hundred and seven feet. As it clears the top of the building, it rests first on an octagonal base; above that it is enclosed by columns twenty-seven feet high, surmounted by a balustrade. At the apex is the lantern, fifty feet in height, surrounded by another row of pillars, and on the top of the lantern is Crawford's colossal bronze statue of Freedom.

"This dome is entirely of iron, painted white, and weighs a little more than eight million pounds. It is supported by solid masonry, and by forty columns carrying arches which uphold the floor of the rotunda.

"It is not by any means the largest dome in the world. There are four larger; but we doubt if there is any more beautiful, more buoyant and perfect, as you would think if you sometimes saw it early in the morning, with the mist streaming away from it as clouds are stripped from a mountain-side, or at night, when the light burns in the tholus at the summit, and shines over the town, announcing that Congress is in session, and almost giving it a place among the stars.

"In summer, sometimes, when Congress sits in the night, and the radiance gleams from the dome and from all the windows, and the moon shines full upon it, the great white splendor, sitting in the dense greenery of its trees, has seemed the very palace of light itself. One hardly knows whether it is most beautiful then, or when, unlighted above, on a dark night, the lamps twinkle in long distances under the arches of the outer basement, the lines of columns retreat spectrally into the gloom, and the dome soars above, a shadow on the shadow of the midnight heavens; or when, on a spring morning, as one comes up the avenue, one sees it throned above the tree-tops of the western side, that rise from banks that are purple with violets.

"The chief attractions of the Capitol belong to the seasons when Congress holds its most important sessions, but its outward beauty is best displayed in the summer-time."

But the beauty of this building would be greatly marred, indeed almost destroyed, if we would take from it its spacious grounds, with their shade-trees and shrubbery, their winding walks and rustic seats, their flowers and fountains, parks and lakes. Visitors from abroad regard the condition of this building, and these grounds, as an exponent of the public taste of the American people.

The Legislatures of the several States have shown a good degree of taste in the selection of suitable grounds upon which to erect State buildings. But public taste may be more clearly seen, from year to year, in the condition of the grounds connected with these buildings. If, in any State, these grounds, which Nature has made beautiful, are left uncared for until they become uninviting, it is evident that the public taste of the people of that State needs to be improved.

A traveller who visits a county town looks at the court-house and jail, and especially at their location, and at the condition of the public grounds around them, and then forms his opinion of the people of that county. His opinion may possibly be incorrect, but he has used the best public index within his reach.

The rule by which we measure the culture of the people of a nation, State, or county, has not generally been accepted as the true test for measuring the taste of the people of a single school district, because we have all been slow to believe that the average condition of our country school-houses and grounds is a true exponent of the taste and culture of teachers and school officers, parents and pupils. In some sections the people have just cause to be proud of their school-houses and school grounds, while in other places they ought to be ashamed of them. Teachers should lead in matters of taste, and there is no better opportunity for them to do this than for each one, aided by his pupils, to have the grounds around his school-house put into condition of which all interested persons may be proud.

In selecting a site for a country school-house, they who are charged with this responsibility should be as careful to perform their work well, as they would be if they had been appointed to select a situation for a State capitol. The situation of the district school-house may, indeed, be to them and to their children a matter of much more importance than the location of the capitol of the State. The value of the lands and the culture of the people of any community will be increased by erecting a handsome school-house in a prominent place, convenient to all who are entitled to attend. But the value of property and the culture of people will depend quite as much upon the condition of school-grounds as upon the style of school buildings.

Let us take a case for the sake of illustration: An intelligent man desires to purchase a farm as a home for himself and family. He finds one with which he is at first pleased, but he observes that the schoolhouse, which is near by, is situated in a low place on a small lot. This lot is not enclosed, and is entirely bare. He goes into another community and finds a farm which seems, in itself, to be about equal in value to the former farm. He observes, however, that the school-house, which is near by, is beautifully situated, and that it bears many marks of good taste in its construction. It is embellished with a handsome cupola and furnished with a sweet-toned bell. It is surrounded by ample grounds, which are enclosed by a neat fence. A part of this lot is adorned with shade-trees and shrubbery, and the residue is laid off into appropriate places for play. He finds that the former farm can be purchased for less money than the latter. I ask the question, Which of these farms will an intelligent man, under these circumstances, be likely to purchase as a home for himself and family?

Several matters of importance should be carefully considered in the selection of a site for a country school-house. I will name some of these.

1. It should be, as nearly as possible, equally accessible to all who are entitled to attend the school.

2. It should be a healthful situation, and should not be in the vicinity of a swamp.

3. It should be a beautiful situation, sufficiently elevated that the school-house may be seen from afar.

4. It should be large enough to give the sexes separate places for private walks, and to allow considerable space to be planted in shade-trees and shrubbery.

The school lot should be enclosed by a neat and substantial fence. Where there is not a spring of water convenient to the school-house, a well should be dug upon the school lot, and convenient arrangements for procuring water therefrom should be provided. A ladder and two or three extra buckets should be provided for each school-house, and kept in a convenient place on the grounds, so they could be used promptly in case a fire should occur. The absence of anything of this kind has caused the loss of many a school-house.

The planting of shade-trees upon school-grounds is no longer considered, by intelligent people, a mere matter of taste. It is a matter that has much to do with the health, comfort, and progress of pupils. Let us take a case for the sake of illustration: Here are forty or fifty pupils, on a hot day, in a school-house which stands on a bare lot. The walls and windows of the building are heated by the burning rays of the sun, and the flushed faces of pupils indicate that they are far from being comfortable. It is evident that when these pupils are dismissed for dinner they ought not to eat in the school-room. It is also evident that they should not eat in an open lot under a noonday sun. They need, for a few minutes at least, to be in the open air, where they are shielded from the sun by shade-trees.

The physical condition of many pupils in warm weather is such that they should play quiet games and take gentle exercise in the shade, rather than

SCHOOL-GROUNDS AND SHADE-TREES. 175

severe exercise in the sun. This is especially true in the case of girls.

But the benefits arising from shade-trees upon school-grounds are not all to be found in the fact that pupils are thus shielded from the rays of the sun. I will name a few additional advantages.

1. Shade-trees produce constant breezes which are healthful and pleasurable.

2. Shade-trees mitigate the heat in their vicinity by the condensation of moisture upon their leaves by night, and by the vast amount of evaporation that takes place through their leaves by day.

3. Shade-trees either absorb or destroy the poisonous gases and dangerous effluvia which may always be found in or around a crowded building. Shade-trees on school-grounds are, therefore, essential to the public health.

In order to prove that shade has an influence even in preventing the most fearful epidemics, I offer some facts which are matters of history. "In 1859," says a certain historian, "cholera raged in Allahabad. British soldiers whose barracks were exposed most to the sun suffered most from the epidemic; those in barracks surrounded by four rows of trees suffered much less; but not a single case occurred among the soldiers whose barracks were in a thicket."

In order to show the benefits of shade along a public road, I quote further from the same historian: "A certain road in India leads for sixty miles through a dense forest. Further on it runs for ninety miles through a barren plain. Hundreds of persons travel the road daily. Now, in the first or wooded portion, cases of sickness seldom occur, while in the latter, the sick, the dying, and the dead are found lying by the wayside."

In our own country epidemics generally do their worst work where people are crowded in buildings which have neither grass nor shade around them. Our government has recognized the necessity for shade-trees, and has been engaged on a large scale in promoting the planting of forest trees. Our State governments should also take an active part in tree-planting wherever there is a necessity for so doing. In a section that is bare, the planting of trees is now regarded almost as essential to public health as the draining of swamps.

We have now reached the practical part of this subject, and I will attempt to answer the question, How shall school-grounds be supplied with shade-trees? Let me say, first of all, that it is not best for school officers to provide and plant trees. This work, like the ornamentation of the school-room, should be performed by the teacher and pupils of each school. In sections of country which are bare of timber it may be necessary for school officers to furnish trees, but the school should plant them. In sections where forests are accessible, no outlay need be made, as a sufficient variety of trees may be obtained from the forest.

The following plan for improving school-grounds

will, in the hands of a skilful teacher, make the work a matter of real pleasure to all pupils; and the interest created will not cease when their school-days are ended. Let us take a case for the purpose of illustrating the plan: —

A teacher of culture commences a country school in a house which stands upon a bare lot. After the school-room has been made beautiful by pictures and mottoes, furnished by teacher and pupils, the teacher proposes that they proceed to improve the school-grounds. The first thing to be done is to remove all obstructions, such as stumps and stones, if any there be, from the lot. The larger pupils, with mattocks and axes, undertake the work of removing these obstructions, and cheerfully devote the time intended for play to this work, until it is completed. The smaller pupils become interested in the work, and wish that they could do something to aid this improvement.

The teacher now proposes that each pupil shall have the privilege of planting a shade-tree, a shrub, or a flower, upon the school-grounds, and that each tree, shrub, or flower shall be cared for and cultivated by the one who plants it, whose name it shall bear. All the pupils, from the oldest to the youngest, have become deeply interested in the work of improving the school-grounds, and each one is anxious to plant something. The patrons of the school have also become interested in this matter, and are discussing the propriety of planting shade-trees upon school-grounds.

It is a subject that many of them have never before carefully considered, and the more they think of it the better they are pleased with it.

The proper season for planting trees is now at hand. The teacher gives a general invitation to patrons, pupils, and school officers to meet at the school-house next Saturday, to decide what portion of the lot shall be devoted to shade. The mothers of the children are especially invited to be present.

When the day set apart for the meeting arrives, the teacher has the school-house open and in order. The floor is clean, the furniture is free from dust, and the ceiling and corners of the room are clear of cobwebs. The walls are adorned with beautiful pictures and pure mottoes. As the patrons collect, they are invited to take a look at the interior of the school-room. They are all delighted with the homelike appearance which the school-room presents. None of them ever attended a school that was half so inviting, and they do not wonder that their children are pleased with the school.

The teacher, in an informal address, explains the object of the meeting, shows the advantages of shade-trees and shrubbery upon school-grounds, and concludes by stating that the school is willing to do the work of ornamenting the lot. On motion, a committee of ladies and gentlemen of culture is appointed to aid the teacher in deciding what part of the school lot shall be devoted to shade.

This committee, after a careful examination of the

grounds, recommends that one dozen trees shall be planted around the school-house, near enough to shield the house in a degree from the sun's hottest rays, and yet far enough away to allow the sun to dry up any dampness that may collect about the house. Stakes are set where these trees are to be planted, and the people who are present seem pleased with the arrangement. The committee further recommends that about one fourth of an acre, which is suitably located, shall be devoted to shade-trees, shrubs, and flowers, and that the teacher be allowed to judge of the number of trees, shrubs, or flowers that may be planted upon this particular part of the lot. The teacher promises to exercise his best judgment and purest taste in carrying out the wishes of the committee. He announces that next Saturday will be devoted to the planting of trees and shrubs and flowers. He states that each pupil will be allowed to bring a tree, a shrub, or a flower, and that space will be found where each may be planted. He extends a hearty invitation to all who may wish to be present on the day of planting.

Some one present suggests that if the school officers will furnish material for enclosing the lot, the patrons of the school will meet in one week from that time with necessary tools to put up a neat and substantial fence. The suggestion is seconded by the school officers, and approved by all who are present.

The day for planting and fence-building arrives,

and teachers, pupils, and patrons are early on the ground. Mothers have come with their little sons or daughters, in order to plant something in which these little ones will each feel an interest. These cultured women, at the request of the teacher, aid in arranging the points where trees shall be placed, or shrubs planted, or flowers set out. The teacher plants a tree in a prominent place, which is to be called the "teacher's tree." Every pupil who is old enough plants something, and the younger pupils have each something planted by their parents.

Early in the afternoon the fence is finished, and the work of planting is completed. It has been a busy day, but a happy one, because all have been interested. Each one feels that while this work is a permanent improvement for the public good, there is something in it in which he is personally interested. As the patrons prepare to leave the grounds they take occasion to assure the teacher that he will have their hearty co-operation in all his efforts to make the school a success. They go to their homes with the feeling in their hearts that they have never before had a teacher who took so deep an interest in their district school. This feeling is the result of the fact that the teacher has given them all something to do.

The interest in æsthetics created, by this teacher, in the minds of the young people of this school district, will increase as the trees and shrubs and flowers which they have planted grow, but this interest will not cease when these trees and shrubs and flowers shall decay with age. It is impossible to measure the foundations of future healthfulness and happiness, interest and culture, that have this day been laid. Time alone can tell the extent of this teacher's influence in a work which would appear to many teachers to be entirely outside of his profession.

LECTURE XVI.

MUSIC IN COUNTRY SCHOOLS.

*"There is in souls a sympathy with sounds,
And as the mind is pitched, the ear is pleased
With melting air, or martial, brisk, or grave.
Some secret chord in unison with what we hear
Is touched within us, and the heart responds."*

Music should certainly be made a part of the daily programme in all public schools. The want of it has done much to render our country schools uninteresting and tiresome to those who attend them. It would, perhaps, with a single exception, be impossible to find another important organization having no music on its programme. Let us look at this subject long enough to see whether the country school, without music, really is an exception to the rules of civilized society.

All Christian denominations, with a single exception, have music mingled with their sacred services, and all social orders of a high character have music interspersed with their beautiful ceremonies. Music is heard in the Sunday school, and it is heard in the social circle. It is heard in the mass meetings and public processions of all political parties. It is heard in the army upon the land, and in the navy upon the sea. It is heard amidst the din of battle in time of war, and it is heard on the day of thanksgiving, when peace is proclaimed. It forms a part of the solemn ceremonies of the funeral, and it adds to the festivities of the wedding. It is heard in the streets of the city, and along the lanes in the country. It is heard in the palaces of the rich, and in the cabins of the poor. A love of it may be seen in the face of the infant as it listens to the music of its mother's voice. In universities, colleges, and schools of high order, and in the most progressive primary schools of cities and towns, music forms a part of the daily programme. Wherever people — young or old, cheerful or sad, rich or poor, learned or unlearned — are gathered together, having the privilege of making their own programme, there is always music. It seems to be essential to life.

In many of the most progressive countries of Europe, music is made one of the branches in the common-school course of study; and far-off Japan, some time since, undertook to introduce elementary music in all the common schools of that country. The Emperor of Japan sent to the United States and secured the services of Mr. Luther W. Mason, who had been for fourteen years special instructor of music in the schools of Boston. Mr. Mason left this country late in the year 1879, to enter upon the important work of introducing music into all the public schools of Japan.

In this country there is a growing sentiment in favor of making music one of the branches in the common-school course of study. The most progressive step in this direction has been taken in California, where the Legislature has made music a compulsory branch in all the public schools of the State.

In several other States music forms a part of the daily exercise in many of the country schools, but in most cases, where it is found, it is there simply by accident, and is liable to be left out when there is a change of teachers, or upon the complaint of objectors.

It is universally conceded that children should first of all be taught that which they will practise in after life. If this be true, they should be taught to sing. Again, it is generally agreed that they ought first to study that which will afford them most pleasure and profit in after life. If this be true, they should study music along with reading and writing. Music, as a branch of study, should certainly precede in importance English grammar, though both are essential, and neither should be neglected.

Most persons concede the fact that the young people of the country should be taught music, but there are some who maintain that this branch should be studied outside of the school, under instructors who make music a specialty. They insist that there are but few persons who are well fitted to teach music, and that only those who are highly qualified should perform this work. I answer that the same might be said of penmanship. There are persons who make this subject a specialty. They are much better prepared to advance pupils in this art than the average teacher, and yet no one would, for this reason, maintain that writing should not be a branch in the common-school course. Every teacher who has had experience in such matters is aware that the organization of a class of pupils in penmanship or music, outside of the school, has a demoralizing influence upon the work of the school to which these pupils properly belong. I have known schools to be almost broken up by the formation of a "singing class" outside of the school.

I may also say that music taught as a special subject, outside of the school, is so costly that the poor cannot afford it. This of itself, it seems to me, is a sufficient objection to the system of special instruction. Therefore, if we wish the masses to have a knowledge of music, we must make music a part of the work of our common schools.

By some it may be argued that the study of music in country schools is impracticable, from the fact that so few of our teachers have secured a musical training. I answer that this objection may be urged against the introduction of any new branch of study. Let music be made one of the branches of study, and teachers will prepare to give instruction on this subject. I am aware that it may be maintained that there are many teachers who cannot become good singers. I answer that there are many teachers who cannot write a good hand, and some of them cannot read well. Let music stand as other branches, and if the musical qualifications of the teacher are too low, let him be rejected, or let him agree to furnish a substitute for teaching music. We sometimes find among pupils one fully competent, who will cheerfully take charge of the class in music.

I would not propose that music should be taught in country schools as a fine art or a profound science; neither would I be willing that its study should occupy largely the school hours. With fifteen or twenty minutes' instruction and exercise at the opening of the school each morning, a great improvement will be made in a few months, and an interest in music will be created which will become a matter of pleasure to teacher and pupils. This exercise in music each morning will have a tendency to diminish tardiness and increase the attendance of pupils. The exercises of the day should also be concluded with music.

A writer in the Philadelphia "Times," on music in the public schools, gives the following reminiscences of the beginners in Boston fifty years ago: —

"It was my fortune to be a member of the Hawes School, South Boston, in 1831, while Joseph Harrington was its teacher, and through his wonderful tact of introducing new and profitable ideas into that school, music was first taught publicly, an anti-swearing society was formed, a library founded, and other novel works established. By some means the city of Boston was induced to test, in a year's study, the introduction of vocal music into one of its schools as a trial, to see if it in any way interrupted the other teachings. The celebrated teacher and musical composer, Lowell Mason, was our teacher. The first portion of the programme, after Mr. Mason's entering our school, was to grade the scholars as he found them: Good singers, No. 1; not so good, No. 2; so on to No. 6, or no singers. At the start the number in the first class was about fifteen out of a school of three hundred scholars; a very large proportion went in the No. 1 class, and only a very small number were in class No. 6. He perfectly demonstrated four facts:—

"First, that vocal music, with instrumental accompaniment, did not in any way or manner retard scholars from learning their ordinary studies.

"Second, they learned more rapidly and readily than before.

"Third, it increased the size of the respiratory organs, thereby improving their health.

"Fourth, it improved them morally.

"The next year music was introduced into all the public schools of Boston."

According to the method of teaching music in the public schools of Boston, the voice and ear should be thoroughly trained by practice before the pupil attempts to read music. In order that I may not be misunderstood in this statement, I will give the language of Prof. H. E. Holt, musical instructor of the public schools of Boston, which language I copy from "The New England Journal of Education," of that city.

Prof. Holt says: "The object of instruction in music in the primary schools should be to develop the musical nature by training the voice and ear, and developing the sense of rhythm. What the child learns of language during the first five years of its life is a preparation for learning to read. No one would think of attempting to teach a child to read before it could talk. It would be equally absurd to attempt to teach a child to read music before it could sing. Children should first learn to sing, as they first learn language, purely by imitation."

I am aware that the above method of teaching music will not be approved by those who insist that children should be taught to read music before they are trained to sing. But as the people of Boston have given special attention to this subject, and have, probably, made greater proficiency in music than the people of any other city on the continent, the system which they practise in teaching music in primary schools is certainly worthy the consideration of all who feel an interest in this subject.

A class of sixteen girls, from the Boston public schools, led by Prof. Holt, sang before the American Institute of Instruction, at its late meeting at Saratoga, and their singing was, by competent judges, considered excellent. It was there publicly stated that they had been trained under the system of singing by imitation. After the voice and ear have been thoroughly trained, they will, of course, be taught to *read music*. This seems to be the *natural* method of teaching music, and yet there may be some teachers who think they cannot successfully carry it out. Let each teacher, therefore, thoroughly study this subject, and then adopt that plan by which he can best teach his pupils to sing.

The extent and thoroughness of the study of music in each school district depends largely upon the qualifications of the teacher, and the interest which he feels in this subject. In some sections, vocal music alone will not satisfy the wants of the school, and by the contributions of patrons and pupils A CABINET ORGAN WILL BE ADDED TO THE FURNITURE OF THE SCHOOL-ROOM.

An organ can be purchased for a small sum, and the demand for instrumental music in the country is increasing, so I venture to predict that the time is not distant when an instrument will be considered as one of the essentials in every school-room. The sound of an organ in connection with vocal music adds to the interest of the opening and closing exercises of the school. It is well to have the older pupils, who are able to preside at the organ, take this place by turns; and if any pupils play upon other instruments which harmonize with the organ, and which are in good standing with the community, they should be invited to bring these instruments and join in the daily exercise. The more interesting these exercises become, the more anxious will pupils be to attend the school. If the number of instruments should make a " band of music," so much the better, as there will then be no need of a compulsory school law.

I am aware that some of the sweetest-toned instruments, by being often found in bad company, have, in many places, become unpopular. As the choice of company has been made by the owner, I think we could safely admit these instruments into the school-room "on trial," or so long as they produce no disorder. Public sentiment, however, should be consulted on this subject. I believe that the time will come when every musical instrument which man has made will be tuned to the praise of God.

In some sections of the country prejudices exist in the minds of many against music of any kind in public schools. In such cases the teacher should summon to his aid those who favor music in schools, and they can readily create a public sentiment in its favor. It will not, as a rule, be best for the teacher to force music into the school contrary to the wishes of the patrons. It is not, however, a difficult matter to convince most persons that there is no time lost by having music in school, morning and evening.

Let the teacher illustrate this by referring to the fact that when we have but an hour to spend in Sunday school we do not regard it a waste of time to devote one fourth, or even one half, of that hour to music. Let him ask how many would be willing to attend Sunday school if there was no music connected with the exercises from beginning to ending. The time allowed for religious services in Christian churches is almost half devoted to sacred song, and no one regards this time wasted. It is certainly evident to every one that if Sunday schools and churches would exclude all music, superintendents and clergymen would soon feel the need of "compulsory laws and truancy acts," to fill vacant chairs and empty benches.

Music will do more to collect a scattered crowd than the voice of the orator. People, young or old, cultured or uncultured, will come together if called by the sweet strains of music. It is not, therefore, unreasonable to suppose that the introduction of music into all our country schools would do more to increase the attendance of pupils than compulsory laws could do. Indeed I can name no other one thing that would so popularize our system of public instruction as the introduction of music into all our primary schools.

Many of the lower animals will collect in flocks or herds, if called by music. Shepherds, in ancient times, when watching their flocks, were accustomed to play upon the harp to prevent the sheep from wandering. The modern practice is to place a sweet-toned bell upon one of the sheep, and then the entire flock will follow the bell, in order to hear its music. It is said that the boys who are engaged in herding cattle on the great plains in the South have learned that they can save labor by moving quietly all day long among the herds, humming low tunes. Cattle are not inclined to wander away, say these boys, if there is music in the midst of the herd. At night the boys rest with the cattle upon the plains, and in case of a sudden noise, as, for example, a clap of thunder, when the cattle are suddenly startled and when there is prospect of a general fright, the boys rise and commence humming their low tunes. The cattle, upon hearing the accustomed music, suppose all is right, and quietly lie down to rest. History furnishes numerous examples of the power of music over various kinds of animals; but I will not further follow this particular part of my subject.

There is music in a sweet-toned school bell, and it tends to collect pupils just as the bell upon a single sheep tends to call the flock together. "The church-going bell" pays its cost in the additions which it makes to the congregation. So fully is this influence understood, that sometimes, in cities, a set of bells tuned to a musical scale is placed upon the church, and the "chime of bells," the sound of bells in harmony, will collect a congregation even at unseasonable hours.

But the best results arising from music in the school-room do not consist of increased attendance of pupils, but of improved conduct and character. Pure music not only pleases the ear, but it improves the heart. No one can listen to pure music without feeling a desire to be better.

Words which are set to music may be immoral, but music itself is pure, it is divine. The present generation of youth is certainly fortunate in having so many excellent published collections of songs suitable for the school-room, from which to make selection. These song-books are generally cheaper than other school books, and *it is as important for each pupil, who can read, to have his own singing book, as it is for him to have his own reader.*

Most of the studies in the common-school course appeal more to the intellect than to the heart, and, as pure music tends to improve both manners and morals, it should occupy a prominent place upon the programme in all our public schools.

Perhaps I cannot conclude this subject to better advantage than by presenting the following article from "The National Journal of Education," Boston: —

"It has been urged that music is a branch of study more ornamental than useful; which can be dispensed with altogether, or the expenditure in its behalf be greatly reduced. Yet, as a matter of fact, no such claim is made among prominent educators, or by those best informed on matters pertaining to public instruction. On the contrary, here in Massachusetts, music never stood higher on the list of studies than now; was never so thoroughly taught as now, never so justly appreciated as now. Our University, with its professor of music, within the year has found it necessary to employ in addition a tutor in singing, and is granting diplomas to such as successfully complete the course prescribed.

"The Empire of Japan has just concluded a contract with Mr. L. W. Mason, late superintendent of music in the schools of Boston, to introduce our system of musical instruction into that country. Arrangements are making at Tokio, on the most liberal scale, to furnish the means and appliances needed in the line of his profession, to promote his personal comfort, and to add dignity to the office he assumes.

"Music has become, may we not say, the chief amusement of the people? As such it is innocent, it leaves no sting behind; and it is not every amusement of which this can be predicated. The love for it, moreover, in the household is limited only by the amount of talent in that direction possessed by the members of the family, or by their ability to procure for themselves the means of its gratification.

"But it would be taking a partial view of the matter were we to regard it merely in the light of a recreation. As a branch of study its value is beyond question. It cultivates the ear, informs the taste, trains the faculties of the mind, develops and invigorates the powers of the body. Of what other study can this be affirmed in an equal degree? Viewed simply as a resource for earning one's living, it is safe to say that a knowledge of music gives direct support to a vastly greater number of men and women than does an acquaintance with any one of the so-called higher studies pursued in our schools.

"Consider the interests of music in their financial aspect. See the amount of capital invested in the manufacture of pianos, organs, band and orchestral instruments; the printing and engraving of sheet music and music-books; the various newspapers or journals devoted exclusively to musical matters; the fabulous sums lavished upon distinguished singers or players, who fill our largest halls at their concerts with eager listeners.

"There has been heard here, this season, an artist who received for singing a couple of songs more than three hundred dollars; while orchestral players have been paid for an hour's work twenty-five dollars each. Members of church choirs obtain for their services from two dollars up to thirty dollars a Sunday. Boys from our grammar schools, even as low as the fourth class, are engaged in the choirs of Boston and vicinity, where, in addition to the instruction given them, they receive salaries corresponding to the degree of talent they manifest. Five dollars, for a couple of hours spent in church at the organ, is not uncommon.

"A professional man, whose fees amount to one hundred dollars a day, is looked upon as quite successful; a merchant, who clears the like sum of money, may well congratulate himself as being in prosperous circumstances. But there are singers able to command twice as much for every appearance they make before the public. It is within the memory of some of us that Jenny Lind contracted with Mr. Barnum to sing one hundred nights in America for *one hundred thousand dollars*, and he never complained of the bargain.

"A single song, the production of Dr. Arthur Sullivan, which may have cost him only a few hours' labor, has yielded its proprietor an annual income of two thousand five hundred dollars. A second song of his, 'The Lost Chord,' well known in our concert-rooms and parlors, has proved a fortune in itself. 'H. M S. Pinafore,' a work of the same composer, which has gone the length and breadth of the land both here and abroad, — a clean, charming, wholesome composition, admired alike by artist and amateur, — has been a mine of wealth to many a manager and publisher, besides affording delight to thousands of hearers.

"Music-selling and music publishing houses in this country, if we consider the magnitude of their business and the variety of their publications, stand second to none the world over.

"Pianos and parlor organs are almost as common as tables and bureaus; or, at least, it may be said with truth that a house without a musical instrument of some sort is a rarity. A family in which there is no music, and no love for it, must certainly be accounted unfortunate in that respect.

"See how largely dependent we are upon the Germans in filling the ranks of our bands and orchestras; because, music having been so many years a regular study in their common schools, enjoying all the time the highest consideration in the community at large, they have become superior to us in the art, and are, for the present, beyond our competition.

"Look at our conservatories and colleges of music, which already surpass those of Europe in the number of their students, and bid fair, in due time, to rival them also in the excellence of the instruction furnished, as well as in the talent and proficiency of their graduates.

"The complaint is sometimes made against our schools, that children are not taught what will be of practical use in after-life. What is learned of some subjects, it is said, needs to be so modified before it can be available in practice, that, aside from the mental discipline thereby secured, it may be a question whether time so spent could not be better employed in other ways. Such is not the case with music. Whatever is gained in that direction, though it be only the power of singing the scale, is immediately useful, and will form one of the inevitable steps to be taken sooner or later if one desires to become a musician.

"Given the requisite amount of talent, with corresponding application under competent instruction, and the pupil finds himself in the possession of an accomplishment more or less adequate to his support in life, while leaving him opportunity to attend to other business But whether he turn this acquirement to account pecuniarily or not, his knowledge and skill in the art will continue an unfailing source of delight to himself and friends as long as life and health remain.

"Is there one of us who, when his son leaves school

to take his place in society, would not be glad to know that he had gained a taste for music, and some knowledge of it? Should we not consider it, in some sense, as a safeguard to restrain him from the pursuit of other and less salutary modes of enjoyment? Where there is music at home, and an appreciation of it, the various forms of dissipation, to which, for want of something better to occupy their leisure hours, the young are so prone, will lose their charms, and fail to make felt their pernicious attractions. .

"All this goes to show how deep a root music has taken among us, how rapidly it is growing, how widely extending, and how it demands — and reasonably, too — a fostering hand and liberal support from those who are charged with the administration of the interests of public education."

LECTURE XVII.

THE DICTIONARY IN THE SCHOOL-ROOM.

IN the school-room, as on the farm and in the workshop, some things are mere matters of comfort or convenience; some are intended to lessen labor, while others are absolutely essential to success. The patrons of our public schools will agree that, first of all, the furnishments of the school-room should include such things as are indispensable in the work of gaining a thorough knowledge of the common branches.

As a simple illustration of the thought which I desire to present, I may say that on the farm the mowing-machine is an important implement, — a labor-saving machine; but it is not absolutely essential, as the ordinary scythe may do well the work of the mowing-machine. The plough is an *essential implement* on every farm, as nothing else can take its place or do its work. Any sensible farmer who wishes to engage in raising grain and grass, if called upon to decide whether he will do without a plough or a mowing-machine, will at once decide to do without the latter. If he is unable to purchase either, and a friend proposes to make him a present of one or the other — his choice of the two — for his own use, he will choose the plough, although he is aware that the mowing-machine sells for the most money.

In the school-room the blackboard serves a very important purpose; it saves an immense amount of labor, and some may say that it is essential to success. But when we consider the fact that, in the absence of the blackboard, the same work may be done upon slates, we conclude that the blackboard, though important, is not indispensable.

A dictionary, giving the proper pronunciation and a complete definition of all the words of the English language, is not only important, but *absolutely essential,* in every school-room. It is to the school-room what the plough is to the farm, — the foundation of success. No substitute for it has ever been found, and it is evident that much of the work done in any school-room that is without it must necessarily be mere "guess-work."

It is folly to argue, as some have done, that teachers in our country schools ought to be so familiar with the pronunciation and definitions of words, that they may with safety undertake to teach without a dictionary before them. The finest scholars, and the most thorough teachers in the higher institutions of learning throughout the land, tell us that, in their work of instruction, they make the dictionary a constant companion. No well-qualified teacher will claim that he can do first-class work without a dictionary as a book of reference for himself and his pupils. It is the one weapon with which every true scholar, who wishes to be strong, must be constantly armed.

But some of the patrons of our public schools may honestly ask, What benefits are to be derived from a dictionary in the school-room? Among the many advantages which might be named I may rely upon three principal ones, namely: —

1. All members of the school may learn to spell correctly by forming the habit of looking in the dictionary, to see the correct spelling of all words about which they are in doubt, before using them in composition.

2. All members of the school may be led, by the use of the dictionary, to form the habit of pronouncing correctly all words which they see in reading or which they use in writing or in conversation.

3. All members of the school may be led to form the habit of looking to the dictionary in order to learn the exact meaning of the words which they see or hear, about which they are in doubt.

Perhaps no one will doubt the necessity for correct spelling, as the meaning of words in a letter or a contract may depend upon the way these words are spelled. But some persons may ask, Where is the need of such precision in pronunciation?

I may answer that it has been truly said, that "hardly any one thing so publicly marks and distinguishes the unrefined and uncultivated from the refined and cultivated, as inaccurate and inelegant pronunciation." A man whose pronunciation is inaccurate and inelegant may read extensively, he may even become a professional man; but whether he appears in the pulpit, on the platform, or in the social circle, his pronunciation will constantly attract attention, as do stains upon a costly garment.

No one will deny the fact that all young people ought to have a clear knowledge of the meaning of such words as they see in reading or use in writing or in conversation. They cannot read, or write, or converse, or even *think*, to the best advantage, unless they have a correct knowledge of the meaning of the words which are used.

It is the duty of those who are charged with the interests of public education to place a dictionary in every school-house. The discharge of this duty would insure to the nation a higher degree of intelligence and a broader culture. In many places public schools have already been supplied with dictionaries, and there is almost everywhere a growing sentiment in favor of this work.

I suggest that where the school officers decline to furnish a dictionary for the school-room, the teacher may, with propriety, appoint a committee of pupils to solicit contributions from the patrons; or they may arrange an interesting literary entertainment, and charge an admission fee sufficient to purchase a dictionary.

In selecting a dictionary for the school-room, care

should be taken to obtain the *best*. A small dictionary should not be selected, as the vocabulary and definitions in such a book will be incomplete and unsatisfactory. We have, in this country, only two unabridged dictionaries, — WEBSTER's and WORCESTER's, — one of which ought to be placed in every school. It should be a part of the regular furniture of the school-room, for the benefit of the whole school, accessible alike to the teacher, and, under proper regulations, to every scholar capable of deriving benefit from consulting it.

But then, as it is obvious, no one copy, nor several copies of a work of this kind, can meet all the wants of all the pupils, since nearly *every* scholar should find frequent occasion to consult his dictionary on minor points, and will often have occasion to refer to it in his own seat, or to take it home to aid him of an evening there, every scholar past the most elementary branches, and beyond the age of six or eight, should have his or her own dictionary in an abridged, portable form.

In order that I may present this subject in the clearest light possible, I will offer the opinions of some of the foremost thinkers connected with the educational work in this country. The first article which I offer is from the pen of one of the publishers of Webster's Unabridged Dictionary; but this fact will in no way weaken its force with people who think for themselves : —

" Every intelligent teacher will readily concede the

importance of having each of his pupils furnished with a good dictionary of the language. The faculty of *speech*, with which man is endowed by his Creator, and written *language*, are among the crowning excellences which distinguish him from the brute creation. They form the garb in which his rational thoughts are clothed, and constitute the medium through which he communicates those thoughts to the minds of others. Without them, the treasures of knowledge which an individual may acquire must remain forever locked up in his own breast, and his own intellectual stores be limited to his self-obtained and very imperfect acquisitions. The past can make to them no additions, nor can he communicate them to those around him, — much less transmit them to the future.

"Words, therefore, a written and spoken language, form the great instrument to be employed in acquiring or communicating ideas. It becomes, then, obviously important, in order that this instrument may be employed skilfully and successfully, that we possess it in as great perfection as is attainable, and know perfectly how to use it. How can I thoroughly understand the mental conceptions of another, unless I know fully the meaning of the words he employs in giving them expression, and unless his utterances, and my understanding of them, are coincident? Otherwise, errors, confusion of ideas, and blunders interminable, must be the result.

"It follows, therefore, that while the scholar, in

pursuing any other given branch of study, as of mathematics, or natural or mental philosophy, needs, specially, only the text-books appropriate to that particular department, yet, in all his studies, the dictionary should be his constant and intimate companion. From the very first hour when he begins to employ words in combination, — nay, from a still earlier period, since orthography and pronunciation, taught by his dictionary, have to do with words in their isolated forms, — on through every stage of his progress, up to the highest attainments in science of which the human mind is capable, the wise and reflecting scholar will have constant recourse to his standard lexicon, and find its treasures continually available.

"It is related of Daniel Webster, that on being inquired of what authorities he consulted, or what course he adopted, in his preparation for his great forensic efforts, he replied that he consulted his dictionary.

"Yet the opinion has been expressed that, in proportion to the number of pupils, a less number of dictionaries will now be found in our schools than formerly. The introduction of a great number of studies, once unknown in our common and higher schools, may have contributed to this result, if such a result have really followed, and thus important elementary studies, lying at the foundation of all others, be in danger of being overlooked. Does not the introduction of these higher branches, on the other hand, render still more important the possession, by every scholar, of a good English dictionary?

"Let us look at this matter a little more in detail. Is there a single study, in which the scholar can be engaged, above the simple learning of the alphabet, and the spelling of words in their primitive forms, which follows (the spelling book affording for this object a partial substitue for the dictionary), in which he ought not to have a constant reference to the latter?

"Take, first, the reading exercise. No reflecting teacher supposes that reading — giving vocal utterance to the written language of an author, so as to do full justice to that author's conceptions — can be intelligently taught by merely requiring a parrot-like compliance, on the part of the pupil, with certain prescribed *rules for reading*, — here to give the rising and there a falling inflection of his voice, here to pause while you could count one, and there two, etc., and in this manner to indicate all the tones and cadences of the voice by stereotyped, fixed directions. How can the ever-varying emotions of the human soul, and the corresponding expression of those emotions by the human voice, appropriately employed by one in reading aloud the recorded thoughts of another, be thus formally indicated?

"Is not this, rather, the true philosophy? The scholar must first possess himself of the exact thought of his author. He must know the precise meaning of every word in the sense in which that author employs it, and that author, it is to be inferred, will have employed correct and appropriate language. The signification of each word, if not otherwise understood, he must learn from his dictionary. He must also learn the relation of one word to another, or the construction of words in sentences. He must become thus thoroughly imbued with the spirit and meaning of the writer. Then, general, simple rules, the instructions of the living teacher, and practice, must do the rest in forming a graceful, effective reader.

"Take the study of English grammar. Is it not perfectly obvious that a correct knowledge of the precise import of every word is necessary, in order to a correct grammatical analysis of any given sentence? The same word is often used, now as one part of speech, and now as another, — here a noun, and there a verb; in this connection a conjunction, in that a pronoun; here the word is an adverb, there an adjective, and so on. The dictionary, therefore, hardly less frequently than the grammar, must be consulted in the preparation for the parsing exercise.

"And so we might proceed through the whole course of English studies. In *mathematics*, a full and clear perception of the exact meaning of a term is absolutely essential to a right understanding of the chains of reasoning employed, and an error here may be fatal to the whole process. Is not every teacher made often aware that many of his scholars either have no lucid perception, or wholly fail to understand the import of such words as *proportion, cancel, inverse, ratio*, and many other terms employed in the arithmetic they are studying? So in physiology, logic, rhetoric, natural and mental philosophy, history, and every science.

"How many persons, young and old, fail to appreciate the beauties of an author, or entirely misconceive his meaning, from want of a right understanding, in their nice shades of thought, of the words he employs! The gratification they would otherwise experience from a fine composition is thus proportionably lost.

"But not only do many persons, from this cause, fail of a correct appreciation of the thoughts of others, but they likewise have very little power of communicating their own. They at best express vaguely or inaccurately their own ideas, and so have very little power, either by written or spoken language, of influencing their fellow-men; while he who is well skilled in the use of language wields a power and possesses an influence, an ability to persuade or convince men to his own views, entirely unknown to one lacking this qualification. Nor is this a kind of knowledge only occasionally available; it is in daily and constant requisition. Indeed, how could the eloquent orator, as Webster or Clay, or the gifted poet, like Willis, clothe, with 'thoughts that breathe,' 'words that burn,' unless he had entire command, in their full import, of these instruments of thought, the *words* in which they must find expression? How else could he so effectively stir up the deep fountains of feeling in the soul of the reader or listener? What wonder that these men of commanding genius and master minds, as we have seen, have constant reference to the dictionary! Nor is such an attainment as has been described, the power accurately to understand and readily to employ the words of a language, made without effort, constant and protracted. The dictionary is the expositor of words. Its business is to give accurately and unmistakably their orthography, pronunciation, and meaning; and, rightly appreciating the importance of a correct knowledge of words, what work can be more profitably made a daily study? And could a thorough and uniform understanding of the meaning of words become universal, how many discussions would be shortened; how many disputes avoided; how greatly mankind benefited!"

I desire next to present some excellent suggestions, made by Dr. Joseph Emerson, long and extensively known as an accomplished teacher, in his Introduction to Dr. Watts's "Improvement of the Mind." His remarks are earnestly commended to every one having anything to do with the mental training of the young.

"There is," says Dr. Emerson, "probably no other branch of literary education of equal importance that is so neglected, or imperfectly taught, as *defining*,— no other that has now such demands upon the attention of teachers. It is often astonishing and grievous to see how grossly ignorant are children and youth, and even men and women, of the meaning of important words and phrases,— an ignorance which, in general, they are very far from feeling or mistrusting. They cannot express their thoughts, for want of words, and often they express thoughts very different from what they intend, because they do not understand the words they employ. And very frequently, from the same cause, they take no idea, or wrong ideas, from what they read and hear. Probably more than three fourths of the disputes that have troubled the world have arisen from the ignorance or misapprehension of words. No doubt one of the greatest reasons why so little good is effected by preaching is, that the language of the preacher is but very imperfectly understood by most of the hearers. Said a venerable and pious lady to her little grandchild, just recovering from sickness, 'Now you must be thankful.' But the poor child did not know — could not guess — the meaning of *thankful*, and was afraid to ask. So her excellent instruction was lost upon the child, at least for years, till he ascertained the meaning of the word. So it is, no doubt, with a great part of the instructions that parents and teachers, as well as ministers, give to those under their care.

"A remedy for these various and abounding evils is devoutly to be wished and sought. What is it? Proper attention to the exercise of *defining* is doubtless one of the remedies, and perhaps the best of all.

And it would be easy to show that all other methods must be ineffectual to gain an accurate knowledge of words, at least of many words, without this.

"But the exercise of defining may not only prevent much evil, but effect much positive good. When properly attended to, it is one of the best exercises for improving at once the memory and the judgment, and storing the mind with useful knowledge. And when a good acquaintance with language, I mean the vernacular language, is once acquired, this knowledge is one of the best aids ever devised by human ingenuity to assist the reasoning faculty in the search of truth. We make much use of words in thinking, especially in close thinking; and it is perhaps impossible to pursue a train of thought, to any considerable length, without their aid. But how often do we impose upon ourselves, and draw wrong conclusions, by imperfectly understanding the words we silently and perhaps insensibly use, or by using them in different senses. And how often do we think in words, of which we have no definite understanding, flattering ourselves that we are nobly investigating thoughts and things, while, in reality, we are only making progress in pride and darkness. As words are only the signs of thoughts and things, and the relation of things, so it is very important, in order to improve our acquaintance with thoughts, things, and relations, that we should have a very clear and correct knowledge of the meanings of words, or objects which they represent. This cannot be gained by attending to the manner and connection in which words are used, whether written, printed, or spoken. This will often leave the sense very vague and indeterminate, or positively wrong.

"*An acquaintance with other languages will not give us a correct knowledge of English words.* For, in the first place, all the English words derived from these three languages do not constitute one fifth part of our language.

"In the second place, there is scarcely an instance in which a knowledge of the original word can give us any precise idea of the meaning of its derivative. The fact is, that the meaning of almost every word includes several ideas; and when we borrow a word from another language, we scarcely ever use it to signify just the same ideas denoted by its original. For example, our words, *cap, captain, caption, capital, capitol, capitation, decapitate,* all are derived from *caput,* — a head. But they all differ in signification from *caput,* as well as from one another. There is, indeed, some resemblance among the significations of all. This makes it a little easier to learn and to retain their meanings; but an acquaintance with these various meanings cannot be gained, but from other sources. The same might be shown by multitudes of other examples. Hence it has come to pass that *use,* and not derivation, is the law of language; and hence our word *virtue* has by no means the same signification as its original, *virtus.* Hence, too, it has come to pass that a knowledge of the original word has often led the unwary youth to misunderstand and misuse its derivative of different meaning.

"It is the grand object of the *dictionary* to tell us the sense or senses in which our words are used by good writers and speakers. To learn the meaning of words, then, must constitute a capital part of a good education. *It should be begun as soon as the child can distinguish between one word and another*, and continued as long as sight or hearing continue. The chief, study in this pursuit is that of defining, principally in the use of a *dictionary*. The best way of pursuing this study is doubtless in connection with other studies,— to learn and fix in the mind the definitions of the most important words, as they occur. The instructions of the lessons will greatly assist to fix in the mind the definitions, and the definitions to fix the instructions. To promote this exercise it is thought needful to have a large number of questions, to be answered by definitions. But the pupil should not content himself merely with learning these. He should consult his dictionary for the meaning of every word that he does not clearly understand. Let him also consider the connection, and endeavor to gain the exact import, not only of each word, but also of each phrase and sentence, as he proceeds. In this way, though his progress from page to page will be slow, especially at first, yet it will be sure, and exceedingly conducive to mental improvement and the acquisition of knowledge."

The following article from the pen of President

Porter, of Yale College, is so able, appropriate, and convincing, that I present it as the concluding argument upon this subject: —

"It is acknowledged by all to be very desirable that every school and every scholar should be furnished with the best English dictionary. No one doubts that it is well that the large dictionary should lie upon the teacher's table, and that some one of the smaller dictionaries should be in the hands of every scholar.

"But how shall they be used? How can they be used to result in the greatest advantage? Is it enough that the large book should repose in the solitary dignity of an oracle, ready to answer any question that is forced upon its notice, about the spelling, pronunciation, derivation, and meanings of the hard words which come up in the school recitations? Is it enough that the pupil should be taught to resort to the dictionary by his side, whenever, in his private studies, he is at loss in respect to any of the points which we have named? These objects are very good indeed. They are quite sufficient to reward all the pains which is taken to provide our schools with works of this kind.

"Is this enough? Can nothing more be attempted with the hope of success? Does the teacher discharge all his duty when he makes an occasional reference of this kind to the standard before him, or when he exhorts his scholars to do the same? We think not. More than this can be done in the way of systematic efforts to train the scholars to the constant use of these books of reference. Many teachers attempt this. They require of their classes in spelling to give the definitions of a few words in every lesson. Some require very young children, as soon as they are old enough to write, to write out definitions in a copy-book, and to learn these definitions by heart. This is generally a severe and unpleasant task. The young scholar finds *the definition* to be nearly if not quite as unintelligible as the word itself, and both are too often words, and hard words too, — '*dictionary words*,' as they are sometimes expressively termed.

"It requires a mature mind to take very much interest in a dictionary, or to resort to it of its own accord. Special and well-directed efforts are needed in order to make the study of it pleasant and profitable. Such efforts, we are persuaded, may be made, and it is with the hope of leading to such efforts that the following suggestions are offered.

"The great end of studying a dictionary is to train the pupils to the study of words. The teacher should aim, with all his patience and skill, to make his scholars *attend* to the words which they use, — to understand them in all their force and beauty, as expressive of thought and feeling. It is not enough to spell and pronounce them correctly, to apply them to the right objects, to use them in the right connection, and to avoid grammatical blunders. This knowledge is desirable in its place; it is even necessary, but it is not all that is to be aimed at. It is only a preparatory to that which is of greater consequence. Words are living things only when they are parts of the sentence. They cannot be fully understood except as seen in their connection. When they are separated from one another they are no more alive than a bone or blood-vessel is alive when it is cut off from the body of which it was a part; no more alive than a leaf, or a flower, or a twig is alive when it is separated from the tree and scattered upon the earth.

"The dictionary must be used in the study, not of dead, but of living words. The dictionary must teach the scholar how to use words as they occur in *sentences*. To show what can be done in this way, we suggest the following exercise as a daily lesson: Let a word or two be selected as the lesson for the day. Let the scholars be directed to prepare to give us many sentences as there are definitions of the word, in each of which one of the words given as the definition shall be prominent. Let this be done sometimes with preparation and sometimes without preparation. In this way the attention of the class will be directed to the shades of meaning that distinguish the words which are ordinarily considered synonymous. He will see that a difference in the connection makes all the difference conceivable with respect to the use of the word. The greater propriety and beauty of the use made of a word by one scholar over that made by another, will suggest lessons concerning the force and beauty of language in general, and make the exercise teach composition and style. When the lesson is done, and all the suggestions and inquiries about the various senses of the word are finished, then the teacher should open the large dictionary, and read, at length, the extended definitions, and the full illustrations which it contains. In view of all the light suggested by looking at the word in actual use, as a part of a sentence, and as a part of very many sentences, all these definitions will be clear and intelligible, and the word or words which have been studied for the day will be ever after full of interest to the pupils.

"Nor is this all. A few such lessons as this will teach the pupil how to use the dictionary for himself, and how to put meaning into the definitions given in the dictionary. A word separate from its connection, or rows of words looked out in a dictionary, from the columns of a spelling-book, can never excite such interest. Nor is it enough to take words in our school or private reading, in sentences made by others, and search out their meaning. The pupil must construct the sentences for himself, he must create by his own powers, he must apply the word in order fully to appreciate it. Then will it be a living thing. It will be a living sprout with a living root, planted in the moist earth; not a dry twig stuck in the dry sand-heap, to stand for a moment and be soon plucked away.

"This is not all. Every word has a history of its

own, and that history the pupil should learn to trace. It was first used in a simple meaning, probably it was a picture word, representing some familiar object or action in nature. The words *right, wrong, apprehend, comprehend, imagine, resolve,* and thousands like them, were first applied to something seen with the eye and handled with the hand, and by changes easily, but gradually, made, have come to signify the remote and abstract things or acts for which they are so freely used.

"The dictionary gives these meanings somewhat in their order. It traces them from their humble origin and application up to their higher uses. It illustrates the successive steps by which they have advanced in the various uses to which they are applied. The teacher may know something of this history of single words. If his attention has not been directed to it, he may obtain much light on the subject from Trench on the 'Study of Words.' From that book he may learn what treasures of knowledge are hid in his dictionary, and that these treasures only need to be mined for the good of his scholars, with a little patience and skill. There is no exercise more profitable to advanced classes than the lessons in the changes of meanings which words have undergone. They will learn that the history of a single word is a history of the thoughts and feelings of multitudes of men who have used it, and that changes are all the while going on in the words which are in actual use at the present time. The adroit and skilful teacher can show how new words are continually coming into being, such words as *loafer*, *filibuster*, *free-soiler*, *bloomer*, *bloomer-hat*, *propeller*, *young America*, *old fogy*, and what is their origin.

"If scholars reflect on the words which they use, they must learn to think. These living messengers of thought are flying from mouth to mouth every instant that we live. They drop from thousands of pens, in glistening pearls that are woven into bracelets of beauty. They attract or repel. They win or they offend us. They are used by the intelligent and clear-headed thinker to influence thousands of his fellows to good thoughts and useful deeds. Happy is the teacher, and happy the pupil, who are led to the thoughtful study and the intelligent use of the words of his native English tongue."

LECTURE XVIII.

HOW TO HAVE A LIBRARY IN EVERY SCHOOL-ROOM.

The actual wealth and enterprise of the people of each State in the Union are about in proportion to the degree of intelligence and culture which the masses have attained in these several States. Wherever the masses are ignorant and uncultured, there are poverty and want; and wherever the people are intelligent and cultivated, there are enterprise and wealth.

But the study of the text-books used in the common schools of the country can never, of itself, produce that degree of intellectual strength which the masses must possess in order to insure public prosperity. The mind, like the body, demands daily food in order that it may increase in strength, and regular reading is the surest method of producing mental growth. Universal reading, therefore, is the surest method of producing universal intelligence.

In childhood, the desire to gain knowledge is as universal as the desire to take food; and if young people were provided regularly with reading matter to suit their taste, as parents provide their children with suitable food, reading would be to them as pleasurable as eating and drinking. But observation and experience prove that the habit of reading, if formed at all, is generally formed early in life.

When we consider that many homes have no libraries, and that few family libraries contain books suited to the taste of childhood and youth, we can readily account for the fact that, in many places, the masses have not formed the habit of reading. They were not furnished with suitable reading matter while their habits were forming. It is evident, then, that if we wish to lift the masses to a higher level — if we wish to raise up a generation of *readers and thinkers* — we must, in some way, provide suitable reading matter for all young people.

There is no other method by which the masses can be so generally reached, and by which the youth of the country can be so readily induced to read, as the plan of having a library in every school-room.

The question, then, for consideration is, shall we have a library in every school-room, and if so, how can we obtain it? I answer, we should have a library in every school-room, and we can obtain it from patrons and pupils with but little cost to any one and with pleasure to every one. I will present a plan for procuring books which requires only a little skilful management on the part of the teacher. It is this: Let the teacher lay the foundation of a library, just as he would introduce pictures into the school-room, or as he would plant shade trees upon school grounds, namely, by permitting each one who is interested to take stock in the enterprise. To be more specific as to the method, I will say:—

1. Let the teacher contribute one volume to the library.

2. Let the teacher encourage each pupil to contribute one volume.

3. Let the teacher appoint a committee of the larger pupils, ladies and gentlemen, to solicit contributions of books and money from the citizens of the district.

4. Let the school give a public entertainment and charge an admission fee for the purpose of obtaining additional funds.

5. Let all money, contributed or collected, be used in purchasing suitable books and periodicals for the school library.

6. Let the teacher obtain printed labels, and let each book contributed be labelled with the

Name of donor ....
Date of donation ....
Value of book ....
Condition (new, soiled, or shelf-worn) ....

7. Let the teacher use the local paper or papers of the county to make known the names of contributors, and the character and amount of each contribution.

8. Let there be a laudable ambition on the part of the teacher, pupils, and patrons of the school, to have the best school library in the county; and let

this purpose be made known through the public papers.

The foregoing plan, if skilfully carried out, will produce a fair beginning for a school library; and the same method may be repeated with increasing interest and pleasure, from year to year.

During the school term, the library should be mainly under the control of the teacher; but a librarian, and other officers, should be elected, and arrangements should be made to let out books at stated times, embracing the season when the school is not in session. In this way the school library may be made a *permanent institution*, and men of means may be led to contribute liberally to its support.

I find, in "The New England Journal of Education," Boston, a communication from a teacher on the subject, "How to start a School Library"; and I here present it for the consideration of those who wish to study the best methods for accomplishing this work: —

"Noticing the above query in a recent number of 'The Journal,' I thought I might interest its readers by stating how we started our library.

"I first mentioned the matter to the school, and asked the pupils to talk with their parents about it. I told them that all who contributed twenty-five cents should have their names enrolled as founders of the library; that each one should pay a cent a week for the privilege of taking out books, or fifteen cents for six months. I also asked them all to see at home if they had not some books that were old to them, but that would be new to others.

"I contributed a 'School History of England,' a delightful 'Child's History of the United States' (given me by a book agent), and the history of 'Old Abe' (bought at the Centennial). The children contributed over twenty books, all good and in good condition. They contributed and collected $8, and I collected over $2 by asking the different friends whom I met, 'Won't you give me five cents toward our school library?'

"In order to get the most for our money, we first subscribed for 'Wide-Awake' and 'The Nursery' for six months; we then invested about four dollars in cheap reprints of standard works, such as may be found in the Seaside and Franklin Square Libraries, and Harper's 'Half-Hour Series'; also several little paper-backed picture books for the little folks, including a five-cent copy of 'Mother Goose.' The remaining four dollars we spent for books on natural history, travels, etc.

"Our library has now been in operation two months, and, though only in its infancy, is a success. We have over one hundred volumes: among these are several on history and biography; some of Scott's, Dickens's, and Miss Muloch's; 'Arabian Nights,' 'Swiss Family Robinson,' and 'Robinson Crusoe.' Some of the more valuable works are only lent, but we are making good use of them while we have them. Several volumes of old magazines were contributed; these I stitched together by means of an awl and coarse thread, and they are quite in demand.

"In conclusion, I will only add that the best way to accomplish any desirable result is to have faith that you will succeed, and then go to work."

The school law of New Jersey provides that the State treasurer, upon the order of the State superintendent, is authorized to pay $20 to any school that shall raise a like sum, by subscription or entertainment, for the purpose of establishing a school library, and $10 annually thereafter on the same condition. I have before me the last three annual reports (1877, 1878, and 1879) of the State superintendent, containing some important facts and figures concerning the operations of this law, which I offer for consideration.

In his annual report for the year 1877, the superintendent says:—

"The number of school districts in the State is one thousand three hundred and sixty-seven. Three hundred and thirty-four districts have school libraries, sixty-five have made the first addition, forty-three the second, thirty-three the third, fifteen the fourth, and two the fifth."

In his annual report for the year 1878, he says:—

"The number of school districts in the State is one thousand three hundred and sixty-seven. Three hundred and ninety-five schools have established libraries, seventy have made the second application, fifty the third, twenty-two the fourth, twelve the fifth, ten, the sixth, and two the seventh."

In his annual report for the year 1879, the superintendent says: —

"The number of school districts in the State is one thousand three hundred and seventy. Four hundred and thirty-seven schools have established libraries, eighty-two have made the second application, fifty-four the third application, twenty-seven the fourth application, thirteen the fifth application, eleven the sixth application, five the seventh application, and one the eighth application."

From the foregoing official statement, it appears that nearly one third of the schools of the State of New Jersey have already established school libraries, and the number of libraries is annually increasing. This *co-operative plan, which helps those who help themselves*, is a wise arrangement, and I commend it to law-makers in other States.

But law-makers are rarely ever in advance of the people in matters of education. Therefore, if we wish our State legislatures to enact laws encouraging the establishment of school libraries, we must first lift the masses high enough to let them see some of the advantages of such libraries. This our teachers can accomplish by the establishment of libraries all over the land, upon the voluntary plan heretofore presented. In this way our teachers may *widen their work*, and increase their power and influence with the people.

In the selection of books for a school library, care should be taken to embrace a wide range of subjects;

but books which intelligent and cultured parents would be unwilling to place in the hands of their sons and daughters should find no place upon its shelves.

The school library should include, at least, some of the most popular histories, biographies, books of travel, stories, some standard works of fiction, the leading poets, books of reference, an unabridged dictionary, Shakespeare, and the Bible. Many standard works are now furnished by leading publishers at low prices, and a small amount of money will secure a fair library. The local newspapers of the county, and at last a couple of the great weeklies from the city, should also be included in the reading matter furnished for the school. It is the duty of the teacher to assist his pupils in forming a taste for reading. He should also, in a degree, direct them in their reading in connection with school studies and independent of the school course. In this way the teacher may lead his pupils to begin a course of reading which shall become a supplement to the school work, lasting throughout life.

The library should be kept open during school hours, and books of reference should be freely used by pupils in the preparation of their lessons. The teacher should instruct his pupils how to use books of reference, as the master mechanic teaches his apprentices how to use tools.

I find in "The Western Educational Journal," Chicago, an editorial on "The Use of Books of Reference," which is so appropriate that I here present it: —

"There is no doubt that too little use is made of books of reference in schools of all grades. Many teachers do not understand how to use to the best advantage even the unabridged dictionaries; failing in this knowledge themselves, how can they instruct their pupils when and how to use them? One of the most important qualifications of a thorough and successful teacher is the ability to teach pupils how to use other books than their text-books. Mere knowledge of what the text-books says upon any subject is not sufficient; the pupil should be taught how to supplement this knowledge by the constant and proper use of books of reference. Even the peculiar shade of meaning in a single word, as used in one connection rather than another, will often throw a flood of light upon the subject-matter in hand, and this may be had by a single reference to the dictionary.

"The master mechanic does not expect his apprentice to become a thorough workman by verbal instruction alone; he shows him how to use his tools to the best advantage. So with the teacher. To make good scholars they must be taught how to use their books of reference; and these should be provided in every school-room with liberality. The unabridged dictionary, of course, and with this the geographical gazetteer, the large atlas and globe, and the biographical dictionary; and, in the higher grades of schools, one of the best encyclopædias ; and all of these should be consulted by pupils under the teacher's guidance, as often as possible, until their use becomes familiar to all In this way will the pupils' habits of observation be cultivated, their ideas broadened, and a spirit of thoroughness be imparted which will be invaluable in later life. The man who knows how to investigate a subject is the man who will become master of it."

If all the teachers in our public schools would go to work, and, in some way, establish a suitable library in every school-room, and induce young people to form regular habits of reading, they would thereby secure to the masses greater prosperity, higher intelligence, and purer morality. It requires no argument to prove that in this way the work and influence of teachers would become worth, to the public, twice as much as at present. It is equally certain that an enlightened people would acknowledge this increased worth of their teachers by giving them correspondingly increased wages.

A brief editorial in "The American Journal of Education," St. Louis, is so clear upon this point that I present it for the consideration of teachers : —

"What the people need to *know* is, that intelligence begets thrift and enterprise, and coins money out of the land, out of the mine, out of water and out of air, and every other element; and that State which educates her people the best is the strongest State, the richest State, the most prosperous and law-abiding State. Our teachers should be so well posted that, when information is lacking, they can give it to establish the truth of these propositions. A little more reading and study on the part of our teachers would bring to them power and influence, and a rich reward."

LECTURE XIX.

NEWSPAPERS IN THE SCHOOL-ROOM AND FAMILY.

NEWSPAPERS are public teachers of incalculable value. No other public educators visit the family so often, no others are so numerous, or so ready to give instruction on any subject, at any hour. While the pulpit and the platform are using the newspaper to widen their influence and to multiply their power, our country school-teachers ought to be sufficiently progressive to use this same element for a like purpose in the educational work.

The first step to be taken by teachers in utilizing the newspaper is to introduce it into every school-room, and to see that it finds a place in every family. The second step to be taken is to keep the people posted, through its columns, as to what the schools are doing.

Speaking of the newspaper in the school-room, President Gregory, of the Illinois State University, says: "Every editor is a teacher, — a teacher of men as well as of children. The newspaper is the freshest of books. It is the latest history, the newest science treatise, the current political economy, the manual of the arts, the text-book of a living philosophy. That school-room, other things being equal, will be brightest, freshest, and most productive in practical learning into which the newspaper penetrates."

But some one will say, How can the newspaper be used in the school-room? I answer, it may be used in various ways. A very interesting and profitable reading exercise may be had, once or twice a week, by permitting each pupil to read from a newspaper an article of his own selection. It is evident that such an exercise will create an interest, and carry with it a freshness not seen or felt in reading from regular text-books. Pupils who take part in these exercises will search the newspapers for interesting articles, and will take pleasure in making thorough preparation to read them. In this way they will gain information on a variety of subjects, and they will learn to read as they talk, when they have something of importance to tell.

These weekly readings may be made still more profitable by inviting the patrons of the school to be present. The teacher should embrace these occasions to convince parents that newspapers are important aids in the education of a family. The following article, from the "National Journal of Education," Boston, may be of service to the teacher in the presentation of this subject: —

"A school-teacher who had been a long time engaged in his profession, and had witnessed the influence of newspapers on a family of children, writes as follows : —

"'I have found it to be a universal fact, without exception, that those scholars of both sexes, and all ages, who have access to newspapers at home, when compared with those who have not, are, —

"'1. Better readers, excellent in pronunciation, and consequently read more and understandingly.

"'2. They are better spellers; define words with ease and accuracy.

"'3. They obtain practical knowledge of geography in almost half the time required by others, as the newspapers have made them acquainted with the location of important places of all nations, their government and doings, on the globe.

"'4. They are better grammarians; for, having become so familiar with every style in newspapers, from the commonplace advertisement to the finished and classical oration of the statesman, they more readily comprehend the meaning of the text, and consequently analyze its construction with accuracy.

"'5. They write better compositions, using better language, containing more thoughts, more clearly and correctly expressed.

"'6. Those young men who have for years been readers of newspapers are always taking the lead in debating societies, exhibit a more extensive knowledge upon a greater variety of subjects, and express their views with greater fluency, clearness, and correctness.'"

In attempting to introduce papers into the family, the teacher may, in a quiet manner, make a list of the names of patrons who are subscribers to newspapers, and a list of those who take no papers. If he will manage this matter skilfully, the former list may be lengthened and the latter list may be lessened, until a newspaper shall be found in every family. When the list is completed, he should give notice of the fact through the local paper, as an incentive to other teachers to work in a similar manner.

President Hewitt, of one of the normal schools of Illinois, suggests an excellent way of using the knowledge gained from the newspaper, and of keeping the school posted on the news of the day. He says: "Ten minutes a day, for two or three days in the week, may be very profitably spent in our public schools in the way of a general exercise on the news of the day. A good plan is to let a committee of one or more pupils prepare a report giving a brief statement of the affairs that seem to be worthy of mention. Then let the teacher and the other pupils make criticisms, additions, corrections, and comments."

The foregoing method teaches pupils not only to compile, but to compose. It is the easiest and most natural method of teaching composition. Pupils may, in this way, be led to form the habit of writing for the public papers, — a habit which is always pleasurable and often profitable. I have seen this plan thoroughly tested, and I commend it to teachers.

I am clearly convinced that it is the duty of all teachers to engage in the work of circulating public papers. They are indispensable to the highest success in the work of educating the masses, — the fathers, the mothers, the children.

The following forcible suggestions upon this subject, from the "American Journal of Education," St Louis, are earnestly recommended to teachers : —

"If our teachers are wise — and they certainly are growing wiser and stronger and better — they will see to it that the printed page, carrying argument, persuasion, and facts, which ripen into conviction, is circulated continuously among the patrons and taxpayers. Trouble and hindrance come from lack of knowledge. Intelligent, well-posted people sustain the teachers in their work of instruction and discipline. Circulate the printed page among the people.

"Are your plans all laid for more reading in connection with your next school term? Books were never so cheap as now, — good books, too. Circulate good books, magazines, newspapers, and thus help the people outside the school-room as well as the pupils inside. The newspapers were never giving so much information as at present. By all means lay plans for more culture, for more reading with the pupils and the people. Intelligence begets its like, and intelligent people appreciate what and how much our teachers are doing for their children."

The teacher who circulates public papers may

easily avoid the charge of "partisan," by obtaining a list of leading periodicals from which to allow patrons to choose for themselves. The newsdealer is not censured for keeping on hand pure publications of all parties. It is a good plan to appoint a committee of the larger pupils, ladies and gentlemen, to solicit subscriptions, as the young people will in this way become interested in the circulation of papers.

The teacher and pupils may with propriety give the preference to the *local paper*, as it is properly the organ of the people of the county, and ought to find a place in every family. Where there is more than one local paper there is a chance to make choice. On this subject I quote the following article from the "American Journal of Education":—

"First the county newspaper, then the great weeklies from the city, and then the religious newspaper, bring all the world to you, and take you out of yourself into the society of the best and strongest. The newspaper, then, not only increases your intelligence, but your faith in the possibilities of yourself and the great people among whom you dwell. The local county papers are not only very friendly, but very helpful to teachers. They are pleased, always, to note the progress made by the pupils in the schools. They are glad to say good things of the good work done by our teachers. The printed page of the local newspaper should find its way to every home and fireside. Certainly no intelligent father or mother can afford to allow the children to grow up without a glimpse of the outside and out-of-sight world which the newspaper gives. Use, by all means, the local papers, to show the tax-payers what is being done in your school."

Objections are sometimes urged against the circulation of local papers, —

1. Because there is sometimes want of culture in the style of their composition.

2. Because they are not always free from impurity and indecency.

The first objection proves that our system of public education has done its work imperfectly; that the masses have not been thoroughly trained in composition. The remedy is, more thorough culture of the masses, that we may be sure to reach those who will become journalists.

The second objection may be removed by the people if they will refuse to tolerate such impurities in their papers. The easiest way to reach this evil is for the teachers to take it into their hands. Let them, in their annual county educational association, resolve that they will try to place the local paper in every family in the county, upon condition that its columns shall be as free from impurity as the conversation in a refined family. Then let the editor accept this proposition. If, after that, an objectionable article should appear in the paper, the attention of the editor should be called to the subject, and he should be treated as a friend who is at fault. If it should become necessary, these admonitions may be repeated from time to time, until the annual association shall again assemble, when a resolution condemning the paper may, with propriety, be passed, and the teachers may give their influence to a purer paper. It would indeed be a rare case that the teachers of a county, heartily supporting the local paper, could not have sufficient influence with its editor to keep its columns clear of impurity.

So far as the impurity of city papers is concerned, about all that teachers can do is to circulate only those that are pure.

An editorial in the "Mobile Register" presents the proper standard of purity for public papers. It says: —

"There is no reason why a newspaper should not be as free from impurity or indecency as the daily conversation of a refined Christian family. The newspaper should be a publication which a father might place in the hands of his daughter, or a brother in those of his sister; in short, which should enter any household without the necessity of preliminary examination. The plea that it must be a mirror of all things going on in the world, — things base, vile, and disgusting, as well as things pure and honorable, — is the shallow sophistry of a prurient inclination. It will not bear examination, as it would not bear being carried out to its full extent, even in the eyes of those who urge it.

"It is no answer to say that newspapers in general

fall far below the standard we have indicated. It is too true that they do, but this proves only that their actual standard is debased. That it is so is, partly, at least, the fault of the public that tolerate it."

We come, in conclusion, to consider how our teachers are to keep the people posted on what the schools are doing. On this subject I will once more quote from the "American Journal of Education":—

"Keep up a column in the county papers. Keep the people posted. The farmers want to know what corn and wheat and potatoes are worth, how much is produced. They want to see results all along the line. It is right that they should. People want to know what progress the children are making in their studies, what they get for the money they pay. It is right that they should know this. Publish this progress in the columns of the county papers, and let the people know what the schools are doing.

"Let the people know that it costs more to hang a man, to board and lodge a man in the prisons, than it would to teach him the duties and responsibilities of American citizenship, and how to get an honest living; that it costs far more to maintain a system of prisons than of education.

"Let the people know that school facilities add to the value of property; train the pupils to industry, to obedience to law, to order, to economy, to thrift, and they produce more and save more.

"Let the people know that education promotes industry and lessens idleness, that it awakens and intensifies desires, and thus incites and impels man to effort to secure the means of gratification; that it touches both factors in the great law of wealth, and that ignorance dwells in hovels, but intelligence changes the rude hut to the cottage.

"Let the people know that the universal and undisputed testimony is that the hand has the highest skill when guided by an intelligent mind; that education improves the condition of the laborer; gives him greater thrift and economy; lessens his tendency to vice; increases his social and political influence, and otherwise prepares him to meet the obligations and duties of manhood."

All the foregoing facts will appear by a wide comparison of an ignorant and an unintelligent people. But we should also let parents know that the schools are producing more than mere wealth and prosperity. They are imparting culture, Christian culture,— preparing our young people for the enjoyment of a higher degree of happiness, purer pleasures than can possibly be enjoyed by uncultured people.

No teacher need doubt the willingness of the newspaper to aid the educational work. The teacher can find no other friend so influential, and so ready to aid him in every possible manner. In fact, the public press has long been the leader of this great movement,— the education of the masses.

Col. Moore, in an oration before the editorial convention of Missouri, expresses beautifully the sentiment and purposes of the public press. He says: —

"The education and elevation of the masses in every department of knowledge will be the special purpose of the newspaper. It will be a check to the powerful, and an aid to the lowly. It will be stronger than factions and parties, and of necessity independent in the broadest sense of the term. It will make and destroy the rulers of men, for the rulers of men, no more than private individuals, can stand against a concentration of adverse popular opinion, and its audience will be without number, and it will reach them through a thousand different avenues of thought. It will follow the merchant's ship in its course around the world, and, understanding the laws of trade, direct commerce, with its potent voice and prophetic vision, into those channels which enrich nations and build up cities. It will be a friend of art, a friend of science, a friend of every occupation, and labor, and calling, the results of which have a tendency to beautify and ennoble life."

LECTURE XX.

TEACHER'S SALARY, LIBRARY, AND EDUCATIONAL JOURNALS.

TEACHERS of country schools sometimes ask why their calling is not styled a profession, and why they receive for their services so much less than the lawyer and doctor. I propose to consider some of the causes which have created this difference in position and pay, and to suggest the means by which this difference may be diminished.

No one will claim that the work of the teacher is less important than the work of the lawyer, or that the services of the physician are more essential to society than the services of the teacher. If we visit the office of a successful attorney, and inquire into his secret of gaining honors and making money, he will perhaps inform us that, after completing his education, he spent years of study under a learned preceptor, before he began the practice of his profession. He may further inform us that his law library and journals cost as much as an ordinary farm upon which a man might maintain a family. From the preparation he has made, and the capital he has invested, it is evident that he will expect and receive large fees for his services.

If we visit the office of our family physician and examine his medical library and surgical instruments, and learn their cost, and if we ascertain how much time and money he spent in making preparation for the practice of his profession, his charges for attending our sick will seem much more reasonable than we have, heretofore, believed them to be.

If we would call upon several pastors of churches, and learn what preparation each one has made for his sacred calling, if we would look into the library and examine the periodicals of each, and then ascertain the amount of salary which each one receives for his support, we would find, as a rule, that each one is paid about in proportion to his preparation and capital.

If we could call our country teachers together, and learn from each the extent of his special preparation and the cost of his library and educational journals, we would probably find that; among well-informed people, the teacher, considering his special preparation and capital invested, is as well paid for his services as the lawyer and doctor. Then, among well-informed patrons and school officers, the principal cause of difference in position and pay between the country teacher and the professional man arises from difference in preparation made and capital invested, and the surest way to diminish this difference is for the teacher to enlarge his preparation and increase his capital.

The teacher's special preparation does not consist of mere knowledge of text-books, though this knowledge is essential, but it includes the study of the laws that govern the growth of body and mind, and it should, by all means, embrace general information and broad culture. In order to make this preparation, the teacher must have books, he must have a library. It need not be costly. It need not be large at first, but it should increase in size from year to year.

When the library of any teacher gets its growth, its owner will cease to grow also, and he is then no longer suited to the work of the school-room. The following article from the pen of Hon. Wm. A. Bell is so appropriate here, that I present it: —

"When a tree stops growing, it begins to die. In this regard a man resembles a tree. When a person's mind ceases to grow — when it fails to add new thoughts, and thus strengthen itself — it begins to dry up and lose power.

"This principle applies with rare fitness to the teacher. A teacher who does not '*add new wood*' every year falls into ruts, goes backward, *dies* as a teacher. Paradoxical as it may seem, it is nevertheless true that the teacher who stands still goes backwards. It is simply an impossibility that a teacher shall retain, through a number of years, the vigor and freshness of his early teaching unless he study; and this study must not consist in the simple routine of preparing daily recitations, — daily preparations, of course, — the reading of professional literature of course, — but something more.

"The mind must be led out of the narrow routine of school-room duties, and allowed to take in something of what is called 'general culture.' The teacher who does not spend some time in study outside the line of his daily duties, of necessity grows narrow. *One hour* of each twenty-four wisely used for mental growth and culture is salt enough to save from stagnation. The manner in which this one hour (more or less) is used will determine very largely whether or not a teacher will rise in his profession, or continue to 'job round' year after year, and then sink beneath the wave of advancing requirements."

Many of our teachers are men and women of reading and culture, but there are others who possess almost no general information. Too many of them, without any special preparation, enter the school-room armed with no weapons but text-books.

In some sections of the country the special training and general information of teachers are not noted by those who employ them and fix their salaries. In all such cases it is evident that the people have not been clearly shown the superior work of well-trained and well-informed teachers. It is equally evident that it will pay progressive teachers to widen their work, and help the people outside the school to gain correct notions upon this subject. This they can accomplish : —

1. By the superior quality and breadth of their work, inside and outside of the school-room.

2. By circulating educational journals among the people, and especially among school officers who employ teachers and fix their salaries.

Let each teacher see to it that every member of his school board reads regularly a good educational journal.

We have no statistics giving the number of libraries possessed by teachers of country schools, nor the exact number of country teachers who are subscribers to educational journals; but the meagre support given to these periodicals proves that a very large proportion of our teachers take no journals. An editorial in the "Educational Weekly," Chicago, says:

"One would think that, of all classes in the community, teachers would be the first to sustain their papers. Yet we venture to assert that there is no other learned profession that to-day is doing so little for the maintenance of its periodical literature. This may be in part due to the fact that the teacher's profession demands such a wide scope of reading, and such a many-sided culture, that there is little time and money left for journals that are devoted more especially to the interests of our schools. The same may be said, however, of all the other professions, in a degree. They all demand extensive reading and varied information, and all who excel in them must find time for this. Making all due allowance for the requirements of modern learning, we still feel that teachers, as a class, are behind the age in attention to the details of their profession, and in the use of means provided by the press for promoting their success."

An editorial in the "Practical Teacher" suggests that principals and superintendents are largely responsible for the fact that so many teachers fail to read books and to take journals. It says: "Many of our teachers don't read books treating upon their work. They don't take educational periodicals. They don't attend teachers' institutes They don't do a great many other things that they ought to do. True, true, every word of it. But we believe in giving to all their dues, and there is another party to this case who should be included in this indictment, viz.. principals and superintendents. A great many of these don't read books treating upon their work; nor take educational journals; nor attend teachers' institutes; nor do a great many other things they ought to do. And another thing they don't do: although they occupy positions as leaders and guides to their teachers, they not only take no educational journal themselves, but they are too indifferent to bring the subject before their teachers. And we may say further, that when journals, the best in the country, are sent to them, with the request that they distribute them among their teachers, they are too dead and lifeless, or too important, to do even that. Such leaders are a hindrance and a dishonor to their grand work. But for them the cause of education would, to-day, be far in advance of what it is."

An editorial in "Barnes's Educational Monthly,"

New York, asserts that one reason why so many teachers take no educational journals, is to be found in the fact that in some normal schools, where teachers are trained, but little interest is taken in the subject of journals. In proof of this assertion it cites the following fact: —

"In a State normal school receiving and expending over eighteen thousand dollars a year, with a faculty of sixteen teachers, only *two* of these teachers take and pay for any kind of an educational journal. *Only two!* Among the pupils, three hundred young men and women, — our future teachers, — *not one* takes any kind of an educational journal."

I know from personal experience that superintendents sometimes neglect to enforce earnestly upon the minds of their teachers the need of educational journals. I know also that when the subject is properly presented, teachers are ready to respond. I will give a case as an illustration.

When I entered upon the work of superintending schools of Monongalia County, West Virginia, in 1874, I found very few teachers in the county subscribers to educational journals. I took occasion in our institutes, from time to time, to call the attention of teachers to this subject, but I found little, if any, increase in the number of journals taken by teachers. In the autumn of 1878 I concluded that, in visiting the schools the following winter, I would present the subject, privately, to each teacher, in his own school-room. I carried with me specimen copies of several journals, and with little labor, and no loss of time, I was able, at the end of the school term, to report eighty-one out of ninety teachers employed in the county, subscribers to one or more educational journals.

I feel quite certain that our normal schools would rest on a firmer foundation, that they would furnish better teachers, and do better work, if they would require all pupils, before graduation, to become thoroughly acquainted with the spirit and work of our school system, by reading regularly some of the best educational journals. I am sure that our county superintendents and commissioners would greatly increase their efficiency, that they would popularize school supervision, if they would, by personal efforts, place an educational journal in the hands of every teacher. I am confident that our country teachers would widen their usefulness, and increase their salaries, if they would place an educational journal in the hands of every local school officer, and, as far as practicable, in every family. In this way the people would become equally interested, in feeling as well as in fact, with the teacher, and they would become " fellow-laborers " in the educational work.

The influence and usefulness of periodical literature are but beginning to be understood and appreciated by superintendents, principals, and teachers, and it is not strange that, in time past, many of them have neglected to read and circulate educational journals. The reason why these journals were never before so highly appreciated is, they were never so good as at present. Some of them are devoted to special departments in education, while others occupy a very wide field, extending from the kindergarten to the university.

There is, however, one department in education to which no journal, either in this country or in England, has been, heretofore, entirely devoted. This department may be styled higher education, though it does not pertain to high schools alone. It is the science and philosophy of education, — a subject that should be carefully studied by all educators, from the county superintendent to the university president. This field is now occupied by an international magazine, entitled "Education," conducted by Mr. T. W. Bicknell, of Boston. In order to give a fairer view of the field which this magazine proposes to occupy, I present the following extract from its first prospectus: —

"It is the most encouraging sign of the times, educationally, that the science and the art of teaching are coming to be recognized as the foundation of a profession of pedagogics. Hitherto but little attention has been paid to the fact that profound study and investigation were required to develop the laws of good teaching and the philosophy of sound instruction. If we mistake not, the current of thought now seeks to discover the essential spirit of true methods, and the soul of dry formulas. Every method, new or old, is put to the searching test of psychology, and the normal laws of mental growth. Failing to meet the demands of this high tribunal of reason and intelligence, it fails utterly. Our magazine proposes to discuss questions of education on the sides of philosophy and humanity. We hope to secure in our discussions writers of breadth as well as depth, of general as well as special attainments. We hope to bring the studies of our best thinkers and writers within the reach of the middle and higher classes of our profession, and to offer to those ambitious to ascend the means of promotion by the intellectual uplift of superior experienced minds. We hope to show that there is a true harmony in all departments of study, from the lowest grade to the highest, and that the success of each grade is an element in the advancement of every other section. We shall endeavor to recognize in the departments their functions in the related educational organism, the harmony of whose adjustment is the proper and universal study of the true educator. Above all, it will be our purpose to show that a better understanding of the human mind, the laws which govern its growth, and the results to be attained thereby, are but the nearer approach of the human to the divine, and an adaptation of the highest faith to the soul's spiritual needs; in other words, that education and religion are one whole, and not the complement of each other."

The great variety of educational periodicals in this country, and the wide range of subjects discussed in their columns, warrant the conclusion that every educator can find a journal suited to his work. The teacher who, in this age of reading, narrows his natural powers by confining himself to text-books, is not fit for the work, and ought to find some other employment.

Some teachers claim that they are so poorly paid that they cannot afford to buy books or to take papers. These teachers say, "Let the people pay us better, and then we will qualify ourselves to do better work." But this demand is contrary to the laws of trade. Skill, in any business, brings a good price in all the markets of the world, but no one has a right to demand the price which skill brings until he possesses the skill. The teacher's preparation, library, and journals constitute his stock in trade, and no one can reasonably expect large profits from small investments. The following editorial from the "New York School Journal" is so appropriate to this subject, that I present it: —

"1. Remember that in teaching, as well as in any other business, you must have a good deal of capital invested to obtain large proceeds.

"2. Remember that your capital is your health, your education, your library, your determination to brighten and improve yourself, and your power to teach others.

"3. Remember that every good business man seeks to enlarge his business each year, by constantly investing more capital.

"4. Remember that good business men watch the market; they mark what others are doing, note how they do it, and take papers and journals that give specific information. You will be very short-sighted if you do not imitate their example.

"5. Remember that business men often meet and consult. They have exchanges, boards of trade, hold fairs, etc. Teachers who do not pursue a similar line of conduct have themselves to blame when they fail.

"6. Remember that your work is a business, in many respects, and must be conducted on business principles; that it does not consist in keeping your pupils still, and getting replies to questions many of which you could not answer yourself.

"7. Remember that your work, if done right, will make you a competent man or woman; it will, like any business, give you a better judgment, more information, and a wider range of thought.

"8. Remember that you ought to be more deeply interested in it every day, as every business man is in his business."

The time is coming — it is near at hand — when people will ask no clearer proof of the incompetency of any teacher than the fact that he has no library, and that he takes no journals. These are no less essential to the teacher in the school than to the attorney at the bar, to the physician in the sick room, or to the minister in the pulpit.

LECTURE XXI.

TEACHERS' TRAINING-SCHOOLS AND INSTITUTES.

The demand for experienced and well-trained teachers was never so great as at present. In some of the larger towns, and in several cities, no inexperienced person is employed as a teacher, unless he has taken a thorough course in some good training-school. This forward step in the educational work of the city is already indorsed by many of the most intelligent people of the country districts, and it is evident that this must eventually become the rule in the selection of teachers of every grade.

Thorough training is not more essential to the success of the lawyer than to the success of the teacher. No one having a case in court would employ as his counsel a man who has had neither training nor practice in the profession of law. The parent cannot afford to commit the education of his children into the hands of an untrained teacher, any more than he can afford to commit a suit in court into the hands of an untrained lawyer. I am aware that many who have been trained for the work of teaching are not first-class teachers. It is equally true that many who have been trained for the bar are not first-class lawyers. Yet I venture to assert that all trained teachers and trained lawyers are doing far better work than they would have done without this training.

It may be asserted, with some degree of truth, that our normal schools have graduated and sent out too many incompetent teachers. This charge was, perhaps, truer in the past than it is at the present. State Superintendent J. P. Wickersham, of Pennsylvania, lays down the law by which this evil may be avoided. He says: —

"Normal schools rest their claims to the support of the State and the people upon the assumption that they are preparing a more skilful class of practical teachers. Whether or not they do this depends mainly upon the use they make of their model schools. No one should be graduated who is not an *expert* in the school-room. Whatever the character or scholarship, a want of skill in imparting instruction or in handling a class should be fatal to graduation."

Our best educators, almost without exception, maintain that money expended for the support of normal schools is a paying investment. I present, as an example, the opinion of Dr. Barnas Sears, agent of the Peabody Educational Fund. He says: —

"The leading countries of Europe have experimented on this subject, and are unanimous in their opinions of the expediency of normal training and of superintendence. The same is true, for a shorter period, of every State of the Union. I venture the assertion that, in the opinion of competent judges, no school-money in Europe or America has been more advantageously expended than that paid for normal schools."

Normal schools are growing in favor with the American people. As evidence of this, I may refer to the fact that their number is increasing from year to year. The following table from the last report of the Commissioner of Education shows the annual increase in the number of normal schools, instructors, and students, for seven successive years:—

TABLE OF NORMAL SCHOOLS.

	1870.	1871.	1872.	1873.	1874.	1875.	1876.	1877.
No. of Institutions,	63	65	98	113	124	137	151	152
No. of Instructors,	178	445	773	687	960	1,031	1,065	1,189
No. of students..	10,028	10,922	11,778	16,620	24,405	29,105	33,921	37,062

Most of our normal schools are academic in their character. They impart instruction in the branches, and also train persons in the art of teaching. This has been the occasion of complaint on the part of some, who maintain that normal schools should be restricted to the professional course, and should give no instruction in any branches of study. The following article from the pen of Professor Edward Brooks, principal of the State Normal School at

Millersville, Penn., shows why normal schools should teach the branches: —

"The teacher must possess knowledge in order to impart it to others; he cannot teach what he does not know. He also needs to have his own powers cultivated for the power it gives him to think, to originate and modify methods, and to influence and control his pupils. In other words, the ideal teacher should be a person with well-cultured powers and a liberal education. It is thus apparent that thorough scholastic training lies at the foundation of a teacher's education. The normal school must, therefore, require of its pupils a thorough training in the branches of a scholastic course of study. .

"This qualification seems to be equivalent to that afforded by the academy or college, and it has been a question widely discussed whether it should not be obtained at these institutions. It was formerly held that the normal school should not attempt to give this scholastic training, but should restrict itself to the work of the professional course; that any attempt to impart instruction in the branches of knowledge was a departure from the legitimate function of a normal school, and an infringement upon the domain of these other institutions. This opinion was held, not merely by those who were not in sympathy with normal school work, but also by some of the leading normal-school men in the country. It has been found, however, in the practical working of these schools, that the young people who presented themselves for professional instruction were not properly prepared in the branches; and the normal schools were thus compelled to introduce a scholastic department, whether they desired to do so or not.

"Whatever, therefore, be the true theory of normal-school instruction, experience has proved the present necessity of such a scholastic course; and the normal schools of the country to-day, almost if not entirely without exception, have provided for the scholastic training of their pupils. Such a course, however, in my opinion, is not only a present practical necessity, but an essential part of the true theory of normal-school education."

Much as our normal schools have done, and are still doing, statistics show that they are training but a small per cent of the teachers of the whole country. The cause of this will be clearly seen if we consider the fact that a large per cent of the students in academies and colleges pay part of their yearly expenses by teaching in the country during the winter, and the greater number of those who do not teach while taking their college course, turn their attention to teaching after graduation. In order that these may be properly trained, it is necessary that instructions in the art and science of teaching shall be given in all schools of high order.

Some of our foremost colleges have already established chairs of didactics for the thorough training of teachers, and others are moving in this direction. President Magoun, of Iowa College, urges the following reasons for this movement : —

"*First*, A large proportion of the graduates take up teaching, either from necessity, for a time, after graduating, or from choice, making it their profession for life; and this latter class it is, for every reason, desirable to increase.

"*Second*, The colleges, by their trained and experienced teachers, and by their laboratories and museums, are best fitted to meet at once the demand for teachers who are thoroughly educated and up to the times in all branches."

The "Educational Weekly," Chicago, contains an article from the pen of Prof. S. N. Fellows, of Iowa University, in which he briefly recapitulates as follows the reasons for establishing chairs of didactics in colleges and universities. He says: —

"1. It will greatly assist the graduates, who, from their superior culture, will occupy chief places and become teachers of teachers.

"2. A reflex benefit will accrue to the colleges themselves, in the greater success of their graduates and in improved methods of their own work.

"3. Professional educational literature will be improved.

"4. The development of a true science of education will be promoted.

"5. It will be a deserved recognition by the highest educational authorities of the value and need of professional training for teachers of every grade.

"6. Teaching will more justly merit the title of a profession.

"7. Higher institutions will become more closely united with our public-school system.

"8. It will increase and widen the knowledge of the ends and means of education among those who, though not teachers, will hold high official and social positions."

Our educational journals with great unanimity favor professorships of didactics in universities and colleges. Mr. T. W. Bicknell, editor of the New England "Journal of Education," in a late editorial, says: —

"The most pressing want of our day and country is a class of professionally educated teachers. It is not a new want. Horace Mann felt it fifty years ago, and attempted to satisfy it by the establishment of the first normal school in Massachusetts in 1839. All true leaders in education have seen the wisdom of that initiative movement for the supplying of schools with fit and fitly educated teachers, and have labored for the establishment of normal schools, normal institutes, anything and everything that would have any possible influence in lifting teaching out of the low forms of mechanical work to the higher plane of philosophic (because natural) methods of instruction.

"Normal schools have done much, directly and indirectly, in forty years, to make teaching a profession, and to make men and women having the power and scope of educators. But even in the States where normal schools have had the longest life and strongest influence, not over thirty per cent of the teachers have ever seen a normal school, or enjoyed its instruction; in others, the percentage varies from this maximum to two, three, four, and five per cent. It has become evident that something more must be done in this direction of raising up a class of educated teachers, and the colleges are now attempting to supplement the work by the establishment of chairs of pedagogics, of didactics, of theory and practice of teaching, etc.

"How far this move partakes of the nature of a bid to fill vacant school-rooms, boarding-houses, etc., in college-surfeited communities, is not the question with us now. Whatever the end may be, if the means is adequate for the production of teachers, we are satisfied. This addition of teachers' courses to the regular college course may mean much or little; much, if it attempts to make a real professional class by a course of study which shall not be an optional, but an additional college grade of study; much, if it places in these chairs men and women of the best accomplished talent and experience in the theory, the philosophy, and the practice of teaching. The Western colleges are especially alive in the introduction of pedagogics in the regular college curriculum. Its double influence ought and will be to improve the teaching of the colleges themselves, where, if anywhere, normal instruction and methods should have a home, and to prepare a class of young men and women with more thorough finishing for the work of teaching, upon which so many of our newly graduated students are entering."

The following article is from the "Educational News Gleaner," Chicago: —

"It will doubtless be urged that college graduates, by virtue of their higher education, require no professional training as a prerequisite for teaching. It is true that a college course may fit a graduate for some kinds of special teaching, but it certainly fails to prepare one to become a good general teacher of a common school or a high school. If a college diploma should entitle the holder to a teacher's certificate, then why not to a medical diploma, or to admission to the bar?

"It certainly is desirable that colleges and universities, especially those established and maintained by the State, should establish professorships of science and art of education, and provide post-graduate courses for those who intend to become teachers. 'Professors of the Theory, History, and Practice of Education' have been appointed in the Universities of Edinburgh and St. Andrews, Scotland, and such a chair is soon to be established in the University of Cambridge, England. This measure has been urged in our own country by prominent educators, such as Professor Fellows, of the Iowa University, Principal Dunton, of the Boston Normal School, Rev. A. D. Mayo, associate editor of the 'National Journal of Education,' Boston, and many others. The University of Michigan has taken the lead in establishing such a chair, and Professor Payne ably fills it. The universities and colleges, combined with State and city normal schools, and normal classes organized in connection with high schools, could in ten years supply the nation with a corps of trained teachers for every grade of school, — from the country school to the high school."

Gen. John Eaton, Commissioner of the Bureau of Education at Washington, in his last annual report, presents his views upon this subject, and shows that no less than twenty German universities take an interest in the training of teachers. Here is what he says : —

"The science and art of teaching is surely a subject so important that it may well be included in the curricula of our universities and colleges. The State University of Iowa established a chair of didactics in 1873, made it an elective subject for the senior year, and gives the degree of bachelor of didactics to such of its graduates as have taught two years after receiving this instruction. The example seems worthy of imitation.

"The attempt to establish chairs of didactics has been embarrassed by the historic customs of our older colleges. They largely retain the ideas and methods which were brought by the colonists from the mother country, and contemplate the education of a comparatively small number of persons, and this after their minds are measurably mature. Their methods are poorly adapted to instruct immature minds, have been totally abandoned in all intelligent elementary training, and have been modified in secondary instruction.

"Naturally the learned men at the head of our colleges were considered the leaders in our educational affairs. Often they stood aloof from the elementary school, and usually made no effort to modify their own methods for its use. Teaching many other sciences, they omitted the philosophy of education from their curriculum, sometimes, indeed, acting as though there were no such subject in the domain of thought. It has been the same spirit, but not carried to the same extent, which has contended against the teaching of the natural sciences.

"It is this lack of a really comprehensive philosophy of culture, which should include man in all his conditions and relations, that has permitted, if not promoted, foolish prejudices between institutions of learning founded on a religious and a civic basis respectively, and between those founded by the several religious denominations.

"A partial cure for this condition has been found in the various college associations which have been founded from time to time. These cannot be conducted with any marked interest and vigor without making our colleges better acquainted and more sympathetic with each other, and causing them to assume a better relation to all other phases of instruction.

"It is not too much to hope that another result will be a more careful consideration of the philosophy of education, and adequate provision for the sound and thorough teaching of it. Many institutions, whose students defray a large part of their expenses before graduation by teaching, do not give an hour's instruction in this subject, nor make any effort to secure pedagogical works for their libraries.

"In striking contrast with this apathy is the treatment of the philosophy of education by the German universities. In the following German universities pedagogy is taught by means of lectures for the time stated: —

	Hours a week.		Hours a week.
Berlin	6	Jena	6
Bonn	4	Kiel	3
Breslau	3	Leipzig	8
Erlangen	2	Münster	4
Freiburg	2	Tübingen	3
Giessen	2	Würzburg	4
Göttingen	2	Vienna	6
Greifswald	3	Berne	2
Halle	5	Basel	2
Heidelberg	3	Zürich	2

"At Jena the subjects of the lectures are: History of education, scientific principles of educating the child, school discipline, methods of instruction, school hygiene, school legislation, school architecture, ancient and modern languages, comparative philology, logic, metaphysics.

"There are in Germany, besides the ordinary seminaries for the training of elementary teachers, several advanced pedagogic seminaries, whose object is to give the students an opportunity to acquire a more profound scientific knowledge in their specialties before they enter upon their professional duties. These purely scientific institutions are attended only by students and graduates of universities, who aspire to the higher positions in the secondary and superior schools. In some of these seminaries great stress is laid on philology, in others on the philosophy of education."

We may feel assured, from the tests already made, both in Europe and in this country, that in establishing chairs of didactics in colleges and universities, we are trying no uncertain experiment.

Next to the normal school, and near akin to it, is the teachers' institute, held annually, and in some places oftener, in almost every school district, county, and State. The teachers' institute is not intended to dispense with, but rather to supplement the work of the training-school. It aims to bring together educational workers of every grade, from the teacher of the primary school to the president of the university, so as to give teachers of the lowest grade the benefit of the highest instructions.

The value of the teachers' institute is found, not alone in the fact that it imparts instructions in the branches and in the art of teaching, but that it affords opportunities for teachers to become better acquainted; that it brings them into fuller sympathy with each other; and that it has a tendency to harmonize the educational work from the common school to the university. I can point to no higher example of this than the six weeks' State Institute held lately in the Virginia University buildings, at Charlottesville. I offer, in conclusion, an account of this institute from the pen of Rev. A. D. Mayo, of Boston, associate editor of the "National Journal of Education," who was one of the lecturers at the institute. Writing from Charlottesville, he says : —

"The State University offered its entire facilities, in class-rooms, libraries, collections, and boarding-houses, for the whole session, while its leading professors have heartily joined its list of lecturers; and their families, in the spirit of true Virginia hospitality, have opened their own houses, and in every way labored to make the crowd of teachers feel themselves at home. Probably no school institute in the country ever assembled under circumstances more attractive. No group of university buildings in America enjoys an outlook so beautiful, or, on the whole, is so generally pervaded with the true academic atmosphere as the University of Virginia. Its spacious park of nearly five hundred acres, in good cultivation, is crowned by the library, from whose dome the eye sweeps over one of the most enchanting views in this region of enchantment, the Piedmont slopes of the Blue Ridge. Here are now assembled four hundred and fifty teachers, two thirds of them women, the large majority teachers of common schools in the country, and the smaller towns of the State, although there is a fine representation of the superior teachers from the best academies; and many family instructors, and even professors in colleges, have come up to the feast. The number was limited to five hundred, the seating capacity of the university hall, although a little effort would have brought a thousand. This institute includes only the white teachers, another of three hundred colored teachers being in session for the same period at Lynchburg.

"One of the most interesting features of this assemblage is its representative character. Almost every county, and, from the immediate vicinity, every school district, is represented. It is the first time in the history of the State when any number of common-school teachers so large and influential have looked in each other's faces, and been brought in friendly contact with teachers in academical schools and the faculty of a leading university. It is impossible to estimate the effects of a six weeks' intercourse upon this body of teachers. The curse of Southern life is its isolation; and the teacher in the little country school, or the graded school of the village, worried by the thousand obstacles that still beset the common school in this portion of the country, finds herself here in a company which probably represents, in large measure, the educational intelligence and real worth of the Commonwealth. It would probably be difficult to get together five hundred people who, all the way from the university president and the governor out to the district schoolmistress, cover a greater variety of interests, and more truly the most hopeful life of the new dominion. In the reception given by the ladies of the university to the institute, on Friday evening, July 30, a stranger could overlook as brilliant a throng of young people as one is likely to see. There were in the crowd teachers connected with the families of Washington, Jefferson, the Randolphs, Patrick Henry, Governor Nelson, Ex-President Tyler, Jeff. Davis; indeed, a large number of the historical characters of the State there appeared by proxy.

"The instruction in the institute has been admirably arranged by Superintendent Newell, of Maryland, himself one of the best representatives of the new education in all its ins and outs, and an organizer of school work of rare ability. Dr. Ruffner, State Superintendent of Virginia, is also in attendance, and is one of the lecturers. Rev. Wm. B. McGilvray, one of the Richmond masters, and Professor A. L. Funk, until recently an eminent teacher in the State, are daily lecturers on methods. The university professors are giving valuable lectures on science, literature, and teaching, and are always at hand to walk the cabinets, libraries, and laboratory with all who desire their aid. A course of five lectures has also been delivered by A. D. Mayo, associate editor of the 'National Journal of Education.' The institute opens at 8.30 A. M., and is instructed by lectures till 12. Constant attendance is insisted on, and full notes taken. At 12 the main body breaks into nine sections, which, for an hour, are instructed by teachers selected for their special fitness, and examined upon the lectures previously delivered. The afternoon is given to rest, with the exception of a general lecture at the closing hour. There is also a good deal of private, special work going on at odd hours. Indeed we have never seen together a body of young people more thoroughly in earnest, more determined to get at and utilize the principles and methods of the best school-keeping. To large numbers of them it has come with all the force of a 'revival of religion,' a wakening up to the glory and beauty of the new gospel to the children, like the first view from the summit of one of their mountains over the wonderland that lies outspread beneath. It is an education in itself to sit upon the platform and watch the faces of these teachers, as some new point is made, or some home appeal wakes up a great deep of thought and feeling before unknown. These eventful weeks will become an epoch in the life of many an earnest young man or woman, no less than a historical point of departure in the educational life of the State.

"The State University of Virginia has cast the whole weight of its great influence upon the side of the rising common school. In this it only follows in the steps of its founder, Thomas Jefferson, who first outlined the plan of the complete system of free education extending from the district school to the university."

I cannot conclude this subject without referring to the fact that we have a "National Educational Association," embracing teachers of every grade ; a " National Council of Education," composed of fifty-one of the foremost thinkers connected with the educational work ; and an " International Society for Investigating and Promoting the Science of Teaching," which last-named society already includes many of the most progressive and scholarly educators in this country and in Canada.

Taking into consideration the number of institutes held in districts, counties, and States, and the annual national gatherings of teachers, it is certainly safe to say that no other distinct class of men and women meets so often for mutual improvement.

LECTURE XXII.

TEACHERS' EXAMINATIONS AND COURSE OF STUDY.

The annual re-examination of country teachers in the naked primary branches and in nothing else is about as unprogressive a plan as could possibly be devised. It is as discouraging, unwise, and unprogressive as the old custom which required all pupils, at the opening of the school term, to commence each branch of study at the beginning of the book.

The annual re-examination in the bare branches and in nothing else has made the impression upon the minds of many teachers that they need no knowledge outside of text-books. This system gives the well-informed and highly cultivated teacher no better certificate or salary than it gives the teacher whose knowledge is bounded by the narrow limits of text-books. Almost any sprightly youth who has just completed the common branches may, in many of these examinations, measure arms with teachers of information and experience. These facts, which no intelligent person will deny, prove that educators ought to invent a wiser plan for the examination of teachers.

Dr. John Hancock, superintendent of the city

schools of Dayton, Ohio, and ex-president of the National Educational Association, in an article published in the "Public School Journal," Cincinnati, urges a radical change in the present mode of conducting teachers' examinations. His article is so appropriate here, that I present it in full. He says: —

"No department connected with the organization of our public-school system could contribute so much to the efficiency of that system as the boards of county examiners, were they armed by statute with all the powers necessary to a proper discharge of their important duties. That county boards or city boards are, in general, doing the kind of work most conducive to educational progress, few thoughtful educators will assume.

"In the first place, what is the work they are doing? It may be answered: They are everywhere — with honorable exceptions, of course — simply asking questions in arithmetic, geography, and grammar, and hearing candidates read from a text-book. Of the character of these questions nothing further need be said, than that too frequently, instead of being comprehensive and root-striking, they are narrow, technical, pedantic, puzzling, and worthless. Having examined the papers of candidates, and assigned a percentage value to each answer, and footed up the results, the examiners deem their duties ended. It would ill become any one to undervalue any proper means taken to determine, beyond a peradventure, whether or not a candidate has a sufficient knowledge of the branches he shall be required to teach. The possession of such a knowledge is fundamental. And it cannot be denied that the determination of this question is one of the main duties of examiners under the law, as it now stands, but it is not their only duty.

"The marked defect of our present law of examinations, if its purport be correctly indicated by the practice of boards of examiners, is that feature in it which relates to the re-examination of teachers. As applied almost everywhere, its results, so far from being advantageous to schools, are, in the opinion of many intelligent educators, absolutely pernicious.

"The frequency of these re-examinations requires that teachers shall employ a large part of their time in grinding over, in a dreary, cramming way, the one grist of the common branches, — a process stultifying in the extreme. If one were to set out with malice prepense to contrive a scheme that should most effectually quench, on the part of teachers, aspirations for a higher life in their calling, and render them narrow in all their ways of thinking and doing, he could scarcely hit upon one more balefully successful than this. Considering, in addition, the exhausting nature of the teachers' school-room work, how can any mental growth be expected of him? Or is it any wonder that, under such a *régime*, he should at length give up all hope of growth, and sink into a pitiable state of marrowless pedantry, content to spend his leisure hours in nosing over the dry husks of a useless knowledge?

"It may be asked whether we should dispense entirely with re-examinations. Such is not my view. But the re-examinations should be such as to *promote* mental and moral growth, not *retard* it. Let candidates who present themselves for examination the first time be thoroughly tested as to their knowledge of the statutory branches, and if they pass the test fairly well, let that be the last of it. Let a certificate issue for such a time as the rules of the board may prescribe, and let the candidate then be notified what he will be examined in at the expiration of his certificate.

"There are two kinds of reading every teacher ought to do much of, — good books on his profession, and the standard literature of his own language. He may, of course, go much beyond this limit, and read in science, philosophy, and art, with the happiest results; but the reading first mentioned is essential. Suppose, then, the examiners assign the candidate who has just been certificated, for his next examination, one professional book, and one in literature, for it is important the field should not be too wide. What these two books shall be, is a question requiring from the examiners a good deal of judgment. They should already have ascertained, with a fair amount of exactness, their neophyte's mental power and development. (And here it may be parenthetically remarked, our boards of examiners make a mistake in confining themselves, as they now almost universally do, to written examinations. The mental status of a candidate cannot be easily determined by the written examination alone. It needs to be supplemented by an oral one. Five minutes' conversation will sometimes be worth more than a quire of manuscript in settling this question.)

"We will suppose the newly passed teacher to have given evidence of good natural abilities, and of a taste for good books. In this case he may be assigned, as his professional work, 'Education as a Science,' by Prof. Alexander Bain; 'Human Culture,' by Michael Angelo or Garvey; or some other professional work of the higher order; and in literature, the best work of Milton, or Tennyson, or Wordsworth, or two or three plays of Shakespeare, or some of the essays of Emerson, or Carlyle, or Macaulay. A candidate of less natural abilities and reading would of course be assigned easier books of both professional and literary character.

"On the second examination the candidates would receive their old marks on the branches in which they had already passed an examination, and have the grade of their certificates raised or lowered, according to the results of their special examination, — or they might fail altogether. For a third examination other professional and literary books could be assigned in the same way, and the same course be pursued in issuing certificates. Such a plan could, of course, be extended over any number of years.

"It is scarcely necessary to call attention to the advantages of such a scheme of examinations over the one now in vogue, for they must be apparent to the least thoughtful. The energizing power of good books cannot be readily measured, and their retroactive benefits on the schools, through their teachers, will be of incalculable value. This scheme of examination would be one of the strongest incentives possible to continuous self-improvement. Under it, indeed, teachers could scarcely avoid this improvement, if they would.

"City boards already have full power under the State statutes; but to carry out such a plan completely in country districts, county boards would need additional legislation; but such legislation could be readily obtained, should educators make an earnest demand for it. The first thing to be done is to create the right sentiment among teachers; and I make no doubt they will most gladly give in their adherence to any reasonable proposition to relieve them from the dull routine to which they are now subjected."

I heartily indorse what Dr. Hancock has said in the foregoing article, and I suggest that the "Teachers' Course of Study" ought to be made uniform in all the States. This may be accomplished by the following plan: —

1. The several State teachers' associations should submit to the National Council of Education the work of preparing a "Teachers' Course of Study."

2. Leading educators of the several States should use needed effort to secure such legislation as may be necessary to inaugurate and carry out this course of study.

The thought of requiring public teachers to pursue a course of study after they enter the work may, to some persons, appear to be novel, but a similar plan has long been pursued by several ecclesiastical bodies. The Christian minister, in several of the leading churches, is required, after he enters the pastorate, to pursue a course of study running through a number of years, but he is expected to pass only a single satisfactory examination upon each subject of study.

No one need fear that teachers who are *thorough* in the common branches will become "rusty" in these, while pursuing a course of reading and study. Any good book, carefully studied, fits the teacher for better work in any branch from the A, B, C, to the highest subject of study.

Some persons may claim that the "Teachers' Course of Study," running through several years, would create a great number of classes to be examined annually. This, however, need not be the case; as the course of study may be so arranged that when any teacher first enters the course he shall take up studies pursued by the class that year. In a word, all teachers shall study the same lessons at the same time. As an example of this, I may name the Chautauqua Literary and Scientific Circle, which provides a four years' course of study. New members are admitted to the "Circle" at any time, and they take up the course of study at the point where they enter. At the end of the four years' course, those who entered after the course was commenced go back and take up the first year, and pursue the course until they come to the point where they first entered, when, if found worthy, they are graduated. It is simply a four years' course of study arranged in a circle; and one time round the ring, no difference where the member enters, entitles him to graduation.

I can name no higher example of the successful work of a uniform course of study, than the Christian Church, in all Bible lands, studying the international Sunday-school lessons. If public educators are as wise as Bible students, they will provide a uniform course of study for all country teachers.

If we wish to lift the common-school system to higher and healthier grounds, we must first lift the country teachers to a higher level. As a means for the accomplishment of this end, a "Teachers' Course of Study" extending through several years, a system of annual examinations that will measure the height and depth and length and breadth of the intelligence, culture, and true worth of each teacher, and a plan for paying each in proportion to what he is actually worth, will be of incalculable value.

LECTURE XXIII.

TEACHER'S SALARY, AND TENURE OF OFFICE.

Country schools cannot attain the highest degree of perfection unless good teachers are well paid, and permanent in their position. Business men are well aware that it is impossible to secure skilful workmen at starvation prices, or to obtain the best talent for positions that are not permanent.

An excellent authority on educational matters recently expressed himself on the subject of the teacher's salary, in the following sensible and business-like manner: —

"Cheap wages must result in cheap teachers; and cheap teachers will naturally cultivate cheap minds, which will fit the pupil for living a cheap life; that is, not attaining to any occupation above a mediocre. Let the subject of cheap teachers be thoroughly discussed, and it will be found at once that the great majority of the educated minds of the country are not in favor of cheap educators."

The pulpit and the press unite in the opinion that the salaries paid to public school teachers, at present, are insufficient to secure and retain the best teaching talent. I offer the following as representative opinions of the pulpit and press upon this subject. Rev. Henry Ward Beecher says : —

"If salaries ever should be ample, it is in the profession of school-teaching. If there is one place where we ought to induce people to make their profession a life-business, it is in the teaching of schools. Oh, those who are to be taught are nothing but children ! — *your* children, *my* children, *God's* children, — the sweetest and dearest and most sacred ones in life. At the very age when angels would be honored to serve them, that is the time when we put them into the hands of persons who are not prepared by disposition to be teachers, and who are not educated for teaching, and who are continually bribed, as it were, by the miserable wages that are given them, to leave their teaching as soon as they acquire a little experience."

The New York "Tribune" says : —

"There is no question but that the teachers in our public schools should be better paid; and there is also no question that an educated, thorough, and liberal service should be demanded of them. At present, teachers cannot be severely blamed, if, with the poor rewards held out to them, they do not thoroughly prepare themselves for their work. The matter for wonder is, that teachers who are at all qualified should be obtained for such rates of pay, and it is certain that the service of the schools holds out the smallest possible inducements for intelligent and capable men and women to remain in it."

I am convinced that even with our present expenditures for educational purposes, much can be done to induce teachers to make more thorough preparation, and to remain longer in the work. The following rules for the accomplishment of this end are in harmony with the laws of business and common-sense:—

1. There should be a wide difference between the wages of the trained and experienced, and the wages of the untrained and inexperienced teacher.

2. The teacher, when once employed, should hold his position until he resigns, or is formally dismissed.

If a man undertakes to build a house, he makes a wide difference between the wages of the unskilled apprentice and the wages of the master mechanic. The wider the difference between the wages of the skilled and unskilled, in any trade or business, the greater the inducement to become master of it. The reason why teachers, in many places, make so little preparation is, there is no *demand* for preparation.

In many parts of the country trained and experienced teachers are offered but little more for their services than what is paid for untrained and inexperienced teachers. It is evident that this plan, if applied to mechanics and artists, would paralyze every motive to become skilful.

The teacher's salary should depend, not merely upon what he *knows*, but upon what he *does*. It should depend upon his *real worth* to the educational work. Superintendent G. A. Littlefield, of Lawrence, Massachusetts, in speaking of the teacher's salary, says : —

"It seems absolutely right that the main criterion in fixing the salaries of teachers should be their relative ability; and, with a settled public opinion in favor of the system, I see no reason why it should not work well, and excellent results flow from it. It would certainly seem possible to make decisions with regard to the worth of teachers with such care and accuracy as to command the respect of all concerned. The permanent and best part of a teacher's work, to be sure, is of such a nature that we cannot fully estimate it. Its real value will only appear in the matured characters of the pupils. And yet there are unmistakable evidences of even this priceless influence when it is exerted, and no other quality of a teacher should receive greater recognition. 'Children have more need of models than of critics.'"

But the most discouraging feature in the teacher's calling is the disposition on the part of so many school boards to change teachers every term. No other work or business, requiring skill, is subject to so many changes. A sensible farmer having a team for which he employs a driver is too wise to change drivers as often as some school boards change teachers. A man having a flouring-mill, for which he employs a miller, is aware that he cannot increase his custom by frequently changing millers. Successful merchants, employing assistant salesmen, could not be induced to adopt such a system of changes as school boards have introduced in the employment of teachers. The teacher should certainly have as fair a chance as the teamster, the miller, or the merchant's clerk; and the school should not be required to bear a strain that would balk a team, ruin the custom of a mill, and bankrupt a merchant.

If, at the end of the term, the teacher of any school is not to be retained for the coming term, it is but just to him that he should know this, so that he may look out a situation somewhere else. But the laws of many of the States provide for the appointment of teachers so late in the season, that, during the summer months, no teacher can tell whether or not he will have work for the winter. Such laws encourage the teacher to keep one eye on the school and the other on something else. Under such unreasonable arrangements many of the most earnest teachers become disheartened and abandon the teacher's calling. If these unwise enactments were so amended that teachers might be appointed early in the season, say before the beginning of the summer vacation, the cause of education would rest on a more solid basis.

Some of the larger cities have thoroughly tested the "permanent appointment of teachers," and the plan has proved to be so satisfactory to all interested parties, that its adoption in public schools is likely to become universal. Hon. John Swett, ex-State Superintendent of California, and ex-city Superintendent of San Francisco, says: —

"It seems to be assumed by the opponents of the abolition of the plan of electing teachers 'for one year only,' that a change would involve a life-lease of positions. This is a fallacy. In San Francisco, the annual election of teachers was discontinued in 1870. Since that time teachers have been elected subject to immediate removal at any time for incompetence, or for any other good cause. During the past two years, at least a dozen teachers have beeen removed for 'incompetence.' The bugbear of a life-lease of office is a rag-baby, held up by conservatives that cannot tolerate the slightest departure from what 'has been.' In San Francisco, with its corps of seven hundred teachers, the plan is a success. The Board of Education is a unit in favor of it. The people are in favor of it. It is no longer an experiment, but is a determined fact."

Superintendent Elliott, of Boston, in a recent communication to the School Board of that city, says: —

"I am in favor of electing teachers, once and for all, to serve as long as they really do serve the schools. It is plain that the teacher will be benefited, that he has anxieties enough without being anxious concerning his re-election, and that if any trouble outside of teaching can be spared him, its removal will render him better able to meet the trouble inseparable from his personal duty. His largest resources, both moral and intellectual, are burdened without adding a feather's weight of uncertainty about his position or his income. More than all this, it is only by making him feel reasonably sure of his place, and for as long as he is able to fill it, that we encourage him to improve himself. He wants time for study, time for growth, and not only time, but inclination, — say rather desire, — which he can hardly feel if his future is precarious. To give him what he needs is to give his pupils what they need, even more than he. To him his reappointment is a question merely of standing or support; serious matter, to be sure, but not the most serious of all. To his pupils it is a question of example and influence, of the vigor and labor which he stirs in them, of the calmness and patience which they are to see in him if they are to cultivate them in themselves; in short, of the force he is to exert over their natures in order to do them the good for which they have been brought to him.

"There is one other consideration which seems to be of weight against a tenure limited by anything short of good behavior. It is that the best teachers, or very many of them, will neither seek nor accept a place involving re-election. Thus men who would adorn our schools turn from them to colleges whose professorships, once given, are not to be given again; thus women, from whom a public school might draw the very inspiration it requires, pass it by for some private institution where they feel they will be protected as well as employed. Such teachers are to be drawn to the schools, not by raising salaries or multiplying promises, but by making appointments once and for all. There will be no embarrassment as to their termination, when the time to terminate them comes."

Hon. M. A. Newell, State Superintendent of Maryland, in an article published in the "Maryland School Journal," says:—

"The system of annual engagements (where there is the power of dismissal at thirty days' notice) is a useless labor on the part of the employers, and harassing, humiliating, and demoralizing to the employés."

I present, in conclusion, the following extract from an editorial in the "National Journal of Education," Boston:—

"So long as the teacher remains loyal to duty, faithful in service, and capable of exercising the functions of a discreet instructor of youth, he should be retained in the public service *permanently*. In demanding such protection for the teacher, we do not ask for exemption from the liability to be removed by the people. On the other hand, the rule of permanency makes the teacher constantly liable. Under the annual election system, the teacher is subjected to a vote of public approval once a year, and having secured an appointment, is safe for a twelvemonth, crimes and casualties excepted. Un-

MALES.

A Diagram, showing the Average Monthly Pay of Teachers, Males and Females, in the several States.

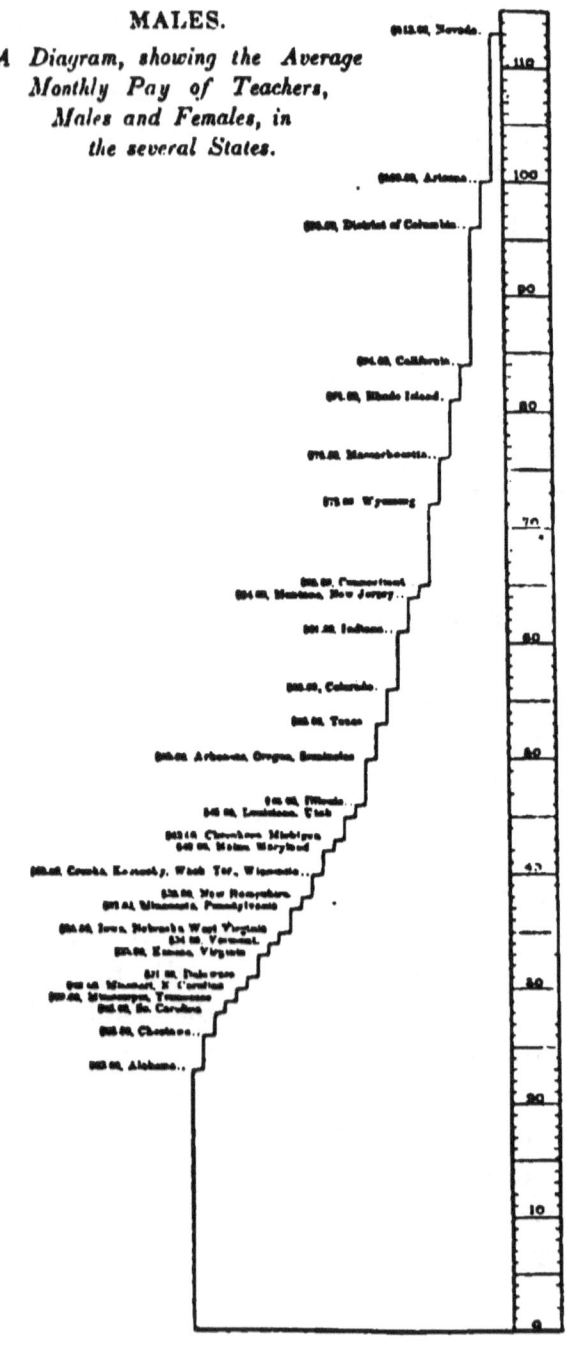

FEMALES.

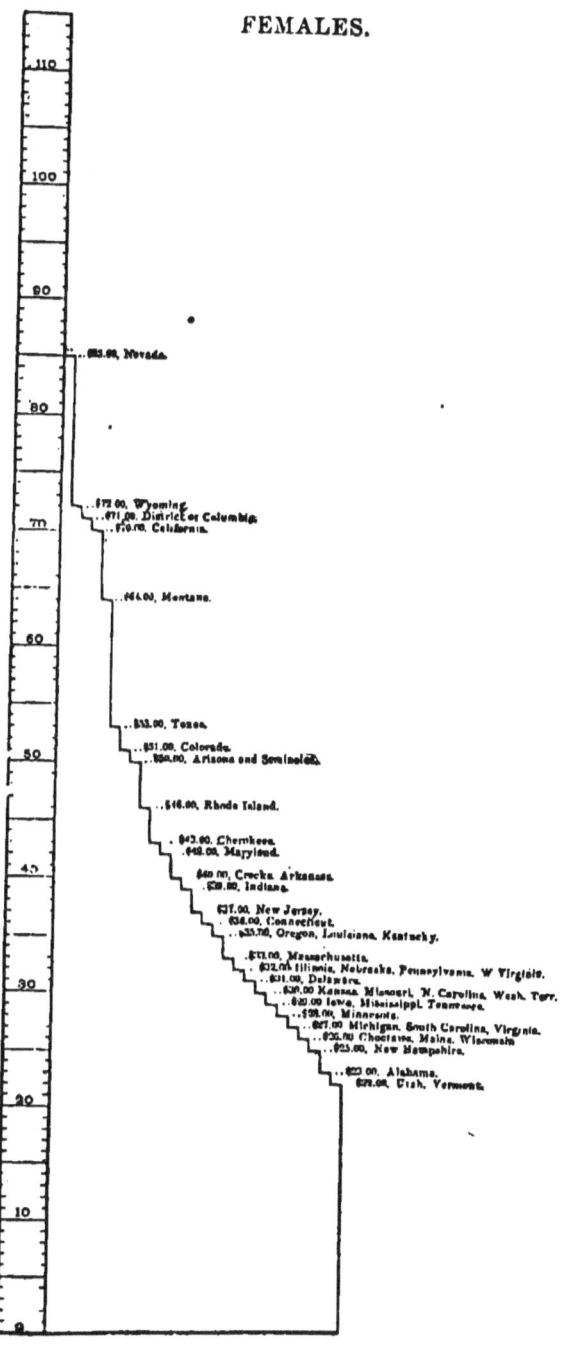

der the tenure-of-office principle, as we hold it, the teacher is constantly subject to the law of fitness and its recognition; and the easy rule of such a law in service is not a yoke of bondage, but one of the most perfect freedom. Should occasion arise, the incumbent may be removed at any time, while, under the annual election principle, the teacher is master of the situation so long as the contract holds. As to precedents, the authorities of Germany, France, and England all favor the idea of permanency founded on good service."

LECTURE XXIV.

FREE TEXT-BOOKS IN FREE SCHOOLS.

SEVERAL cities and some of the States are trying the experiment of furnishing free text-books in free schools. General Eaton, commissioner of the National Bureau of Education, in his last report, gives a brief account of this movement, which I here present: —

"From a desire to extend to every child the full advantages of public instruction, the laws of thirteen of our States make provision for supplying indigent pupils with the needful text-books free of charge. These books are understood to be held by the children as a loan, to be returned in the best condition possible to the school boards after use, and to be passed on from session to session, and from child to child. The benefits derived from this arrangement have been so many and so various as to give rise to considerable discussion of the question whether the system of a free supply of books by school boards would not better be made universal, instead of partial and discriminating, as it is.

"The advocates of a system of free supply urge in favor of it that it saves expense, the books being purchased at wholesale; that it saves time, enough books for every scholar being thus available at the opening of each term; that it secures for a district a desirable uniformity of text-books, making the work of teachers greatly easier and more effective than in other cases; that it thus promotes better classification of pupils, so that more time can be given to each class; that it increases the attendance on the schools; and, finally, that it prevents expense and annoyance when a pupil goes from one district to another.

"In view of these advantages, our two largest cities, New York and Philadelphia, have, for a long time, furnished free books; and smaller cities, such as Bath and Lewiston in Maine, Fall River in Massachusetts, Newark and Paterson in New Jersey, have followed their example, with the happiest results. Four of the States, too, now explicitly provide for allowing the system of free supply. Maine, Massachusetts, and Wisconsin leave the matter to be decided by district or town meetings and city councils and the local school boards; and New York authorizes city boards to furnish books to pupils out of any money provided for the purpose. In most of the remaining States the laws are silent on this point, except, as before mentioned, where a supply for poor pupils is allowed. But in California, Iowa, Michigan, New Jersey, and Pennsylvania the State superintendents express themselves as decidedly in favor of furnishing free all the books needed. Superintendent Carr, of California, further ventures the opinion that in the silence of the law there is no obstacle in the way of the adoption by any district of the free plan; and probably, in almost any State, districts would be allowed to decide the matter for themselves, provided that proper notice be given beforehand to the people of the intention to discuss and determine the question at a specified time."

State Superintendent E. A. Apgar, of New Jersey, after thoroughly testing the system of furnishing text-books by district taxation, in his annual report of 1877, gives the following reasons in favor of the plan : —

"*First.* The largest discount can be secured. Parents pay fifty per cent more for the books they purchase than the district would be obliged to give.

"*Second.* The books, when owned by the district, continue in use until they are worn out They pass from class to class. There is a very great saving in this. A single child, or the children of a family, seldom wear a book out. Every parent knows how frequently he is obliged to purchase new books, to take the place of others still in a good or fair condition, which his children have finished.

"*Third.* Changes in school books are too frequent. These changes are too often made at the request of the teacher, who, upon entering a new school, finds the books used are not those he is most familiar with, and others he is most accustomed to are recommended. If the district furnishes the books, the teacher has not the same opportunity to secure changes, and they will, therefore, be less frequent. These changes are not necessary. A good teacher will do as good work with one series of books as with another. More depends upon who is behind the book, than what is in it.

"*Fourth.* The most important saving is in the time of the children. If the district owns the books, a child, upon entering school, is assigned his place in his classes, and furnished with all the books he needs, without delay. He at once enters upon his work. Where this is not the case, the teacher first ascertains what books the child requires; he sends the list to the parent. Then there is more or less delay in purchasing the books. Several days may elapse before the father becomes entirely satisfied that the books are actually required; then he finds they cannot be had in the district store, and the child must wait until some business necessitates a visit to the city. Thus the child is unable to take his proper place in his classes, and valuable time is lost."

State Superintendent J. P. Wickersham, of Pennsylvania, in his annual report to the Legislature, in 1878, renews his former recommendation of free text-books, as follows: —

"Boards of school directors are required to adopt books for the schools under their care, and to see that these and no others are used. But there is some doubt as to whether the law now authorizes them to furnish text-books to the pupils without charge, as they furnish globes, maps, charts, and dictionaries. The plan of free text-books has so many advantages, and has worked so well wherever fairly tried, that I have no hesitation in asking the Legislature to remove whatever uncertainty there may be with reference to the power of school boards in the premises."

The system of free text-books may be liable to some abuses, but it certainly has many advantages. The subject should be fully and fairly discussed in State and county institutes, and in the public papers, so that the people may understand it and decide for themselves.

LECTURE XXV.

METHODS FOR SECURING ATTENDANCE.

How to have a complete attendance upon public schools is a problem yet unsolved by the American people. After experimenting for more than a century upon this question, we have, now, an average attendance of but little more than one third of the school population of the States and Territories.

No other obstacle so formidable as non-attendance stands in the way of educating the masses. It is evident to every one, that universal education is attainable only by universal attendance. How to so manage the masses that all children may be brought into school is, perhaps, the highest problem of the present age.

Compulsory laws have been enacted in several States, and wherever they have been enforced the attendance has increased. This enforcement, however, has been confined almost entirely to cities and towns. There has been very little disposition to carry out compulsion in country districts. In some of the States where compulsory laws were enacted years ago, no attempt has ever been made to enforce them, either in town or country, and if not repealed, they remain as dead letters upon statute-books. If we may judge the future by the past, it is unwise to depend upon compulsory laws for securing a full attendance in country schools. I may further say that if we can, by pleasurable methods, bring pupils into school, it is far better than to compel them to come.

The most sensible plan for securing attendance that has yet been tried in country schools, is that which makes the teacher personally interested in the per cent of attendance. The two principal methods for accomplishing this end are here presented:

1. Let the amount of the teacher's monthly salary depend, in some degree, upon the average per cent of attendance.

2. Let the teacher's tenure of office depend, in some degree, upon a reasonable per cent of attendance.

The first method will increase the salaries of live teachers and diminish the salaries of dead ones. The second method will retain live teachers and dismiss dead ones. Both methods should be made a part of the school law of every State. This plan makes the teacher the *paid agent* for bringing pupils into school. It is cheaper and more *pleasurable* than compulsion, and is near akin to the laws which govern men in business and in the professions.

The merchant's clerk commands a salary, great or small, in proportion to his ability to win and retain custom. The fees of the attorney and the physician depend largely upon the number of their clients and patients. The salary of the Christian minister is somewhat dependent upon his ability to command a good congregation.

The active teacher who can secure an average attendance of seventy-five or eighty per cent of all who are entitled to attend his school is, all else being equal, worth twice as much as the teacher who sits down satisfied with an attendance of thirty or forty per cent. As a rule, to which there may be some exceptions, the attendance upon a school is a fair index to the quality of its inside work. If the per cent of attendance is low, there is generally a lack of interest in the work of the school.

Whether the position and pay of the teacher are made to depend upon attendance or not, the work of securing a full attendance in each school must, in many places, be done mainly by the teacher, or it will not be done at all. In order to aid teachers in the work of increasing attendance, I offer some suggestions founded on the customs of political parties and religious denominations. Let us take a case for the sake of illustration.

Here is a district or township containing half a dozen country school-houses, and the teachers for these several schools have just received their appointments. It is evident that the highest success in each school cannot be reached unless all who are entitled to attend can be present at the beginning of the term. Now let these teachers learn wisdom from politicians; let them take the same pains to bring pupils into their schools that politicians take to bring people to the polls, and then see what the result will be.

Let us look at the methods which politicians use in securing a full attendance at the polls, and see if the same methods will not secure a full attendance in the schools. What methods do politicians use for this purpose? I answer, —

1. They list all the names and see all the "doubtful ones."

2. They hold mass meetings, have banners and music, make earnest speeches, create emulation, and circulate papers. They spare no pains in trying to convince people that the success of their cause is essential to public prosperity.

Now if the teachers of the district or township, directed by the county superintendent or commissioner, will spend one week, before the school term begins, working as earnestly, skilfully, and harmoniously as politicians of the same party work, they will find a full attendance on the first day of the term. But as schools are not like elections, which last for one day only, teachers cannot, like politicians, cease their public efforts after securing one day's full attendance. They should, therefore, adopt the custom of the churches, and hold public meetings at stated periods. No religious or moral enterprise will long retain its interest without holding meetings at stated periods.

Our educational work in the country provides for a great many meetings, but most of them are "teachers' meetings." We need more educational mass meetings, in which the *people* may take part.

In order to have a full attendance on the first day of the term, some teachers adopt the plan of offering, beforehand, a reward to all who may be present on that day. This plan, though a good one, offers no inducements to pupils after the first day of the school term. A still better method — one that has worked with admirable success wherever tried — is, for the teacher to offer, before school begins, a handsome diploma of honor, to be presented, at the end of the term, to each pupil who may be entitled to it. I present here a miniature form of this diploma.

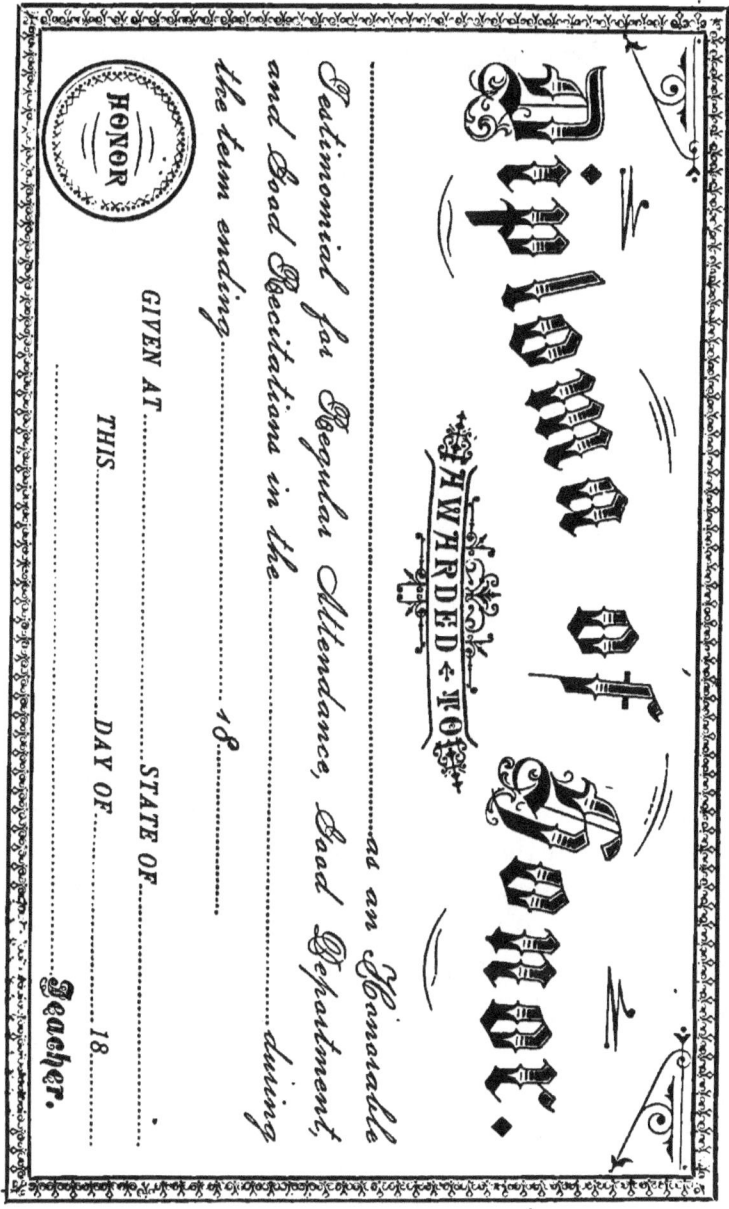

It will be observed that this diploma requires not only regular attendance, but good deportment and good recitations. The effect of this plan upon the attendance, conduct, and diligence of pupils can be realized only by those who have tried it.

But the most successful method for securing a full attendance upon the schools of any county in any State is a system of beautiful banners. This system embraces a county banner and a banner for each township or magisterial district. The county banner is publicly presented, at the end of the school year, by the county superintendent or commissioner, to the township having the highest per cent of attendance for the past year, and the name of the township, and the year in which the banner is presented, are inscribed upon it. But this banner is presented with the understanding that if at the end of the next year the township holding it should not show the highest per cent of attendance of all the townships in the county, then the banner shall be surrendered and presented to the township having the highest per cent, and the name of the township receiving it, and the year in which the banner is surrendered and presented, shall be inscribed underneath the name of the township which surrenders it. Should any township obtain this banner a second time, the year of its second presentation may be inscribed opposite the former inscription.

Each township banner is publicly presented, at the end of the school year, to the school in its township having the highest per cent of attendance for the past year, and the name of the school, and the year in which the banner is presented, are inscribed thereon.

Each township banner is held and surrendered upon the same conditions as the county banner.

The county banner, in the course of time, may be obtained and surrendered by every township in the county; and each township banner, in the course of time, may be won and lost by every school in its township. These changes, however, will be made only through mighty struggles, some striving to hold and others to obtain the banner. Parents, pupils, and teachers will voluntarily become recruiting agents to bring absentees into school.

This system of school banners should be extended so as to create an emulation between the several counties of a State, and between the several States of the Union.

A beautiful banner, suitably inscribed, seems to be Nature's choice method for creating a high degree of interest. Every nation under the sun has its ensign, which it keeps before its subjects, whether they are on land or sea. No great political party, in any country, could be induced to dispense with banners in its mass meetings and marches. Great armies, mixing in fierce encounter, are cheered when, amidst the smoke of battle, they even get a glimpse of the flag of their country.

Late experiments have proven that the banner is as essential, and may be made as powerful in the educational work, as it is in an army, a political party, or a nation. Its influence may be easily tested in a single township, county, or State.

As this system of school banners for securing attendance is a new plan, a brief account of its origin may not be inappropriate. While superintendent of the schools of Monongalia County, West Virginia, I introduced several new methods for securing attendance. Early in January, 1878, I offered a beautiful banner, suitably inscribed, to be presented to the district (township) that would produce the highest average per cent of attendance of its entire school population for the year ending Aug. 31. In order to show the inscription, I present here a representation of both sides of this banner.

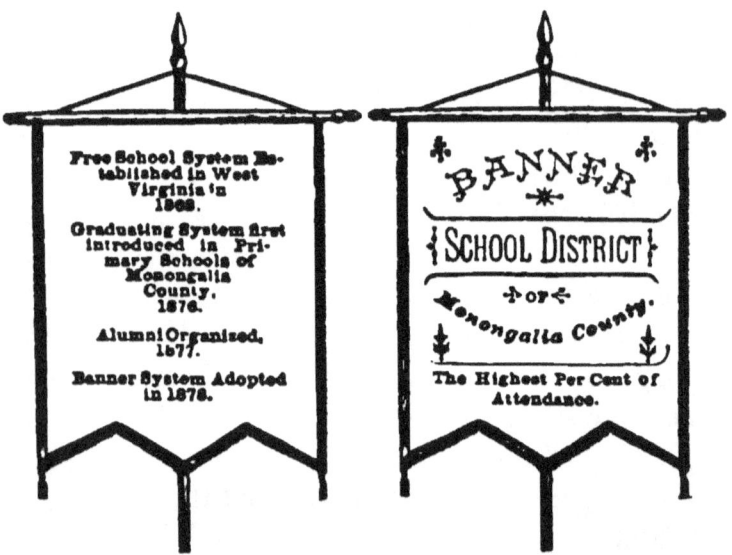

COUNTY SCHOOL BANNER.

I carried this banner wherever I went in my work of visiting schools, and placed it on exhibition in the educational mass meetings which were held each evening. Many parents who had never before taken an interest in education, commenced sending their children to school, and urging others to send, as they said, " for the purpose of obtaining the county banner." Several teachers said to me, " If we had only known of this plan beforehand, we would have had all our pupils in school on the first day of the term."

Finding that the county banner was working so admirably, I offered seven district banners, one to each of the seven country districts of the county, each banner to be presented to the school in its district that would produce the highest average per cent of attendance. These banners were all to be presented with the understanding, and to be held upon the conditions already stated. The influence of these district banners was like local elections in a State campaign, — stirring every nook and corner of each community in the county.

In order to show how carefully this banner system was carried out in the county, I present the following extract from the published report of the presidents of the several school boards of the county, made at their annual meeting held at the court-house.

"MORGANTOWN, WEST VA.,
June 24th, 1878.

" At a meeting of the county banner committee of the free schools of Monongalia County, to ascertain the per cent of attendance attained by the several districts of said county, we, the undersigned committee, find, from the reports of the district committees, the average to be as follows: —

"Clinton district, sixty per cent of attendance; Morgan district, fifty-three per cent of attendance; Union district, sixty-seven per cent of attendance; Grant district, sixty-one per cent of attendance; Cass district, sixty-one per cent of attendance; Battelle district, sixty-one per cent of attendance; Clay district, fifty-five per cent of attendance.

"We, therefore, award the county banner to Union district, to be held one year, or till it shall be excelled by some other district.

"We find, also, from the reports of the district committees, that the following schools are entitled to district banners for the ensuing year: —

"Battelle district, West Warren school, J. Milton Shriver, teacher, — eighty per cent.

"Cass district, Jimtown school, D. Weidman, teacher, — seventy-three per cent.

"Clay district, McCurdysville school, Otis W. Waters, teacher, — seventy-five per cent.

"Clinton district, Martin's school, Wm. J. King, teacher, — eighty per cent

"Grant district, Stewart's Run school, A. J. Arnett, teacher, — eighty-six per cent.

"Morgan district, Chestnut Ridge school, John D. Gans, teacher, — sixty-nine per cent.

"Union district, Pleasant Hill school, Adis Zearley, teacher, — seventy-two per cent.

"We find, further, that the average per cent of attendance in the county is about sixty per cent.
(Signed)
"JAMES S. WATSON,
S. H. SHRIVER,
JAMES HARE,
A. W. BROWN,
COLEMAN VANDERVORT,
Committee."

In the autumn of 1878, before the schools were opened, many of our teachers visited their patrons and obtained promises that they would send their children promptly. Several of our schools had a full attendance on the first day of the term; and the efforts of each district to merit the county banner, and of each school to merit its district banner, were even greater than the previous winter. In some parts of the county, clothing and books were quietly provided for poor children, and they were brought into school for the purpose of increasing the attendance.

At the end of the school year the county banner was again awarded to the district that had he'd it the previous year; two district banners were retained by the schools that already held them, and all the other banners changed places. We had expected to reach, that year, an average attendance of seventy-five per cent, but "mumps" and "measles" prevailed, during the school term, to such an extent, that our attendance was but little over sixty per cent. This, however, is about as high an average attendance as a country district, where the school population embraces all ages, from six to twenty-one, can reasonably be expected to reach. It is folly to say, as some have said, that our schools are a failure unless we have an attendance of one hundred per cent of the entire school population. Many persons who are entitled to attend school have already completed the common branches, some are sick or distant, some are learning trades or working on farms, some are doing housework, and some are married.

It is the duty of the friends of popular education to see that all young people obtain, at the very least, a fair knowledge of the common branches. In order to accomplish this, we should adopt the best methods for securing attendance.

The newspaper may be made a powerful agent for increasing the attendance upon our public schools. If in this work we can create an emulation among the several schools of each township, among the several townships of each county, among the several counties of each State, and among the several States of the Union, and then use the newspaper to promptly make known the results, as we do in matters pertaining to elections, we will greatly increase the interest of the people in the work of securing attendance. Our school statistics lack *freshness*, because they come so late.

The National Bureau of Education furnishes much

valuable information, but it comes one or two years after the time we ought to have it. The delay is, however, not the fault of the Cmmissioner of Education, but want of facilities. I present an interesting diagram from his last report. This diagram, which shows the relation of enrolment and average attendance to the school population of the United States, ought to be presented in every newspaper in the land. A like diagram could be made to show the attendance of the several counties in a State, or the several townships in a county.

The following explanation of this diagram is from the "New England Journal of Education," Boston: —

"AVERAGE ATTENDANCE. — The percentage of daily average attendance is here based on the total shcool population of each State, as given in the State census, and is subject to the same variable element as appears in the total enrolment table. Another variable element appears in addition, — the differing lengths of the school year in the general States. No two are alike. The school year varies from sixty days, the minimum, in North and South Carolina and Missouri, to one hundred and eighty-eight days, the maximum, in the District of Columbia. The percentage of daily average attendance is not given in the States of Arkansas, Delaware, Minnesota, South Carolina, Texas, and Wisconsin, and in the Territories of Dakota, Idaho, Montana, New Mexico, Washington, and Wyoming.

"ENROLMENT. — The central column represents

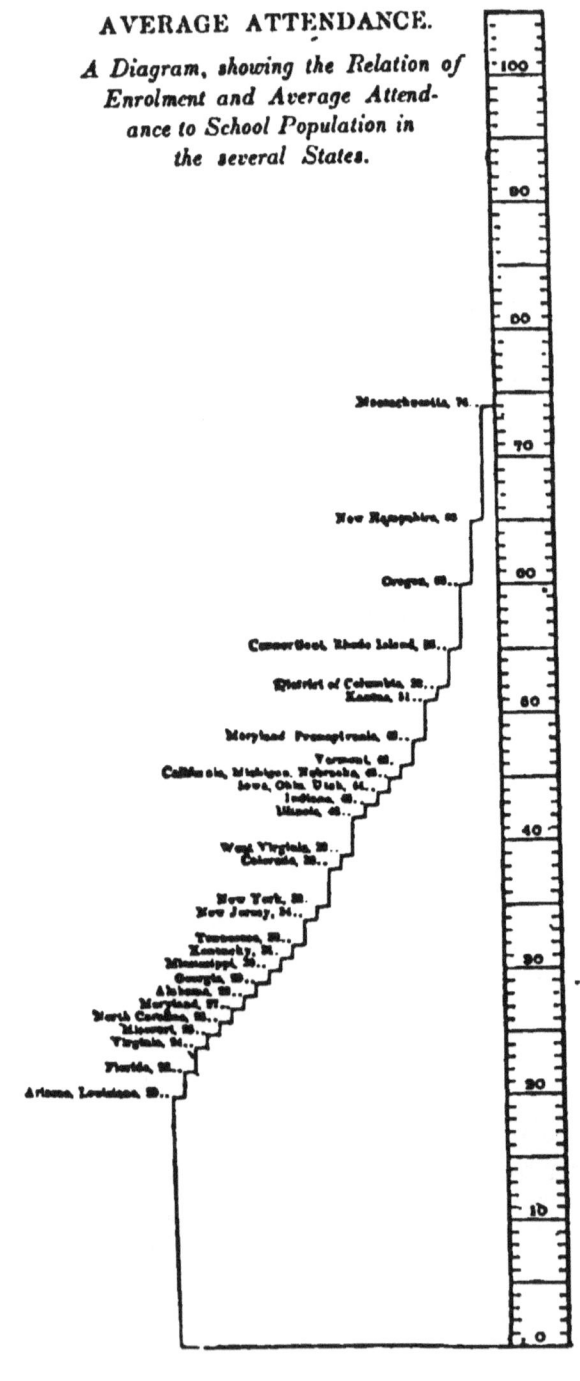

AVERAGE ATTENDANCE.

A Diagram, showing the Relation of Enrolment and Average Attendance to School Population in the several States.

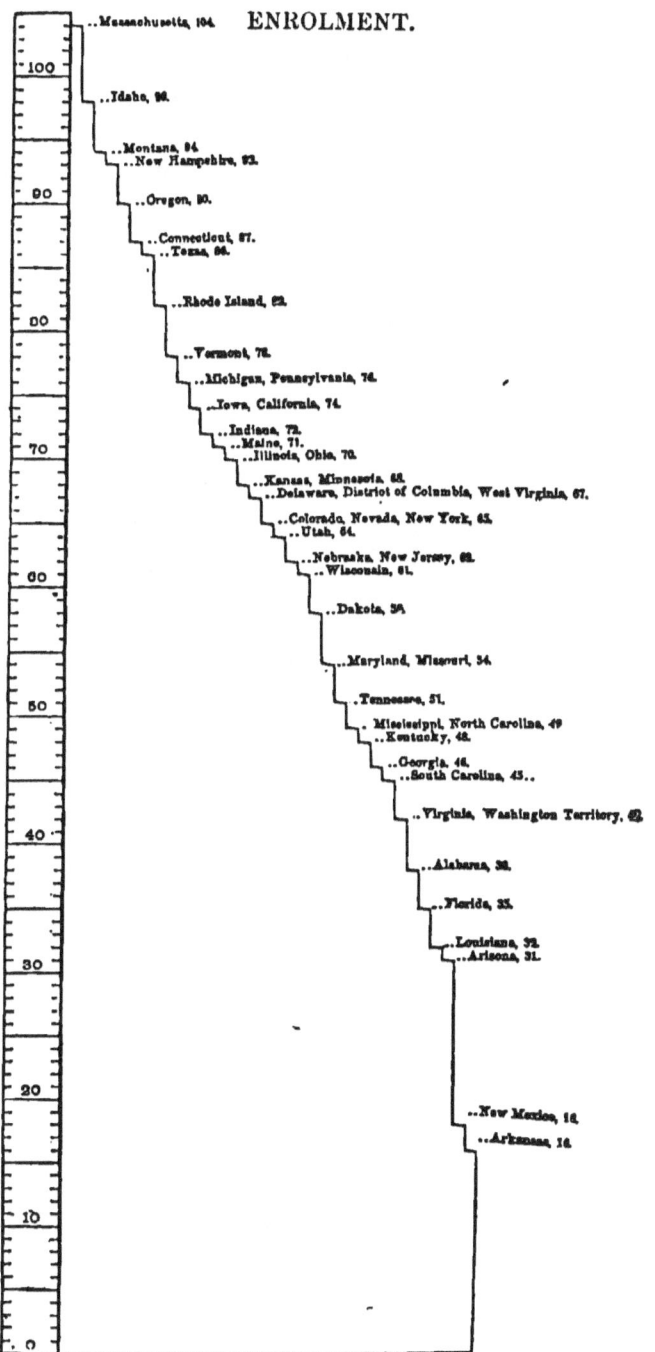

the total school population of each State, and is divided into one hundred parts. The census of the school population varies in the several States, affording seventeen different standards of school age. In the longest the age extends from the fourth to the twenty-first year, covering seventeen years; the shortest extends from eight to fourteen years, covering a period of six years. The figures on the right show the percentage of the school population of each State that is enrolled in the schools. Arkansas has only sixteen per cent of her school population enrolled, but the school age is from six to twenty-one years. Massachusetts has one hundred and four per cent in enrolment, while her school age is from five to eighteen years. Persons using this table must bear in mind this important fact of the variable school age of the school population of each State."

LECTURE XXVI.

FIRST LESSONS IN THE COMMON BRANCHES.

In this age of steam and lightning, while railroad and telegraph companies are extending their lines, and farmers and mechanics are introducing improved implements and machinery for the purpose of accomplishing more work in less time, progressive teachers are introducing improved educational methods for a like purpose. It was once the custom in country schools for the teacher to hear each pupil recite singly. It is now evident to every one, that under the present plan of placing all pupils of like grade in the same class, the teacher's ability to hear recitations, and his opportunity to throw light upon lessons, are infinitely greater than under the former method. Country teachers, in former times, were unanimous in the opinion that children should learn all the letters before beginning to spell, that they should become good spellers before attempting to read, and that they should be able to read well before undertaking to write. Progressive teachers of the present day have proven, however, that all these branches may, with profit, be taken up and studied together.

Paradoxical as it may appear to those who have not thought upon this subject, if we will but take the hints which nature gives us we will see that children should begin to read before they begin to spell, and they should begin to learn words before they begin to learn letters. For proof of this declaration we have but to look at the method by which the child learns the names of its playthings, and all their parts. Take, as an illustration, a toy-wagon. We find that the child learns first the name,—*wagon*,—and its use; then the names of its principal parts,—wheels, bed, tongue, axles, spokes, hubs, linch-pins, etc. And notwithstanding the fact that the primary school has attempted to reverse this order of nature by requiring the pupil to learn first the names of the several parts, the mature man adopts, in his practice, the methods of infancy. Take, as an example, a man who wishes to gain a clear knowledge of a steam-engine; he studies first the engine as a whole, then the several parts.

In order to test the practicability of the old-time school method, let us try it in teaching a child the names of the several parts of its toy-wagon. Let us take the wagon to pieces and show the child the separate parts, and require it to learn their names before it sees their use, and before it has any conception of their combined beauty. It is evident that this process would be slow and laborious; while under the child's own method it soon learns all these, and we can scarcely tell how or when it learns them.

If we try the school method on the mature man, and undertake to give him a clear understanding of all the parts of a steam-engine, the plan will prove equally unsatisfactory.

For some time past the freshest writers and the foremost thinkers connected with primary education have been urging the universal adoption of the "child's method" in primary schools, and practical teachers have proven that the plan works with wonderful success. I offer the opinions of some standard authorities on this subject. Mrs. Rebecca D. Rickoff, of Toledo, Ohio, who recently read a paper before the National Educational Association, entitled "First School Days," and who is author of a primer on primary school work, says: "The child should be taught —

"*First*, To read sentences.

"*Secondly*, To read words.

"*Thirdly*, To analyze spoken words into sounds.

"*Fourthly*, To analyze written words into symbols of elementary sounds, beginning with such words as cat, rat, not, etc.; then such words as that, them, ship; then words with new sounds to the symbols, as thin, caper, no; finally, words with silent letters, as cate, rate, noble, etc."

The "National Journal of Education," Boston, in reviewing a new book for primary schools, by Col. Francis W. Parker, supervisor of the public schools of that city, says:—

"The lessons are simple, but based upon a definite

plan — and that an admirable one — of teaching the child a vocabulary of words, the signs of ideas, and repeating them in such association as to open to it new thoughts as well as new words. A few words should first be taught thoroughly as the nucleus of a vocabulary, and then plenty of good reading will give the child facility in expression, as well as an understanding of the thought conveyed by the words read. Nothing better has been put into print."

The following appropriate article is taken from the "Primary Teacher," Boston: —

"In starting little folks in reading, it is not quite clear that, at the outset, it is best to trouble them much with letters, and the sounds they represent, or to try to have them derive the word from its phonetic or alphabetic elements. The theory seems to be very good, too, but we find that, in practice, children learn many things contrary to our wise theories. In learning to speak the language they skip over the elementary laws that govern speech, and are only bothered with them when they reach the school. It is pretty much the same in learning to sing, indeed in learning most things, — the scientific principles do not confront the young learner on the start. So in learning to read, the normal method, as we view it, is to let beginners, if young, go on for a time without spelling out the words either by sounds or letters. We should teach them words, — *dog, cat, chair,* — precisely as we would the real objects which these words represent.

"We all know how rapidly children learn the names of things about them, becoming acquainted with hundreds before they are old enough to be sent to school; and they learn them, too, for the most part, without being directly taught by any one. Then, too, in recognizing objects and speaking their names, they do not fix the eye upon each separate part, — as, for example, the object *chair*, and speak each part of the chair before naming the object itself. They see the object as a whole, and speak it at once. Indeed, in adult age we all do the same. We speak words addressed to the eye in the same way, whatever method was pursued by our teachers in giving us the start.

"Since children learn the names of things so readily, why should they not be able to acquire words readily? It is found that they will. They will acquire them surprisingly fast if teachers will make the work equally simple, not load the words down with *elements*, which to the little learners of reading are not elements. It is best, then, or at least as it appears to us, to keep beginners upon words for some time, — two or three months, perhaps. Starting out with the phonetic elements complicates the matter greatly, and confuses little learners more than one is aware of. Besides, it is not necessary. All this fine word-analysis and nice training in the discrimination of sounds are proper enough, introduced incidentally, or further along in the course, but nothing of the sort is essentially needed at the outset.

"By commencing with words, as the child does in learning to talk, omitting the elementary sounds, teachers find that their pupils become interested in their work almost at once, since in a few days they are able to read phrases and short sentences at sight, and this newly acquired power pleases them greatly. With slate and pencil and proper encouragement they begin to imitate the words they have learned, and write *boy*, *cat*, *good*, etc., with supreme delight."

It is now the almost universal practice of the foremost teachers in primary schools to introduce writing along with reading, at the very beginning. The child is thus trained to express thought on slate and blackboard in written words, as soon as it can have word forms in which to express it. It is found that good penmanship can be more easily acquired early than later in life; and it is evident that its acquisition in early life will leave more room for other studies, demanding reason, in later years.

The following extract from a lecture by Superintendent Parker, of Boston, cannot be too highly commended: —

"Everything should be learned by doing. The best way to get a correct idea of any form is to attempt to draw it, so have the children draw the words, — for writing and drawing are the same thing; the purpose is not to picture the words upon the board, but by often picturing them upon the board to produce a correct picture in the brain of the child; hundreds of children spell well orally who cannot write the simplest words without blundering; of what use is such spelling? There should be no oral spelling in the first two years of school, no reproduction of words from memory in that time either, but faithful copying from well-written patterns. *Wait for things to grow in the mind; ideas grow slowly*, and if you force a child to a single utterance before he is ready you do him an injury.

"*If the first year's work is done*, IF THE FIRST YEAR'S WORK IS DONE, IF THE FIRST YEAR'S WORK IS DONE, there is no trouble with the rest.

"Begin written compositions in the second year. A good beginning is to do something, and ask the child to write what you did, upon his slate. Never allow a word to be written wrong; never allow a sentence to be begun except with a capital; never let a child *guess* at the spelling of a word; if he mistakes once, don't let him try again; write the word correctly for him at once, or have another pupil do it; guesses confuse the mind. Say nothing about rules for punctuation and capitals in a primary department, but write your sentences correctly, and insist upon correct copies from the pupil."

Teachers who are not skilful in "printing" upon the blackboard, may adopt the method of teaching beginners to use script, even before they learn Roman letters. Indeed it is now maintained by some eminent educators that this is the easier and more natural method for beginners. A writer in the "New England Journal of Education," Boston, in answer to the inquiry, "Should script be taught before Roman?" says:—

"No practical difficulty arises from the use of two forms, if the child uses script alone for its first hundred or two hundred words, and is given its new words in script for some time thereafter. The child does have difficulty in passing from print to script at any period of school-life, and it suffers almost irremediable injury by use of print first. The infant languages of the world are script languages. The untaught little child writes (?) continuously across its slate or paper. In teaching we purpose giving the child *ideas* as fast as he can use them. The compact and much-used print-form the child gets and masters (with no perceptible effort) as soon as he needs it. We avoid weakening, even to destruction, the child's fondness for using what he knows, and his power of thinking and of expressing his thoughts in the symbols he at any given time possesses. To read and not to write is questionable gain for the child. We have not only watched both processes — the script-print and the print-script — in scores of classes, but have tried both ourselves, and have seen no reason to abate our preference for the prior use of script, and its abundant use throughout school-life."

Another correspondent of the same journal says:—

"In teaching beginners to read we would not teach the *names* of the letters, whether made in script or in Roman character; because, 1. *It is not necessary.* If the children have escaped learning them before attending school, they will learn them incidentally, and without pains for anybody. 2. *It is not desirable.* A knowledge of the names of the letters of the English alphabet is an obstacle to a child beginning to learn to read. It interferes with the process of teaching reading. The aim of the teacher is to teach a word, and, as soon as may be, a phrase or sentence in which it is used. His success is hindered if the pupil's attention is distracted from the whole word by any antecedent interest in its parts. The child tries in vain to transmute the sound of the name he has learned into the sound he does not, and cannot know that he ought to give for each letter in the word or words before him.

"In teaching beginners to read we present words, phrases, sentences, on the blackboard in script. We continue to present in that way all words whose form or significance we wish to impress accurately and durably, until at least one hundred script words can be read by the pupil in any sentences that can be made from them; we withhold the printed page of chart or primer. The script form of a word is significant of an idea already alive in the child's mind through object-presentation. The letter-parts of that form are not significant, with rare exceptions, of anything useful or comprehensible to the child. At first we do not teach the *forms* of the script letters. We do not take these forms separately and teach them, nor do we call attention to them in the words. The child copies all his words as wholes. Gradually he becomes conscious of the forms composing them, and his drill in penmanship fixes correct perceptions of those forms, and habits of executing them exactly. We wish the pupil from the start to make on slate, blackboard, separately and in sentences, that he may surely know, on paper, all his new words, and to continue making them, and know how to use them. Of course we give him his copy in the form in which we wish him to make his words. Besides, the continuous form of the script-form assists the teacher to impress, and the child to receive, the word as a whole. The disjoined form in which the word appears in Roman tempts the eye, until thoroughly accustomed to reading words, to dwell upon its parts, and confuses the child's mental picture of the word. Its components stand apart from each other. The impression received is a broken one. It lacks unity, whereas it stands for a unit-idea. It is best that the child feel that each word is not a combination of characters, but a character to represent the idea he has in mind.

"Moreover, it is easier for both teacher and pupil to make words in script form well and rapidly than to make them well and rapidly in Roman character. A modified Roman character resembling Italic is sometimes used effectively, but it also breaks the word into parts, and its acquirement mars progress in chirography. Furthermore, as is well known, children do not pass easily from understanding, reading, and making print, to doing the same with script; while it is a fact that they do pass with extreme ease from script to print. A child who knows his hundred or two of words in script will at once detect them in print. Taught to read three or four readers without using script, he can with difficulty read a line of it. So we, at first, teach no letters, neither by names nor by form, neither in Roman nor in script. We teach words, phrases, and sentences in script; and the children make them in script, from copy the first year, from copy and from memory afterwards; and we very carefully and very slowly advance from the first through a regular drill in penmanship. We do so not only because we believe the process well based in theory, but because we have found it to yield better results than we have known to be reached otherwise."

Pupils, when further advanced, should, of course, become familiar with the names and sounds of all the letters; but whether they should be kept constantly repeating these names in order to learn how to spell, is, to say the least, a matter of very grave doubt. The fact that so much time has been spent in learning to spell, and so few good spellers have been produced, is certainly proof that our system of teaching spelling has not been a success. Teachers who stand in the front ranks tell us that we have been on the wrong track; that in teaching spelling we have used mainly the tongue and ears of the child, whereas the mature man in practice uses his hand and eyes. I present, in this connection, the following from a correspondent of "The Teacher," Philadelphia: —

"It fell to my lot to examine the pupils of our seventh grade, at the close of last term, and I tested them in spelling, both orally and on slates. Most of these pupils were thirteen to fourteen years old, and had been going to school about seven years. They spelled fairly orally, but all, of course, missing some words, as everybody does in oral spelling. In the test by writing, they failed much more. Evidently they had not yet finished learning to spell. One who missed two words orally missed ten with the pencil. Oral spelling had not enabled them to spell practically.

"I am strongly inclined to believe that oral spelling is an actual detriment, and that the immense amount of time given to it is wasted. It may be different with children; but we adults never think of the letter-names when spelling a new word, fresh in the papers. Suppose it is a name in the Afghan war, — say Gen. Phayre. If we want to write it, we recall the eye-picture of it, and copy that. Now, children excel us in this sort of photography. Their eye-galleries are less crowded with images, and their apparatus clearer and fresher, and impressions firmer. If we do not need to go over the jumble of *pee-aitch-ay-wy-ar-ee*, for writing Phayre as seen in print, it does not seem likely that children need to; but, on the contrary, it seems very likely that requiring them to learn the oral jingle for each word is an enormous imposition, a stumbling-block that only few ever surmount, and one that, in most cases, prevents education instead of aiding it.

"Why, indeed, should we keep children through all their childhood incessantly repeating, like so many parrots, these separate and senseless jingles — one for each word — until each is thought to be fastened in the dull and faithless ear? The eye is vastly quicker, more retentive, and better placed; and *the hand alone uses spelling.*

"When we consider these wonderful powers of the eye, and how quick the child is in catching and keeping all the details of a scene, we may fairly expect that spelling can be met and mastered by employing the eye, from the first, to note all word-forms, and to guide the hand in shaping them, taking care that the eye is not impressed and confused by any spurious forms. No other school improvement could compare with this in beneficial results. It would be the lifting of a heavy, smothering weight off every school and every child of all the millions that are learning English."

Reading in country schools is as unsatisfactory as spelling, because the habit of halting to examine the several parts of each word in spelling clings to the pupil when he attempts to read. A more rational method of spelling will therefore produce a better class of readers. Pupils should be trained to write sentences and repeat them as part of their reading exercises. They will read well their own composition because they understand it, and they should be encouraged to read the writings of others, as they find them in books, just as they would read their own. Pupils should not be loaded down with "rules for reading," but they should be as free as at home or out in the open air. The following rules on reading are laid down by Superintendent Parker, of Boston. These rules, it will be observed, are for teachers, not for pupils: —

"1. Pupils should not be required to express a thought (read a sentence aloud) until the thought is in their minds; that is, until the sentence is mentally read.

"2. If the thought is in the mind, it will *control expression*, thus making attention to punctuation, mechanical emphasis, and inflection not only unnecessary, but a great hindrance to the proper expression of thought. Capitals and punctuation aid the eye in taking the thought, but have nothing whatever to do with the expression of it."

Arithmetic, or exercises in numbers, may be taken up along with the first lessons in reading and writing. Each beginner should be provided with balls placed on a wire by which to learn to count, add, subtract, multiply, and divide. The following article on primary arithmetic is from "Barnes' Educational Monthly." New York: —

"1. The pupil should be taught to count at first only to 12 or 15. But he should *never* count without counting something. Let there always be objects before him to be counted. Adhere strictly to this.

"2. Teach him to make the Arabic figures as far as he has counted. When he has counted to five, and has five pieces of chalk (for instance) before him, then have him make the figure five. Do likewise with the other numbers, carrying the same plan to hundreds when they are more advanced.

"3. When he can write numbers to four or five, teach him to add and subtract these, both mentally and upon slates or board. Continue until he can perform the operations very rapidly. When he can count and write to ten, teach him to add and subtract all numbers below ten, and in this manner continue. At length derive multiplication, addition, and division from subtraction, and drill him in these operations.

"4. An hour before recitation, which should occur just preceding the 11 A. M. intermission, place upon the board examples in addition, subtraction, etc., omitting the answers, for the class to solve at their seats upon slates, and have the work brought to the class for the correction of answers and other criticisms. During the recitation some work should be done on the board by them, and a very brief analysis required. Examples may be both abstract and concrete.

"5. Intersperse the above work with drill in rapid combination, in counting by twos and threes, etc., by requiring them to invent and solve concrete examples, and by occasional work in Roman notation up to one hundred.

"6. The common errors of method in this branch are such as the omission, for a long time, of any written work; the attempt to teach counting in the abstract to a thousand, perhaps, without having them count *things;* the attempt to teach them to write numbers to billions before they can add to hundreds; the omission of any written work at seats between recitations."

Geography and history are inseparably connected, and should always be studied together. The first step in teaching these branches is to give pupils a clear conception of the earth, as a whole, — its form and motions. It is evident that a good globe is essential to success at this point.

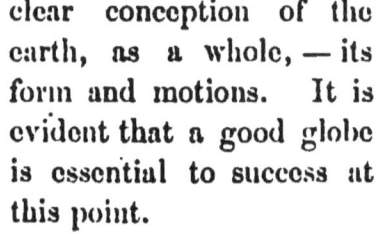

The latest and simplest apparatus for impressing the form and daily motion of the earth upon the minds of pupils is the "Time Globe." In order to give a clear idea of this globe, I present the following description and cut: —

"The 'Time Globe' is a globe apparently endowed with life, having a diurnal revolution exactly corresponding to that of the earth. It is a miniature representation of the earth in position and daily motion, revolving once in twenty-four hours upon its own axis by means of chronometer works located in its interior. It gives local time on dial above the north pole, and the time of any and all parts of the world is read at a glance on the equatorial zone. It shows at all times the position of different parts of the earth, with reference to midday, midnight, morning, or evening twilight. It measures the comparative, and, by simple computation, the exact size of any country on the globe as it passes the meridian ring and equatorial dial. It illustrates the difference in time between any two or more places. It can without injury be put in sidereal position or placed horizontally to be used as a clock. All parts of its surface can be readily examined. It runs several days, is a stem-winder, and regulates from the outside."

After pupils have become acquainted with the earth as a complete body, they will enjoy learning something of its several parts. The several grand divisions, oceans, and most important island, should then be pointed out on the globe. No books should be used in the study of this subject until after pupils have become familiar with the most important places marked on the globe. If all our school-maps were placed on globes, pupils could certainly gain a clearer idea of the relative position of the most important places on the earth's surface. Books should be introduced, therefore, only when the class needs information which the school-globe does not furnish.

While assigning lessons in either geography or history, the teacher should see that each member of the class has, before commencing to study the lesson, a clear understanding of the direction and distance of the place or places referred to in the lessons. Without this understanding pupils might as well study lessons in "dreamland."

Free-hand map-drawing should be practised daily in connection with the study of geography and history. The child's first efforts may produce only rough sketches, but the countries sketched will be thereby photographed in the memory. State Superintendent J. W. Dickenson, of Massachusetts, in a circular letter to teachers, says:—

"Every map as studied should be drawn in outline, upon slates or paper. With a little practice such drawings can be made in very little time. There is no method comparable with map-drawing for fixing geographical knowledge in the memory. Have exercises in representing the various natural features quickly and accurately upon the blackboard. Recitations in geography should be largely guided by a special outline previously written on the blackboard. This practice saves much talking on the part of the teacher, and cultivates independence in the pupil."

But pupils should study the people and products of the several countries on the face of the earth more than they should the boundary lines of these countries. They should learn the names and location of the most important places only. Learning long lists of names and location of unimportant places is time worse than wasted. It is burdening the mind with knowledge that is not needed, and nature will throw it off as soon as possible. There is so much life on the land and in the sea, that geography ought to be a *living* subject rather than a dead one.

If we undertake to teach universal history, we should first present the world in its most perfect form, — the present. If we undertake to teach the history of a nation or country, we should first present its current history; then we may, with profit, study the past. It is true that this plan rather reverses the usual order of studying history. Too many commence with the past, and never come up to the present. This is too true, even of teachers. Professor Saulsbery, an experienced conductor of normal institutes, says, in the Wisconsin " Journal of Education " : —

"Teachers, with rare exceptions, do not read nor greatly interest themselves in the history of the present. They know something of Jackson's administration, and more of Washington's, but nothing at all of Grant's or Hayes's. Events of a hundred years ago are more familiar to them than those of the past ten or fifteen prolific years. The ancient history of our country, and of the world, is better attended to than the modern or recent. Whatever may be the cause of this, the fact itself is lamentable. It indicates such a state of immaturity and mental childhood on the part of those who assume to teach, or such a degree of dead indifference as to the world's ongoings, as ought in either case to startle those who come in contact with it."

Beginners should have lessons in current history presented on the blackboard, until they become familiar with the present, before they undertake to study the history of the past.

The bare mention of English grammar is almost enough to frighten beginners, therefore children should be trained in speaking and writing correctly without any intimation that this is English grammar. They should be early impressed with the fact of the wonderful beauty of language when written and spoken in its best form. The best method of teaching beginners *how* to speak and write correctly, is to *have* them speak and write correctly.

Professor Greene, author of Greene's English Grammar, in an address before the Rhode Island Institute of Instruction, said:—

"I believe in writing very early, and having children taught at an early age to put their thoughts into writing. Then you can point out improvements, and show the child why the improvements are made, and why they are improvements. If I were a teacher in the primary school, I would adopt this motto from beginning to end: 'Every lesson shall be a language lesson.'"

Hon. E. E. White, ex-State school commissioner of Ohio, but now president of Purdue University, Indiana, says:—

"The study of the English language, though it is the most difficult of all the school studies, ought to be the most interesting. Pupils should not be required to memorize pages of dry, wearisome notes and observations as found in text-books. A knowledge of the meaning and relation of words is of first importance in all reading lessons, and this study of language must be commenced long before a grammatical text-book is used. The reading lesson should be made the prominent exercise of the day.

"The correct use of language is a matter of habit rather than of technical study of the rules of grammar. It should be a part of the work of the teacher, either in classes of higher or lower grade, daily to correct the inaccuracies of speech resulting from bad habits of pronunciation, and in the use of language. No provincialisms, no slang or careless pronunciation, should be allowed to pass unnoticed. Questions should be direct, answers concise. Every answer should be a complete sentence."

A thoughtful teacher can readily see that while he is training his pupils in speaking and writing, their inquisitive natures desire an acquaintance with the source from which he obtains his information. Suppose, for example, the teacher has occasion often to correct his pupils in their use of certain irregular verbs; a list of these verbs, and exercises illustrating the proper method of using them, will prove interesting and profitable to the entire school. So all the several parts of English grammar may be made pleasurable, provided each part is presented just when pupils feel their need of it.

Constant exercises in writing, together with corrections made by the teacher, will convince pupils that they need a more thorough knowledge of the laws of language, and by the time they are old enough they will be anxious to take up English grammar as a branch of study. When each pupil, by careful study, has become acquainted with his English grammar, he should be encouraged to use it as he does his dictionary, as a book of reference.

LECTURE XXVII.

HINTS UPON TEACHING WRITING.

PENMANSHIP, in this the latter part of the nineteenth century, is, perhaps, more generally neglected in country schools than any other branch in the common school course. In many parts of the country *good* penmanship appears to be reckoned among the "lost arts."

Writing, as a medium for the communication of thought, is almost as important as speaking. For this reason, it has been said that "writing is a secondary power of speech, and they who cannot write are in part dumb. Scrawls that cannot be read may be compared to talking that cannot be understood; and writing difficult to decipher, to stammering speech."

Feeling anxious to offer the highest helps of the ablest instructors, I applied to Prof. D. T. Ames, editor of "Penman's Art Journal," New York City, asking him to prepare an article that might be both an incentive and an aid to better penmanship. This he consented to do. The cuts for the illustrations of his article are chiefly from "The Spencerian Theory of Penmanship," and inserted by courtesy of the publishers, Messrs. Ivison, Blakeman, Taylor & Co., New York. The remaining cuts were kindly furnished by Prof. Ames. I here present Prof. Ames's article, without further comment.

Of the great importance to all classes of a rapid, graceful, and legible handwriting, I scarcely need speak. To the young man it opens more avenues to desirable and lucrative employment than any other one qualification. To a young lady it is not only a rare accomplishment, but to such as are required to earn their own livelihood, it is the one most ready and available.

To be able to awaken and maintain earnest thought and study on the part of the pupil, and skilfully direct the same, is a paramount qualification for successful teaching. Indeed, the power to do this is the real secret of the wonderful success that has attended the labors and immortalized the names of our greatest teachers, not of writing alone, but of all departments of education. The interested and attentive pupil is always a success, while the indifferent pupil is a certain failure; the former seems almost to drink in knowledge, while the latter receives it as by force. Many teachers of writing rely mainly upon the imitative power of pupils for their success, which is a fatal error; writing should be taught mechanically more than by imitation.

An imitative pupil may manifest remarkable progress, and be able to imitate with the greatest fidelity the most perfect copy, so long as it is before him, and yet write most awkwardly when it is removed, from the fact that there remains no correct mental conception or ideal of writing to guide his practice. It is not so with the pupil who has been taught mechanically, and has learned the correct analysis of each letter, studied its form and construction, at the same time that the errors in his own writing have been criticised and corrected according to established rules and principles; though he may, at the outset, be greatly distanced by the imitative genius, he will, in the end, become much the more skilful. The removal of the copy matters little to him, its form having become so completely impressed upon his mind that it continues, as it were, constantly before him, a perfect ideal, to reproduce which the hand will ever strive, and ultimately attain. Writing, in all its grace, ease, and perfection, must first clearly exist in the mind before the hand can, by any amount of exercise, be taught to produce it. The hand can never transcribe a form more perfect or beautiful than the ideal of its master, — the mind. Hence the vital importance of preceding and accompanying all practice, in writing, with a careful study of its mechanical construction. The exercise or copy for each lesson should be short, embracing but a few letters; and they should be systematically arranged so as to present, forcibly and concisely, at each lesson, some important feature of writing.

The observation and experience of more than

twenty-five years as student, teacher, and author of writing, have led me to believe that every person possessed of ordinary faculties can and should learn to write with facility, at least, a legible hand. That they do not, is due alike to the faults in our methods of teaching and practice. The first great fault has been with the teachers and authors of systems of writing, that they have given to the pupil too many and too complicated forms for letters, apparently in the belief that the more numerous and fanciful were their forms, the greater the evidence of their own skill and deserved popularity. Not unfrequently in a single copy-book, or a short course of twelve or twenty lessons, has the pupil been required to practise upon from two to four distinct and radically different types or forms for all the capitals and many of the small letters of the alphabet, and all or most of these forms much too complicated to be practical for rapid business writing. I will here illustrate in the case of one letter, and this is no fancy sketch, but from a case of actual observataion. I have found all the following types of the letter R in a single copy-book, and have seen them all, and others, taught or attempted, by a teacher of writing, in a short course of ten lessons : —

This method carried through the alphabet would require the pupils to practise upon *one hundred and eighty* different forms for the capitals alone, and a corresponding, though necessarily less, number for the small letters, all given and practised often without any sort of system or science. Is it any wonder that the pupil is a discouraged failure at the end of a course of such diversified practice upon complex and multitudinous forms?

The labor and practice necessary to become skilful in making such a multitude of difficult forms is too great to be overcome except by rare genius, or the most persistent and prolonged practice. The multitude must fail; while, if required to make but twenty-six of the most simple forms, and those reduced by system to seven elementary principles, the multitude can and will succeed.

Another fruitful cause of failure is found in the effort of many, perhaps most, teachers to teach writing almost or quite wholly by imitation, by which method pupils acquire little or no absolute or permanent idea of the true form or construction of letters or the general style and excellence of writing. They may succeed well at imitating their copy so long as it is before them, but fail utterly to write well when it is removed. This will not be the case when it is systematically and analytically taught; each letter being accurately analyzed, its correct form and manner of construction explained by the teacher, and understood by the pupil, at the same time that his writing is thoroughly criticised and its faults pointed out and corrected according to well-established principles. Where this is done the eye and understanding are disciplined and taught as well as the hand, and there remains impressed vividly upon the mind of the pupil a clear and well-defined conception of the form and construction of his copy, so that, though literally absent, to the mind's eye it is ever present, and is a perpetual copy, for the mastery of which the hand will ever strive and will ultimately accomplish. Unlike the pupil who practises without system or principle by imitation, and who not only ceases to improve, but actually goes backward, when the instruction ends, and the copy is removed, the analytic pupil will continue ever to advance, and is certain, ultimately, to become a good writer.

HOW WRITING SHOULD BE TAUGHT.

POSITIONS.

The first care is to secure and maintain the correct positions of body, arm, hand, and pen. The position at the desk or table will be governed somewhat by circumstances. In the school-room, where desks are small and narrow, we think a position with the right side to the desk will be the best, thus:

In business colleges and writing academies, where the table or desk is more spacious, and especially in the study and practice of bookkeeping, where the books are often large and numerous, also by artists and penmen working upon large pieces of work, the front position will be found the best, thus:

In this position the same relative position of hand, pen, and paper should be maintained as described in the former one.

Another position at the desk, sometimes advocated by authors and teachers, is the right oblique, which is a position between the front and side.

In our opinion, which of these positions is to be adopted should be governed by the circumstances of the writer or the class-room.

HINTS UPON TEACHING WRITING. 343

Some authors and teachers have also advocated a position of presenting the left side to the desk, in favor of which we have nothing to offer, for we believe either of those above described entirely preferable; yet the position at the desk is of much less importance than that the proper relative positions of the pen, hand, and paper should be sustained and observed.

PENHOLDING.

Take the pen between the first and second fingers and thumb, letting it cross the forefinger just forward of the knuckle (A) and the second finger at the root of the nail (B) ¾ of an inch from the pen's point. Bring the point (C) squarely to the paper, and let the tip of the holder (D) point toward the right shoulder.

The *thumb* should be bent outward at the first joint, and (E) touch the holder opposite the first joint of the forefinger.

The *first and second fingers* should touch each other as far as the first joint of the first finger; the *third and fourth* must be slightly curved and separate from the others at the middle joint, and rest upon the paper at the tips of the nails. The *wrist* must always be elevated a little above the desk.

These positions should be rigidly maintained, thus keeping the nibs of the pen flat upon the paper, and both always under the same degree of pressure, when the pen will give a smooth, clear line, and move smoothly and easily upon the paper.

MOVEMENTS.

These positions secured, attention should be directed to movements, all of which should be explained and illustrated, and the peculiar advantages and disadvantages of each set forth.

There are four different movements more or less employed in writing.

The First, or Finger Movement, is most generally used and taught by unprofessional teachers, and practised by most unskilful writers, and is so called because the fingers alone are employed in giving motion to the pen. Writing by this movement is less rapid and graceful than that by either of the other movements. . It is more of a drawing process, it seems to be the most easy and natural to acquire, and, being the only movement known or taught in a large majority of our public schools, it is practised by a very large proportion of people outside of the mercantile and professional pursuits. Most of the latter have found it necessary to gain some further knowledge of writing than that acquired in our public schools, so they have either attended a commercial school or received instructions from some professional teacher of writing, and have been instructed in other movements.

The second is the *Fore-arm, or Muscular Movement.* By some teachers it is called the Spencerian, and by others the Carstairian, being so called after the names of two of its most noted and skilful teachers and advocates; this movement is obtained by resting the fleshy or muscular part of the fore-arm upon the desk, and then by simply contracting or relaxing the muscles of the fore-arm a very rapid, graceful, and tireless motion is imparted to the hand and pen; but it is only when combined with the finger, producing what is known as the *Third, or Combination Movement*, that it is employed to the greatest advantage. In this movement the muscles impart rapidity and endurance, the fingers accuracy of form, and ease in making the extended letters, thus rendering it, as a whole, by far the best and most desirable movement for practical writing.

The *Fourth, or Whole Arm Movement*, is the most graceful and rapid of all the movements; it is also, when employed on a small scale, much less accurate, and hence less desirable for practical writing. It is used to advantage only where considerable license is allowable, as, for instance, in writing dates, signatures, superscriptions, blackboard writing, etc. To be able to employ this movement with skill requires much and continued practice. Its proper and skilful use is, however, an important accomplishment to the professional penman. It is obtained by raising the entire arm free from the table, resting the hand lightly upon the nails of the third and fourth fingers, and then striking the letters with a full sweep of the whole arm. This movement is also used in all offhand flourishing.

MOVEMENT EXERCISES

should be frequently and extensively practised, and a short exercise should precede the regular practice of every lesson. The object is threefold. *First*, to secure a free, graceful, and rapid general movement to the fingers, muscles, and fore-arm. *Second*, a special upward and downward motion; and *Third*, a lateral movement of the hand. To secure the first two, exercises like the following should be practised:

To secure the lateral movement, the following or similar exercises should be practised:

The major part of the time for the first, considerable of the second and third, and a part of the time for every lesson of a course, should be devoted to careful movement exercises.

These exercises, as well as all the copies of the course, should be either engraved or written upon short movable slips, and passed to each pupil of the class with the opening of each lesson.

We are now prepared to present the principles and begin the analysis and practice of writing, which we do by placing upon the blackboard the principles.

At the same time we briefly illustrate to the class

their use and importance in learning to write, by rapidly making a few monograms embracing the entire alphabet, capitals and small letters; showing the close resemblance between the form and construction of many of the letters of the alphabet, and how very simple and easy is their construction from these principles.

This can be very clearly and strikingly illustrated in the case of the small letters by a monogram representing them all as follows:

We then combine the capitals in three monograms, those having the fifth principle for their base, thus:

Making the letters and subsequently arranging them in groups, each embracing those letters that most resemble each other in their form and manner of construction, thus:

Monogram embracing the letters having the sixth principle as base is made as follows:

and the letters separately, thus:

Monogram of seventh-principle letters would be made thus:

and the letters, thus:

By this method the great simplicity and practicability of this plan of teaching and practising writing is fully brought home to the mind and understanding of the pupil, and also the great importance of mastering thoroughly, at the outset, these elementary forms or principles of writing. I will briefly define these principles.

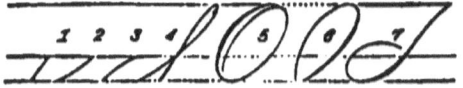

No. 1 is simply a straight line, shaded or unshaded. No. 2 is a right curve. No. 3 a left curve. No. 4 combines a right and left curve to form the loop. Principle No. 5 is a direct oval, whose length is twice its width. No. 6 is an inverted egg-shaped oval. No. 7 consists of an unshaded left and shaded right curve of equal length and degree of curvature, forming a compound curve variously called capital stem, master stroke, chirographic curve, line of beauty, etc., to which is added a left curve which intersects the other two curves at the point of their union, forming an oval. The stem slanting on an angle of fifty-two degrees, and the oval on an angle of fifteen degrees; the oval should be twice as long as it is broad, so, if divided into sections, it would have four spaces in length and two in width.

The correct angle of slope will be best illustrated, thus:

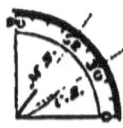

The class will now make this principle after a few

moments' practice. Robert, and several others, are found to be making it thus:

While James, and others, are making it thus:

Other members of the class are also making equally conspicuous faults. We now make upon the blackboard strokes representing the most prominent faults of the class, and illustrate. Robert has made the left curve too long and the right curve too short, and not on same degree of curvature; while the second left curve defines more nearly a circle than an oval, and intersects the downward stroke below the centre, and would be corrected, as indicated by the dotted lines.

After sufficient attention has been given to the analysis and practice of the capital stem, we add to it a line to make the

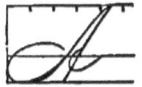

which we practise briefly, and then add the small letters forming a short word for a copy, all of which is written upon the blackboard and analyzed before being practised by the class. Follow this in the same manner by the

and so on through the alphabet, — presenting the capitals in groups most similar in their construction and analysis.

By thus using a short copy we are better enabled to concentrate the entire thoughts and practice of the pupil upon a few points in writing at a time, which will be more clearly understood and thoroughly mastered than if he were to practise upon a copy embracing most of the alphabet and all the principles and characters of writing. If such a copy were fully analyzed, so much would be said, and so many points presented, as to cause utter confusion, and its entire effect would be lost, and the corrections of faults too numerous to be either remembered or guarded against in subsequent practice.

Where copy-books are used having long copies, they should, in the early stages of practice, be written down the page by sections of not more than one fourth its length, thus concentrating the practice and criticism upon a few letters at a time. The leading faults of the class while practising the copy should be pointed out and corrected at the blackboard. General faults in writing would be corrected by writing the copy upon the blackboard in such a manner as to magnify the fault, and then show how it can be

HINTS UPON TEACHING WRITING. 353

best corrected. For instance, the bad effect of disproportion in size of letters can be strikingly illustrated by writing the copy, thus:

Auction

Having care to make each letter, by itself, as nearly perfect as possible, showing, thereby, that perfect letters alone cannot make good writing. The correction of this fault can be greatly aided by ruling a guide line for the top of the letters.

At the next lesson illustrate the bad effect of uneven spacing, thus:

communication

At the following lesson we would present the special beauty of a variety in slant in writing, thus:

Willing

Slant, though quite different, will not be specially conspicuous in the contracted letters, but may be made to appear strikingly so by drawing extended lines through the parts of the letters, thus:

Willing

We then illustrate all the essential qualities of correct writing, by writing the copy correctly upon a scale, thus:

Steadfastly

This method pursued earnestly through a course of even twenty lessons will not fail to secure to the attentive pupil not only marked improvement, but will so discipline his eye, and idea of the correct forms and characteristics of good writing, that he can scarcely fail of ultimately writing, with facility, a legible and graceful hand.

LECTURE XXVIII.

HINTS UPON TEACHING MAP-DRAWING.

DRAWING is now regarded, by the foremost teachers, as the most effective method of fixing the form of any object in the mind. It is practised with profit in the study of all the common branches, and in no other is it found to be more helpful than in the study of geography. The old method of learning geography by memorizing boundary lines, and long lists of names of places, is giving way to the more sensible method, — map-drawing.

As the object of this lecture is simply to help those who have had no instructions in map-drawing, I shall not attempt to fully discuss this subject, but rather to give some helpful hints, hoping thereby to lead teachers and pupils to form such a taste for map-drawing that they will wish to follow it further. The method that I present is known as " Apgar's System of Free-Hand Map-Drawing," which is a plain method, a method well suited to the work of our country schools. The illustrations presented are taken from " Apgars' Geographical Drawing Book." They are original, and have been patented, but are used here by permission of the patentees and authors, Messrs. E. A. and A. C. Apgar, of Trenton, New Jersey. The cuts for these illustrations were furnished by the publishers of the above-named book, — Messrs. Cowperthwait & Co., Philadelphia. Most of the suggestions which follow are also taken from the foregoing work, but neither suggestions nor illustrations are arranged in the exact order in which the authors placed them.

The study of geography consists largely in a study of the form and locality of the features of the earth's surface. Maps give a much better idea of the form and locality of geographical features than can be obtained from descriptions only; hence maps should be among the principal objects of study in geography. That form is easiest remembered which the hand is taught to trace. The exercise of the mind, needed to teach the hand to trace a form, impresses that form upon the mind. As the study of maps is a study of form, the manner of studying them should be by map-drawing. In learning to draw maps, the pupil needs some rule or guide to assist him in drawing them correctly, and also to enable him to judge of their accuracy when drawn. This assistance is best afforded by the use of geometrical figures or diagrams. The diagram used in each case, in order to answer the purpose intended, should be so constructed as to coincide as nearly as possible in its outline with the boundaries of the map to be drawn. By the relative lengths of the lines of which it is composed, it should express the general laws of form of the map it is intended to accompany, and

HINTS UPON TEACHING MAP-DRAWING. 357

by its angles and division marks the position of prominent features should be determined. However complex and irregular the map may be, the diagram should be so simple that it can be readily constructed and easily remembered by the pupils. In the construction of the diagrams used for drawing the continents, the first line in each case serves as a measure for determining the lengths of the other lines.

I present here a diagram of North America, with directions for drawing it. By comparing this diagram with a map of North America it will be seen that they nearly agree in outlines.

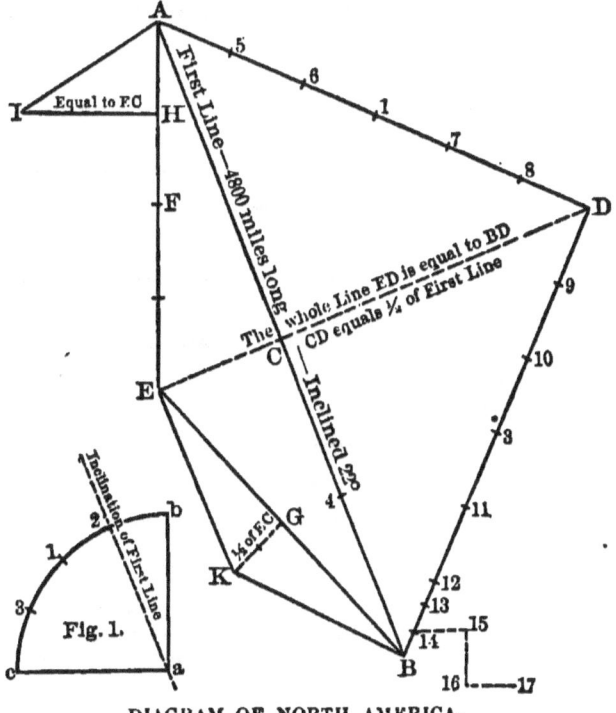

DIAGRAM OF NORTH AMERICA.

358 GRADUATING SYSTEM FOR COUNTRY SCHOOLS.

DIRECTIONS FOR DRAWING.— *Diagram.* —1. Draw a quadrant, and divide it into four equal parts, as represented in Fig. 1. Through the first division point at 2, and the right angle at a, draw the first line of the diagram the length desired for the map.

2. From the centre of this line draw the line CD at right angles with it, and one half its length. Connect A and D, and B and D.

3. Extend the line CD toward E, making the whole length, DE, equal to AD or BD, and draw lines from A to E and from E to B.

4. Divide the line AE into four equal parts, and from the upper division point, at H, draw the line HI at right angles with AE, and equal to EC in length. Connect A and I.

5. Divide the line EB into two equal parts, and from its centre, and at right angles with it, draw the line GK one half the length of EC.

6. Divide the lines CD and CB each into two equal parts, and the lines AD and DB each into six equal parts.

7. Subdivide the lower division of the line DB into three equal parts, and from the division point at 14 draw a line to the right to 15; and from 15 draw one toward the south to 16; and from 16 draw another to the right to 17,— making the length of each equal to two thirds of the distance from 12 to B.

It will be observed that if the diagram is correctly drawn, the lines AD, ED, and BD are equal in length, and the line AE is vertical.

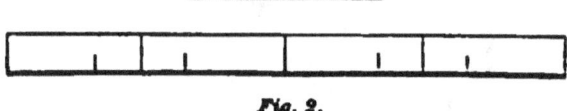

Fig. 2.

Fig. 2 represents a convenient ruler for pupils to use in drawing maps upon the blackboard. It is twenty inches long, and divided into halves, thirds, fourths, and sixths. A similar one, six inches long, may be used for drawing on slate or paper.

HINTS UPON TEACHING MAP-DRAWING. 359

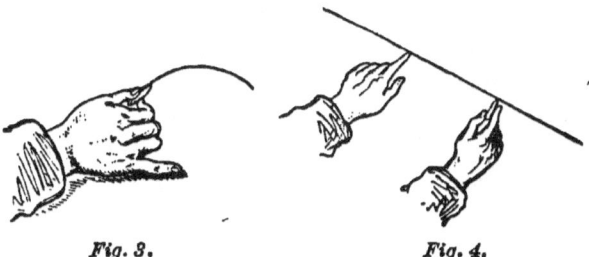

Fig. 3.   *Fig. 4.*

Fig. 3 represents an easy method for drawing a Quadrant. | Fig. 4 represents an easy method for trisecting a line.

NOTE. — In the construction of diagrams, and in the division of lines, the pupils should at first be allowed to use a ruler, such as the one represented in Fig. 2. This is important, in order to insure accuracy. After some practice, however, the ruler should be dispensed with, and the figures should be drawn by hand, guided only by the eye.

In drawing a quadrant, a piece of crayon held between the thumb and first finger may be made to describe the arc around the end of the fourth finger, as represented in Fig. 3. A vertical and a horizontal line drawn from the centre to the arc will complete the quadrant. Instead of the hand, a short string, with a piece of crayon tied to the end of it, may be used ; or each pupil may be furnished with a quarter of a circle, cut out of a piece of writing-paper, having the divisions of quarters and sixths marked upon it.

In dividing a line into three equal parts, use the finger of one hand and a crayon in the other, and place them so that the three parts appear equal, as represented in Fig. 4.

In dividing a line into four or six parts, first bisect it, and then bisect or trisect each half.

It will be observed that the different lines of the diagrams are drawn in the order they are lettered, and that the divisions are made in the order they are numbered.

In drawing upon paper or slate, the diagram should be in very light lines. For blackboard work, the figure should be drawn with a slate-pencil. At each board should hang a rule, a triangle, a rubber, and a pointer.

POSITION. — North America is situated north of the Equator, and is joined to South America by the Isthmus of Panama.

EXTENT. — The greatest length of the continent, extending from Point Barrow, on the north, to the Port of Guatemala, on the south, is 4,800 miles. This length is represented by the first line of the diagram.

GENERAL FORM.—The general form of North America is triangular. It is wide toward the north, and narrow toward the south. The Arctic and Atlantic coast lines are nearly straight in their general directions, while the Pacific coast line is curved.

POINTS OF COINCIDENCE.—The position of Point Barrow is determined by the northern angle of the diagram; Cape Charles by the eastern angle; port of Guatemala by the southern angle; Bay of San Francisco by the western angle; and the western extremity of Alaska peninsula by the northwestern angle.

DRAWING THE MAP.—*Arctic Coast.*—Commence at Point Barrow. Make the mouth of the Mackenzie River opposite to the first division; Victoria Land on the second; the mouth of Hudson Bay between the third and fourth, and Ungava Bay and Cape Chidley near the fifth division. The southern extremity of James Bay touches the line CD, near its centre.

Atlantic Coast.—On the line DB, between Cape Charles and the first division, draw the Gulf of St. Lawrence. Make the peninsula of Nova Scotia without the line, and opposite the first division; Cape Cod north of the second, and Cape Fear at the third. The western shore of Florida peninsula crosses at the fourth division. The mouth of the Gulf of Mexico is between the fourth and fifth divisions; the northern shore crosses the line CB near its centre, and the western shore is on the line EB. Cape Catoche is near the fifth division and the shore of Central America, and the Isthmus of Panama follows closely the zigzag line extending from 12 to 17.

Pacific Coast.—Commence at Point Barrow. Draw Kotzebue and Norton Sounds without the line, and Bristol Bay within. Norton Sound is near the centre of the line. The southern shore of Alaska follows closely the line IH, and the remaining portion of the western shore of the continent deviates but little at any one point from the lines of the diagram. California peninsula extends nearly as far south as the angle at K, and the eastern shore of the Gulf of California crosses the line $K\,G$ near its centre.

NOTE. — It will be observed that the Lake of the Woods is on the line CD, midway between the centre and C; also that Lake Erie is midway between the centres of the lines CD and BD, or between the points 2 and 3 on the diagram.

In map-drawing exercises the pupils may either be required to describe their work in full, without the assistance of questions, or the lessons may consist of a series of questions and answers. After the diagram is made the class is prepared to draw the map, — first with the atlas in hand, and afterwards from memory. Every order given by the teacher should be executed by the class simultaneously, and with military promptness and precision. The execution should commence immediately after the last word of the order is given. Each pupil is supposed to have his own diagram on the board upon which he draws his map.

For the States *no additional diagram is used*, because the bounding lines are generally straight, and they themselves, when taken together, form a geometrical figure. In drawing the States, therefore, it is only necessary to select one of the straight lines forming the boundary for a measuring unit. The line selected should be a convenient measure or multiple of the other lines.

In conducting exercises in map-drawing, the class

should be practised, *first*, in drawing upon the blackboard, under the immediate direction of the teacher; *second*, in drawing upon slates, their work to be submitted to the teacher; and *third*, in executing maps upon paper, to be presented for the criticism of both the teacher and the class.

Either the teacher or one of the more skilful pupils should execute a well-finished and accurate map upon the blackboard. From this drawing — which is much to be preferred to any printed outline map — the class may recite their lesson; and upon it each of the new features, as they are learned from day to day, may be represented.

It is well to accompany every lesson in map-drawing with more or less practice in rapid sketching. In order to excite emulation for quick work, the lesson may be drawn on the board and the exercise timed by the teacher. Pupils, by practice, will soon be able to draw a diagram in half a minute, a State in from half a minute to two minutes, and a continent in from three to five minutes. Concert recitations should frequently accompany rapid sketching.

An exercise called *talking and chalking* will be found both interesting and valuable. The pupil, while he is drawing a map, briefly, and in a lively manner, describes the features as he represents them; his verbal explanations all the while keeping pace with his illustrations made with the chalk.

All directions and exercises in map-drawing should

be such as to prepare the pupil to draw rapidly, accurately, and *without the copy*.

After the pupils have learned to draw a map with sufficient accuracy, and are able to describe satisfactorily the features it contains, they may, with the use of colors and India ink, be taught to draw and embellish one for preservation. Not much time, however, should be spent in producing highly ornamented maps. A slate-pencil and slate, lead-pencil and paper, white crayon and blackboard, are all the materials usually needed in map-drawing exercises. Rapid work, and much of it, should be the motto.

Special attention should be directed to the method employed for representing the population of cities and the heights of elevations. The symbols used will greatly assist the memory in retaining these facts. Special lessons may be given to teach their meaning. Their use should be required in all map-drawing exercises.

I will conclude this subject by presenting two pages of symbols; one showing the signs used to represent the population of cities and towns, and the other the signs used to represent the elevation of mountains.

EXPLANATION OF THE SIGNS
USED TO REPRESENT THE POPULATION OF THE
CITIES AND TOWNS.

FIRST CLASS.

In the First Class only one Sign is used viz. a round dot.
● represents under 10,000 Inhabitants.

SECOND CLASS.

Each Line of the Second Class represents a population of 10,000.

THIRD CLASS.

The markings of the Third Class have a Dot in the centre. Each Line upon this Dot represents 100,000 population.

Second Class		Third Class	
○	10,000	●	100,000
╬	20,000	╬	200,000
╫	30,000	╫	300,000
╪	40,000	╪	400,000
╫╫	50,000	╫╫	500,000
╫╫	60,000	╫╫	600,000
╫╫╫	70,000	╫╫╫	700,000
╫╫╫	80,000	╫╫╫	800,000
╫╫╫	90,000	╫╫╫	900,000

FOURTH CLASS.

The markings of the Fourth Class have a Dot and Circle (◉) in the centre. Each Line upon this Dot and Circle represents 1,000,000 Inhabitants.

◉	1,000,000	╫	3,000,000
╬	2,000,000	╪	4,000,000

System Patented October 16th, 1866.

EXPLANATION OF THE SIGNS
USED TO REPRÉSENT THE
ELEVATION OF THE MOUNTAINS.

RANGES.

Hill and Mountain Ranges, Like the Cities, are divided into Four classes. The First is represented by a series of Parallel Curves; the Second by a series of Interlocking Curves; the Third by a Waved Line; and the Fourth by a Zigzag Line; as follows:

)))))))))))))))))))   *First Class or Hills,*—Under 2000 ft. high.

Second Class,—Between 2000 & 8000 ft. high, or Between ½ and 1½ miles high.

Third Class,—Between 8000 & 16,000 ft. high, or Between 1½ and 3 miles high.

Fourth Class,—Over 16,000 feet high, or over 3 miles high.

PEAKS.

For Peaks under one mile high each Curve upon the right represents One-Fourth of a mile Elevation; for those one mile high or more, each Line upon the right represents One Mile in Elevation and the Dash underneath One Half a Mile.

⌒ ¼ of a mile high.   ◮ 2½ miles high.
⌒ ½   ,,   ,,   ◭ 3   ,,   ,,
⌒ ¾   ,,   ,,   ◭ 3½   ,,   ,,
∧ 1   ,,   ,,   ◭ 4   ,,   ,,
△ 1½ miles high.   ◭ 4½   ,,   ,,
▲ 2   ,,   ,,   ◭ 5   ,,   ,,

System Patented October 16 Ch., 1866.

LECTURE XXIX.

HINTS UPON TEACHING LETTER-WRITING AND BOOK-KEEPING.

The pen is seldom used by country people except in writing letters and keeping accounts. If it be true that children ought to learn, in school, what they will practise in later life, then it is evident that they should there learn how to write letters and keep accounts. The slipshod style of writing and directing letters, and the unsystematic and unsatisfactory manner of keeping accounts, seen and practised in all parts of the country, prove that these subjects have not received sufficient attention in public schools. In many schools the subject of letter-writing and book-keeping is not so much as hinted at by the teacher.

In order to present, forcibly, the importance of a knowledge of letter-writing viewed from a business, social, and intellectual standpoint, I offer the following extract from Westlake's admirable book, "How to Write Letters," published by Sower, Potts & Co., Philadelphia: —

"As letter-writing is the most generally practised,

so also it is the most important, practically considered, of all kinds of composition. This will more fully appear from the following considerations: —

"1. *Letter-writing is indispensable in business.* All persons have business of some kind to transact, and much of it must be done by means of letters. To be able to write a good letter is greatly to a person's advantage in any occupation. Many good situations are obtained by teachers, clerks, and others, on account of this ability, and quite as many are lost for the want of it.

"2. *It is a social obligation.* We are naturally social beings; and pleasure, interest, and duty equally demand that our friendships and other social ties should be maintained and strengthened. In many cases this can be done only by means of letters. No one would willingly lose out of his life the joy of receiving letters from absent friends, nor withhold from others the same exquisite pleasure. It may be stated, also, that a person's social, intellectual, and moral culture is indicated in his letters as plainly as in his manners, dress, and conversation; and it is as great a violation of propriety to send an awkward, careless, badly written letter, as it is to appear in a company of refined people with swaggering gait, soiled linen, and unkempt hair.

"3. *It gives intellectual culture.* Letter-writing is one of the most practical and interesting exercises in English composition, — one that is suitable for persons of all grades, from the child just learning to write, to the man of highest attainments. It affords exercise in penmanship, spelling, grammar, diction, invention, — in short, in all the elements of composition; and gives ease, grace, and vivacity of style. Many who have become distinguished in other kinds of writing, have acquired much of their power and fluency of expression by their practice of writing letters. Of these Robert Burns is a notable example. In fact the letters of distinguished men and women form a distinct and important department of literature; and some who are recognized as standard authors would long ago have been forgotten but for their admirable correspondence."

It is not my purpose to suggest that letter-writing should be made a branch of study in the common school course, but rather to insist that the teacher should be familiar with the best forms of directing, heading, introducing, and concluding letters, and that he should occasionally present these forms for the benefit of his pupils. A pleasing and profitable exercise of fifteen or twenty minutes may be had in the school-room, once a week, by presenting upon the blackboard any separate part of the subject of letter-writing. In order to make this matter clear, I offer some illustrations of the method by which letter-writing may be taught. The quotations which I make, and the models which I present, were all taken, by permission, from Westlake's "How to Write Letters." The cuts for the models were furnished by Messrs. Sower, Potts & Co., Philadelphia, publishers of the above-named book.

Let the teacher take up, for the first lesson, the subject of the "*superscription*," which is the outside address that is put upon the envelope. In order that the lesson may seem to be a reality, each pupil should have several envelopes. The teacher may then draw upon the blackboard the form of three or four envelopes, with directions upon each, and accompany the same with instructions, while his pupils direct and stamp real envelopes. Old stamps may be used for this purpose. The following instructions and forms may be presented.

If the person addressed lives in the country or in a small town, the following form should be used: —

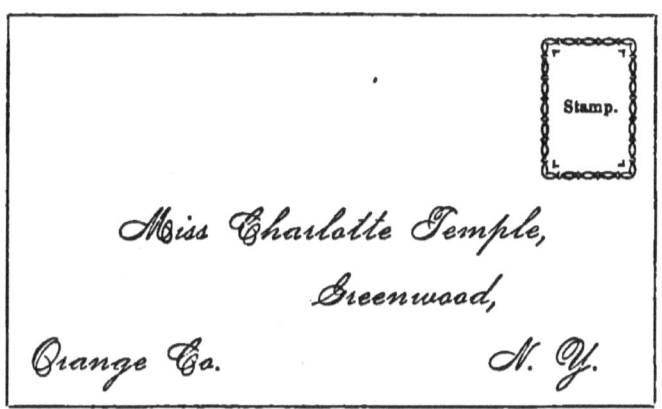

Whenever it is desirable that, in case the letter should not be called for within a certain period, it shall be returned to the writer, the following form may be used: —

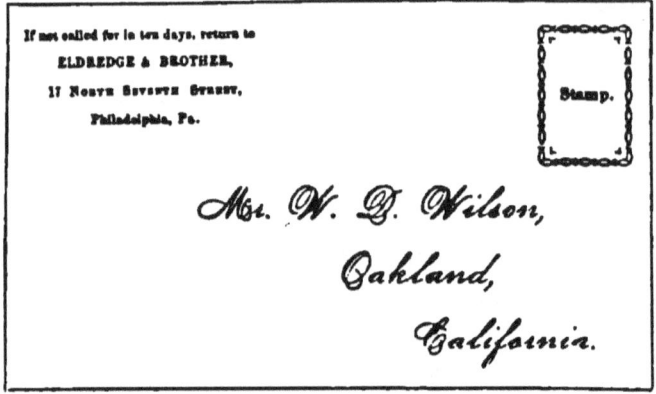

If the person addressed lives in a city, this form should be used.

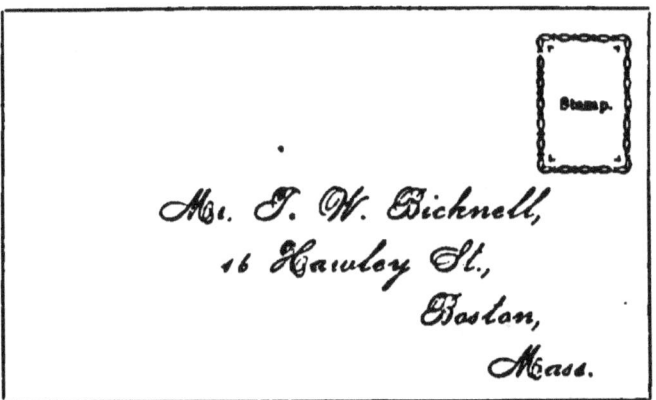

The following rules and suggestions for directing letters, punctuating the superscription, and affixing the stamp upon the envelope may be either placed upon the blackboard or read aloud to the pupils: —

"1. The name should be a trifle below the middle of the envelope, and should begin near the left edge, sometimes close to the edge, sometimes one or two inches from it, according to circumstances; and the other parts should be written at equal distances under it, each a little farther to the right, so that the last part (State) shall come near the lower right-hand corner.

"2. Put a period after every abbreviation and after the last word. Put a comma after each item (that is, each line if properly written), except the last. If a title is added to the name, put a comma between the name and the title; if two titles are added put a comma between them.

"3. Place the stamp on the upper right-hand corner of the envelope at about one eighth of an inch from the end and half as far from the top. It does not look well when placed close to either edge. *Why* this is so we cannot tell, but *that* it is so is undeniable. Perhaps it is for the same reason that a picture looks best with a white margin all around. The stamp is a picture, and should, of course, be right end up."

The following note of warning cannot be too carefully impressed upon the minds of pupils: —

"A letter will not be forwarded unless it is prepaid at least three cents. About 400,000 letters are every year sent to the dead-letter office because they are not properly stamped. The superscription should be plainly and legibly written, especially the name of the post-office and the State. If the name of the State is short, write it in full; and if abbreviations are used, take care to form the letters correctly. Pa. and Va., Penn. and Tenn., N. Y. and N. J., are particularly liable to be confounded. Hundreds of letters are sent to Trenton, N. Y., that were intended for Trenton, N. J., and *vice versa*. Often letters are missent on account of sheer carelessness on the part of the writer. Of the 3,000,000 or 4,000,000 letters that go to the dead-letter office every year, about 70,000 are not properly directed, and between 3,000 and 4,000 have no directions whatever."

At the conclusion of the lesson each pupil, after writing his name upon the back of his envelopes, should deliver them to the teacher, who may examine them at his leisure and use the time of the next week's lesson in commendations and criticisms upon these envelopes, after which they may be returned to the pupils.

The teacher may take, at another lesson, the subject of the "Heading of Letters," which is a statement of the place where, and the time when, the letter is written. Each pupil, for this lesson, should be supplied with several sheets of letter-paper. The teacher may then place upon the blackboard the following: —

MODELS OF HEADING.

Model 1.

Troy, N. Y., Aug. 5, 1860.

Model 2.

*Gettysburg, Adams Co., Pa.,
Monday, May 20, 1860.*

Model 3.

*Mt. Holyoke Seminary,
South Hadley, Mass.,
July 22, 1860.*

Model 4.

*222 Madison Av., New York,
June 30, 1860.*

If preferred, this heading may be arranged as follows: —

Model 5.

*222 Madison Avenue,
New York, June 30, 1860.*

Model 6.

Residence and date at the bottom.

Place of signature.

*17 Nahant Street,
Lynn, Mass., May 1 1860.*

These several models of heading should be copied by each pupil, on as many sheets of letter-paper, according to the following directions: —

"On ruled paper, the heading should begin on the first line, a little to the left of the middle; and it may occupy one, two, or three lines (never more than three), according to circumstances. If the paper is not ruled, the positions should be the same. The parts of the heading should be separated by commas, and a period should be placed at the end of the heading, and after each abbreviation."

While the pupils are copying the foregoing models the teacher may go among them and give needed instructions. At the conclusion of this lesson, pupils should be directed to preserve carefully the sheets of paper containing these models to be used at several subsequent lessons.

At another time the teacher may take up the subject of the "Introduction of Letters," which consists of the address and the salutation. The address, when complete, consists of the name and title of the person written to and his directions. The salutation is the term of politeness, respect, or affection with which we introduce a letter; such as, *Dear Sir*, *My dear Friend*, *My dear and honored Father*, etc.

In order to make the matter more clear, let the teacher place upon the blackboard, for the pupils to copy, several of the following models of introduction. Pupils should use the paper which contains the headings presented in the last lesson.

MODELS OF INTRODUCTION.

Model 1.—*Business Form.*

Messrs. Franklin & Hall,
   58 Market St.,
      Philadelphia.
Dear Sirs,
         Your favor, etc.

NOTE.—The body of the letter usually begins under the end of the salutation, but when the address is long, as in the above model, it may begin in the same line as the salutation, in which case a dash must precede it. Thus:—

Model 2.—*Business Form.*

Messrs. Tiffany & Co.,
   550 Broadway,
      New York.
Dear Sirs,—Please send by return, etc.

NOTE.—It will be observed that in Model 1 the salutation begins under the initial figure of the second line, while in Model 2 it begins under the initial letter of the first.

Model 3.—*Business Form.*

Messrs. Samuel Gilbert & Sons,
   Boston, Mass.
      Gentlemen,—I have the honor to acknowledge the receipt, etc.

Or it may be arranged as follows:—

Model 4.—*Business Form.*

Messrs. Samuel Gilbert & Sons,
    Boston, Mass.
Gentlemen,
        I have the honor, etc.

Model 5.—*Business Form (to a Lady).*

Miss Clara F. Abbott,
    Newport, R. I.
        We acknowledge with pleasure the receipt of your manuscript, etc.

If the lady were married, *Madam*, or *Dear Madam*, would follow the address, as in Model 8.

Model 6.—*Official Form.*

Major-General M. C. Meigs,
    Quartermaster-General,
        Washington, D. C.
General (or Sir):
        I have the honor to transmit herewith my report, etc.

Model 7.—*Social Form.*

Respected Friend,
   Thy kind favor was very gratefully received, etc.

When the name of the correspondent is not given at the top (as in Models 7, 9, and 10), it should be written at the bottom.

In addressing a member of the religious society of Friends, no title is used.

Model 8.—*Social Form (Formal).*

Mrs. Hannah More.
Dear Madam,
   Accept my sincere thanks for the beautiful book, etc.

Model 9.—*Social Form (Domestic).*

My dear Daughter,
   Since I last wrote to you, strange things have occurred, etc.

Model 10.—*Social Form (Familiar).*

Your most welcome letter, my very dear friend, arrived to-day, etc.

The teacher, at another time, may take up the subject of the "Conclusion of Letters." The following definitions and suggestions may aid him in presenting this subject:—

"What is technically known as the conclusion of a letter is that which is added after the communication itself is finished. It consists of the complimentary close, the signature, and sometimes (when not at the top) the address of the person written to. The complimentary close is the phrase of courtesy, respect, or endearment used at the end of a letter. As in the salutation, the particular words used vary according to circumstances. Social letters admit of an almost infinite variety of forms of complimentary close. In business letters, or letters of any kind written to strangers or mere acquaintances, the customary form is 'Yours truly,' or 'Yours respectfully.' These may be emphasized by very, as 'Yours very truly,' or varied by inversion, as 'Truly yours.' Official letters have a more stately and formal close.

"Every letter should be signed in a plain, clear hand, and if it contains anything of importance, the name should be written in full. If the writer is a lady, she should, in writing to a stranger, so sign her name as to indicate not only her sex, but also whether she is married or single.

"The complimentary close is written on the next line below the end of the letter proper. If too long to look well in one line, it may occupy two, or even three lines. The signature is written on the next line below the complimentary close, near the right-hand edge of the sheet. The close and signature must be arranged similar to the parts of the heading and introduction; that is, they must present a regular slope downward and to the right. A comma is required after the complimentary close, and a period after the signature. If the close is long, other points may be required, as may be seen by consulting the models given below. The address, when placed at the bottom, is punctuated the same as when placed at the top of the letter."

In order that the forms of concluding letters may be fully impressed upon the minds of pupils, the teacher may write upon the blackboard, and allow his pupils to copy, upon the lower part of the sheets used at the former lessons, the following : —

MODELS OF CONCLUSION.

(The dotted line stands for the last line of the letter.)

Model 1.

Yours respectfully,
Henry F. Adams.

Model 2.

We remain, dear Sir,
    Your obedient servants,
        John Hancock & Co.

Model 3.—With Address.

Your loving daughter,
    Evelyn Williams.
Dr. John Williams,
    Providence, R. I.

Model 4.—Official.

Very respectfully,
    Your obedient servant,
        Oliver Warren,
    Secretary of the Commonwealth.

Model 5.—With Date.

Very truly yours,
    Clara Hawthorne.
The Arlington, Washington, D. C.,
    Sept. 20, 1875.

The teacher may take, at another time, the subject of the "Body of Letters." The following definitions and suggestions are intended to aid in the presentation of this subject: —

"The body of the letter is the communication itself, exclusive of the heading, introduction, and conclusion." This part of the letter is an original composition, and the writer ought not to be hampered by stereotyped phrases. The pupil, however, needs instructions in this as in other kinds of composition, and may be greatly aided by the following directions: —

"A blank margin should always be left on the left-hand side of each page, — not on the right. The width of this margin should vary with the width of the page. On large letter-paper it should be about an inch; on note-paper, about three eighths of an inch. Indeed, if the sheet is quite small, a quarter of an inch will answer. A margin that is too wide looks worse than one that is too narrow. The margin should be perfectly even. Letters, as well as other compositions, should be divided into paragraphs, if they speak of different and disconnected things. For example, if, after speaking of affairs at home, the writer turns to speak of himself, he should make a new paragraph. Do not make too many paragraphs. Sometimes persons make the mistake of making a paragraph of every sentence. It is a matter that depends wholly on the sense. A letter may consist of only a single paragraph. On a large letter-sheet, the paragraphs should begin about an inch to the right of the marginal line, that is, the line of writing; on note-paper, they should begin about three fourths of an inch to the right of this line.

"Letter-writing presupposes the ability to write a legible hand. But we should not be satisfied with mere legibility; we should endeavor to attain to neatness and elegance. A letter should be regarded not merely as a medium for the communication of intelligence, but also as a work of art. As beauty of words, tone, and manner adds a charm to speech, so elegance of materials, writing, and general appearance enhances the pleasure bestowed by a letter."

At the conclusion of these suggestions each pupil may be requested to write, within the coming week, a letter directed to the teacher, using one of the forms heretofore given, and these several letters should form the subject of the next lesson.

I have given a glimpse of the subject of letter-writing in hope that teachers and pupils may be led, thereby, to follow it further. Several interesting features connected with the subject of correspondence have not been named, among which I merely mention notes of ceremony and compliment, and cards of invitation. I shall now offer a few suggestions on the subject of book-keeping.

That all young people should receive, in school, at least sufficient instructions on the subject of book-keeping to enable each one to keep his own accounts, no fair-minded person will deny. The want of this knowledge has produced dissensions in communities and furnished work for the courts.

It is not my purpose to discuss book-keeping in its broadest sense, but rather to suggest the method by which teachers may give their pupils a practical knowledge of this subject without interfering with other studies. Every thoughtful teacher is aware that there are times when pupils become tired of the regular recitations, — times when it is better to depart a little from the daily programme. Such occasions may be used by the skilful teacher in presenting practical lessons in the work of keeping accounts.

Suppose, as the first lesson, each pupil is permitted to open an account with his teacher. The teacher may present upon the blackboard the form of keeping accounts in a ledger, by single entry, and each pupil may rule a sheet of paper for the purpose. The teacher may then write upon the board the names and number of the several articles which he wishes to purchase of each pupil, and the names and number of the several articles which he wishes to sell to each pupil, and the price of each article. Each pupil may copy the charges and credits and carry out the amounts. The teacher may then call for settlement in order to see how his account stands with each pupil. Such a lesson will, to children, appear to be almost a reality, and they will exercise great care in their calculations. After each pupil states how his account stands, the several sheets may be handed to the teacher for inspection and criticism.

At another time the teacher may present the method of keeping the day-book; at another the method of posting the book, and at another time the mode of properly indexing the ledger. Blank books with paper backs may be procured at very little cost, and used by the pupils as though they were actively engaged in business. Pupils may, by this method, under the training of a skilful teacher, soon gain a practical knowledge of the subject of single-entry book-keeping.

Teachers may, by a like method, give their pupils a fair knowledge of the forms of written instruments in business, such as receipts, promissory-notes, agreements, deeds, and wills.

The common people cannot well afford to send their children away from home to commercial colleges, therefore the country school should furnish a fair business education.

LECTURE XXX.

HINTS UPON GRADING COUNTRY SCHOOLS.

In offering suggestions upon the subject of grading country schools, I shall not attempt to present a stereotyped form, suitable for all the States, but rather to point out a flexible method by which all schools may be graded.

As the method of gaining knowledge in infancy and the method of gaining knowledge in mature manhood ought to be one and the same, so the method of grading colleges and country schools ought to be alike. The country school is, indeed, sometimes called the "People's College." In a college the course of study is prescribed by officials, and the classification of pupils is made and carried out by instructors. While the courses of study in various colleges may be somewhat similar, and the methods of grading in all of them may be nearly alike, yet this work, in each one, is performed by its own officers and teachers. Neither Harvard nor Yale would undertake to prescribe a curriculum for the Virginia University, or insist upon indicating a specified method of grading its classes. Each school maintains its own individuality.

If we wish to make all the country schools of a State as one working school, then there should be a uniform course of study and system of grading in all the country schools of the State. And this is the plan that is now finding favor in the eyes of the foremost educators.

The National Educational Association, at its meeting in Philadelphia, July 31, 1879, passed a resolution calling the attention of State superintendents of public instruction throughout the United States to the propriety of adopting a graduating system for country schools, since which time initiatory steps have been taken in several States for the grading of country schools. The first outline of a graded course for country schools, published after the passage of the above resolution, was prepared for the schools of the State of Tennessee, and appeared in the June number, 1880, of the "American Journal of Education," St. Louis. This outline, or circular, which was furnished by Hon. Leon. Trousdale, State superintendent of Tennessee, provides not only for the grading of country schools, but for the graduation of pupils who satisfactorily complete the common school course of study. This outline is too long to be here presented in full, but I offer Superintendent Trousdale's introduction to this circular, which is entitled "Graded Course of Study for Country Schools." He says: "What the schools desire and need is a plan,— a system, a model, a guide-post. This we now endeavor to supply in the following well-matured schedule, which has been prepared by Professor S. Y. Caldwell, superintendent of the Nashville public schools, after many earnest and anxious conferences and comparisons of views with myself. It has been my earnest desire, for the last four years, to present such a working plan for the schools, and the one here presented seems to be sufficiently practical to adapt itself to the scope and genius of every teacher who is sufficiently interested and earnestly alive to its great utility, and to the new and progressive life it will infuse into our public school system. It furnishes a sliding scale, so to speak, of sufficient margin for practical working, which promises to adapt it to the diversified circumstances and attainments of the pupils in all the schools, while there is definiteness and system enough to supply a standard by which each teacher may be guided while giving scope to his peculiar ingenuity, tact, and common-sense. The general qualifications of the teacher himself, his ability, skill, and judgment, must mainly be relied on to execute successfully the design. These suggestions are especially commended to those who agree to introduce the proposed plan of grading and granting certificates to those who complete the course. It is suggested that the studies authorized to be taught in public schools as found in the school law, be arranged under the following heads."

(Then follows a carefully prepared course, in the common branches, arranged after the order of a college curriculum.)

The editor of the "American Journal of Education," St. Louis, in the number from which the foregoing extract is taken, says:—

"The great want constantly felt in country schools, and which has heretofore been regarded as most difficult of attainment, indeed, which has not yet met with an accepted solution in any of the States, is the regular gradation of the course established by law for our public schools, so as to admit of flexibility and margin enough to bring within the limits of classification rural schools of pupils of uneven attainments. That exact grading cannot be attained in small schools, where the terms are short and attendance irregular, seems to be the greatest difficulty to be surmounted. This can only be done by allowing a large margin in the possible adjustment of the grades, by permitting pupils of unequal attainments in the different branches to alternate their studies in different grades until they have brought up their attainments to an even standard.

"The overwhelming importance of making a beginning in this direction justifies the essay we publish in this number of the 'Journal,' by Hon. Leon. Trousdale, State superintendent of public schools in Tennessee, who has, with the assistance of a number of the leading educators of the State, wrought out a graded system for the country schools which is so suggestive and valuable that our teachers in all the States will find it of great value.

"There may be obstacles which will confront the

teacher in maintaining a systematic grading, partial and disjointed though it may be, yet he should persevere in an effort so well worthy of a triumph, and which will render his work so much more satisfactory and fruitful of good results. He should meet each of these obstacles with tact, patience, and conciliatory firmness, bringing to bear upon it his knowledge of human nature, acquired training, and, above all, common-sense. But he should never despair, and should constantly persevere in the effort to systematize the course of study prescribed by law into a well-rounded and successive development of mental training and knowledge. He may not immediately succeed in a thorough grading of his whole school, but he may approximate so near to this standard that the greater number of his pupils shall be drawn into the plan at once, and those who are left straggling in a vain and obstinate effort to direct their own studies and pursue their own undigested schemes, will, after a while, fall into line, and the final result will justify the task he has proposed to accomplish."

A movement somewhat similar to that in Tennessee has recently been made in several other States. I find in a late issue of the "Educational Weekly," Chicago, an official circular from the State superintendent of Illinois, accompanied by a carefully graded course of study for the country schools of the State. This circular shows how the subject of grading country schools was introduced in that State, and how thoroughly the work is to be carried out, so I present it here, hoping that teachers and school officers in other States may be induced thereby to do likewise.

ILLINOIS CIRCULAR 15.

OUTLINE OF STUDY FOR THE UNGRADED SCHOOLS OF ILLINOIS.

DEPARTMENT OF PUBLIC INSTRUCTION,
SPRINGFIELD, ILL., Sept. 1, 1880.

The subject of a course of study for the ungraded schools of this State was discussed at the meeting of the County Superintendents' Association of Illinois, held at Bloomington, December, 1879. After the discussion, a committee was appointed to prepare an outline of such a course of study, and the State superintendent was requested to have it printed, when prepared, and to send a copy of it through the county superintendents to the teacher and board of school directors of each ungraded school in the State.

The committee have prepared the following outline of study. This outline is earnestly commended to county superintendents, school directors and teachers, in the belief that it will contribute to the usefulness and efficiency of the ungraded schools of the State.

JAMES P. SLADE,
Superintendent of Public Instruction.

Then follows a graded course of study, signed by James P. Slade, Albert G. Lane, and Mary L. Carpenter, committee. This course is somewhat similar to, but in some respects different from, the course prescribed for the schools of Tennessee.

I am in possession of a circular dated "River Falls, Pierce County, Wisconsin, July 31, 1880," issued by James T. McCleary, county superintendent, which indicates that the subject of grading country schools is receiving careful attention in the State of Wisconsin. I quote the following items from the foregoing circular: —

"*To all Friends of the Common Schools:* —

" Having felt, as a teacher, the need of some such arrangement, we have spent considerable time and thought in mapping out, for the common schools of Pierce County, the following course of study. It is based upon the course for the ungraded schools of Wisconsin, outlined by a committee from the State Teachers' Association, headed by our faithful and efficient State superintendent. We propose to adapt to the ungraded schools a system that has long been in successful operation in schools of higher grade, the two main features of the system being: 1. A definite course of study; 2. An honorable graduation of those who complete the course. ' Those pupils in the several schools of a town (township), who are recommended for graduation by their respective teachers, are to be examined by the county superintendent, assisted by two competent persons. To those found qualified, the common school diploma will be granted. An examination will take place annually in each town, except that in certain cases the pupils from two towns may be examined together. We offer the following reasons for adopting the course of study and graduation plan : —

"1. The course contains such studies as the pupils should pursue.

"2. There being an objective point, pupils will work more faithfully, attend more regularly, and remain longer in school than they would otherwise do.

"3. The schools can be governed more easily and by better means.

"4. The tendency will be to make the teacher's tenure of position more certain and lasting, and thus to induce persons of ability to remain in the profession.

"5. A better standard of success will be established.

"6. Better work can be done at teachers' meetings.

"7. We shall be preparing to take advantage of the high-school law.

"8. Pupils moving from one place in the county to another will 'fit into' the new school."

In several States the work of grading country schools has been carried on by counties working singly and separately. This method is good as far as it goes, but it is fragmentary, and slow to reach all the counties of the State. The method adopted in Tennessee, Illinois, and Wisconsin makes the work of grading uniform throughout the State.

The subject of grading country schools should be discussed in every State association and in every county institute, and a committee, consisting of the foremost educators in each, should be appointed to further consider and report upon this subject. To aid them in their work these committees should procure from State superintendents where gradation has been adopted, copies of the several graded courses of study for country schools. The reports of these committees will give teachers the best light that can be obtained, and will be likely to lead them to favor the universal adoption of the graded system in country schools.

Hon. W. K. Pendleton, State superintendent of West Virginia, occupies high ground upon the subject of grading country schools. In his official report to the State Legislature, under the head of "Graded Primary Instruction," he says:—

"There ought to be a beginning, a regular order of progress, and an end to the primary course of instruction. This has been felt by some of our best county superintendents, and Superintendent Wade, of Monongalia County, has succeeded in introducing a method in the schools of his county that has worked with admirable success. But so long as it is left to each teacher to do as he lists with respect to the organization and conduct of school work, we can have but little system or uniformity in it. I suggest that authority be given to prescribe a regular course of primary instruction, to be generally followed in the schools, with provision for the examination and graduation of all pupils who satisfactorily complete it."

It requires no prophetic eye to see that the country schools of the several States are yet to be as universally graded as colleges and universities. The importance of this gradation is clearly stated by Superintendent Parish, of New Haven, Conn., in the following paragraph, which I copy from the "National Journal of Education," Boston: —

"Nothing, perhaps, contributes more effectually to secure unity of purpose and action to the administration of our school system, than the thorough gradation of studies and careful classification of pupils according to capacity. Let it not be inferred, however, that there is, necessarily, what is often charged upon public schools when working systematically, anything like 'machine work,' to the exclusion or hindrance of the mental culture of the pupils. Concert of action is appropriate in the school-room as elsewhere, when considerable numbers are to be treated, both as a physical and mental drill; and experience has proved that it is beneficial to the bodies and minds of the pupils. Naturally dull minds are specially benefited by acting with others quicker than themselves, stimulated by the combined influence of compulsion and interest in a pleasurable exercise."

LECTURE XXXI.

SCHOOL GOVERNMENT, MANNERS, AND MORALS.

GOVERNMENT, manners, and morals are so near akin that I shall not try to separate them. Where manners and morals are bad, good government is unattainable; but where manners and morals are good, government will take care of itself.

I have heretofore, at various times, spoken of the power of motives in maintaining order; I shall now speak of penalties, and the purposes for which they should or should not be used. I may as well begin with the use of the rod.

The clear-headed educators of to-day, with few exceptions, agree that the use of the rod in the schoolroom, as in a well-regulated family, should generally be permitted but seldom practised. In case of a downright rebellion in the family the rod may be necessary, but a wise parent never uses it for the purpose of producing mental or moral growth. We have but to open our eyes in order to see that the best forms of family government are neither established nor maintained by the frequent use of the rod.

The school is the supplement to the family, and

what is true of the one is true of the other. The rod, in cases of emergency, may be applied in the government of pupils, but it should never be used as an incentive to study. Close observation will convince any sensible teacher or parent that lessons learned under the fear of the lash, like food forced upon the stomach, will be, by nature's law, thrown off undigested. This driving method cannot be long continued without producing mental dyspepsia. Mental dyspeptics may be seen all over the land.

What has been said of the rod, is in some degree applicable to all school-room penalties. They should be used only in the government of the school. The rod, I may further say, should be placed at the far end of the list of penalities. Even in the government of pupils penalties should be used sparingly, and the teacher who is not sufficiently skilful to govern without frequently resorting to penalties, ought to seek some other employment.

But some one may here say, if the teacher cannot *compel* his pupils to study, by what method can he induce them to do so? I answer this question by quoting the language of Herbert Spencer. In his book entitled "Education," he says: —

"The direct gratification consequent on activity, is the normal stimulus [to the acquisition of knowledge], and under good management the only needful stimulus. When we are obliged to fall back upon some other, we must take the fact as evidence that we are on the wrong track. Experience is daily showing with greater clearness that there is always a method to be found productive of interest, — even of delight; and it ever turns out that this is the method proved by all other tests to be the right one."

I come now to consider the subject of manners and morals. Of the importance of these I scarcely need speak. The State provides a system of schools for the purpose of so training its youths that they may become good citizens. Now if good manners and morals are as essential to the citizen as good scholarship is, then the former should be as carefully taught as the latter. That this is seldom done is evident to every careful observer. Superintendent W. F. Phelps, Winona, Minn., says: —

"The experience of each day in the management of our public schools serves only to deepen the conviction that their efficiency is crippled and their highest usefulness greatly restrained by their omission to give proper attention to the morals, manners, and general behavior of their pupils. The good name of the schools, the welfare of the children, and the good order of the community alike demand that this department of instruction should be elevated to its full rank in the administration of the system. We hear much said about the lack of moral instruction in our schools, and the same tongues wax eloquent frequently in their glorification of so-called 'scholarship' as the chief end of education, without offering a single practical suggestion as to how we are to teach morals and manners. When the boast is made that all the elements of excellence except scholarship have been excluded from the estimate of our school work, it is time for all thoughtful men to pause and reflect. Scholarship, when genuine, is good; but character is better. No school ever yet made a great scholar. That is the work of a lifetime of self-application. But schools can do much toward laying the foundations of a noble, useful, virtuous character, and that should be their supreme aim."

Prof. B. F. Shaub, president of the Pennsylvania State Teachers' Association, says: —

"The moral nature should receive more culture in the schools than it generally does; and just in proportion as parents are careless in this particular should the schools be more careful. Is it safe to leave moral culture to chance? Would it not be much less dangerous to leave the culture of the intellect to chance? Perhaps the best way to give this culture is to do so informally, but persistently and continuously, at every suitable opportunity. In every school, from the highest to the lowest, in every association of teachers, this subject should receive emphatic recognition, and should be lifted up into that prominence which its supreme importance demands."

The following editorial, from "Barnes' Educational Monthly," New York, is so appropriate that I present it for the benefit of the boys in our public schools: —

"A philosopher has said that true education for

boys is to 'teach them what they ought to know when they become men.' What is it they ought to know then? *First*, To be true, to be genuine. No education is worth anything that does not include this. A man had better not know how to read, — he had better never learn a letter in the alphabet, and be true and genuine in intention, in action, — rather than being learned in all sciences and all languages, to be at the same time false in heart and counterfeit in life. Above all things teach the boy that truth is more than culture, more than earthly power or position. *Second*, To be pure in thought, language, and life, — pure in mind and body. An impure man, young or old, poisoning the society where he moves with smutty stories and impure examples, is a moral ulcer, a plague spot, a leper, who ought to be treated as the lepers of old, who were banished from society and compelled to cry 'unclean,' as a warning to save others from the pestilence. *Third*, To be unselfish, to care for the comforts and feelings of others ; to be polite, to be genuine, noble, and manly. This will include a genuine reverence for the aged, and things sacred. *Fourth*, To be self-reliant and self-helpful, even from early childhood, — to be industrious always, and self-supporting, at the earliest proper age. Teach them that all honest work is honorable, and that an idle, useless life of dependence on others is disgraceful. When a boy has learned these four things, — when he has made these ideas a part of his being, — however young he may be, however poor, or however rich, he has learned some of the most important things he ought to know when he becomes a man."

But I am asked what qualifications the teacher needs in order to fit him for giving instructions in manners and morals. I answer by quoting the language of Rev. A. D. Mayo, associate editor of the "New England Journal of Education," Boston. In his address before the National Educational Association, in 1880, Mr. Mayo said:—

"The true teacher is the central object in all moral instruction. Unless he is the incarnation of all his pupils should be, it will be in vain that he attempts to give formal instruction in morality. Every school is really a committee of investigation of the teacher, and every instructor who combines high character and teaching ability cannot fail to be a powerful spiritual force in the school-room. The people must insist that only teachers of the most positive moral character shall stand before the children. In proportion as the level of moral power in the teacher can be raised, will character be shaped in the school-room."

Again, I am asked to name the text-book from which the teacher may draw lessons in morals. I answer, there is but one *standard work* on this subject, and that is the BIBLE.

I am aware that in some places the Bible is, by law, excluded from the school. The inconsistency of such legislation is seen in the fact that the same law which excludes the Bible from the youth in the school recognizes it as the seal of the citizen's oath before the court.

The school should be in no sense sectarian. But the use of the Bible in the school-room need no more constitute a sectarian school than the use of the Bible in the court-room constitutes a sectarian court. And this view of the subject has been sustained by the Supreme Court in several States. I offer as an example the late decision of the Supreme Court of Illinois, namely: "A few minutes' reading of the Bible each morning in a public school is not sectarian religious instruction."

Perhaps it is not best to prescribe a formal reading from the Scriptures each day in the school-room. Let the Bible be laid upon the teacher's desk by the side of the dictionary, to be used by the discreet teacher, just as the dictionary is used, — whenever it is needed. It should be used, mainly, as an aid in discipline and character training, and no intelligent parent can object to having his child bear in its character and conduct the seal of the Ten Commandments, the Sermon on the Mount, the Lord's Prayer, and the Golden Rule.

The leading educational journals of the land heartily favor the Bible in the public schools. As an index to their sentiment, I quote from the editorial columns of the two leading weekly journals. The "Educational Weekly," Chicago, says: —

"We believe that the Bible should be retained in the schools as the basis of moral instruction, and that certain portions of it, such as the Ten Commandments, the Lord's Prayer, and the Sermon on the Mount, should be made familiar to all pupils. The Bible is used as a sanction to oaths in the courts, and all citizens should be educated to reverence it. The schools should not undertake, of course, to expound its theology."

The "National Journal of Education," Boston, says: —

"The State of Massachusetts, in providing for instruction in morals and piety, and the reading of the Bible in school, expressly disclaims all indorsement of anybody's theory of inspiration, philosophy of morals, or religious creed. It forbids all teachers from entering on this debatable ground, and simply requires such instruction in morals and religion as every citizen fit to be outside of the State prison must acknowledge to be necessary, and lays the Bible, in any good version, on the teacher's desk as the best known, most honored, and least objectional handbook of youthful discipline. Inasmuch as the State builds its whole structure of criminal legislation on the foundations of that Christian morality common to all civilized lands, and punishes the citizen even with death for transgression of the moral law, it is difficult to see how religious liberty is assailed by instructing school-children in the principles of good morals and unsectarian religion, and reading the Ten Commandments, Beatitudes, and the Sermon on the Mount as a help in such discipline. We should say a State that was so dainty that it could not enforce the instruction of fundamental Christian morals in its common schools was a State in the air. To build a republic on the everlasting corner-stone of the Christian morality, to incorporate the very soul of the Christian idea of man, his rights and duties, in constitution and law, and to enforce that morality, through precept and discipline, in public schools, is neither to establish a State religion, to unite Church and State, nor to trench on any freedom of a parent except the liberty to make a criminal of his child. The American people regard religion, morality, and the Bible as the great common basis of American society on which our whole civil, social, ecclesiastical, and educational fabric is built; without which such a nation as this Republic would be simply impossible. The vast majority of the American people who support the common school believe in the absolute necessity of planting the common Christian morality in the very heart of its discipline and instruction."

LECTURE XXXII.

INDUSTRIAL EDUCATION IN COUNTRY SCHOOLS.

It is universally conceded that the country school ought to furnish an education extending beyond the school-room to the family, the farm, and the workshop; but how such an education can best be given is a question which is still unsettled even among the foremost thinkers.

In many of the great cities of Europe, and in some of the cities of the United States, workshops are attached to school buildings, and pupils are trained in various trades. It is evident, however, that the erection of workshops in connection with country school-houses is not feasible.

Although the country school, as it seems to me, cannot consistently undertake to train young people in various kinds of work, it can do that which is evidently of equal importance; it can inspire the children with a love for the callings which they are likely to pursue in later life. Most of the girls in our country schools are to be wives and housekeepers, and most of the boys are to be husbands and farmers, or mechanics, and they should be taught not only that labor is honorable, but that there is no nobler calling anywhere than that of the accomplished housekeeper, the complete farmer, or the finished mechanic. They should be taught that these are the most independent pursuits, and that they may be made not only very profitable, but also very pleasurable. They should be taught that to be ignorant of work is worse than to be ignorant of books; that to refuse to help their parents is worse than to fail in their recitations; and that to be a poor housekeeper, farmer, or mechanic is a greater misfortune than to be otherwise poorly educated.

The schools are sometimes charged with creating a sentiment unfavorable to industry. We have but to open our eyes, however, to see that wherever the schools are most flourishing the several industries are most prosperous. It is true that many of the schools have devoted themselves almost entirely to the cultivation of the brain, and have failed to create any sentiment at all upon the subject of industry. This is a very unfortunate omission, because a sentiment in favor of educating the hand is as important as a sentiment in favor of educating the head.

Prof. W. M. Barbour, of Yale College and Seminary, says, " Our seminaries and colleges are suffering from congestion of the brain; too much thought and too little putting it into practice. We need to diffuse the blood from the head into the extremities." This complaint of our seminaries and colleges, I am sorry to say, has been contracted in some of our country schools.

Pupils in country schools should be taught that one object in giving them an education is to enable the boys to become better farmers and mechanics than their fathers, and to enable the girls to become better cooks and housekeepers than their mothers. Teachers should point out methods by which children may hope to excel their parents in whatever pursuits they enter in life. For a single illustration, I may say that the teacher should impress upon his pupils the fact that if they desire to excel their parents in ability to do work, either of the hand or brain, they ought to have better health than their fathers and mothers have had. This they may hope to enjoy by giving closer attention than their parents have given to the subject of comfortable clothing, well-prepared food, eaten at regular hours, government of the appetite and temper, healthful situations for houses, thorough ventilation of sleeping apartments, and many other matters pertaining to the laws of life.

Pupils should be taught to use neither intoxicating liquors nor tobacco, but to save their earnings, spending money only for such things as are needful. They should be encouraged to study and use labor-saving machinery, and to employ some of the time so saved in the cultivation of their minds and in the ornamentation of their homes.

Boys should be taught that the work of enriching the soil, improving stock, and producing the best grades of grain and grass, requires a working brain as well as a willing hand. They should be taught that the mechanic needs a refined taste as well as a trained hand, so that his work may embody beauty of form and elegance of finish.

Girls should be taught that a complete knowledge of housekeeping, from the kitchen to the parlor, is the finest art, — an art which requires not only industry and skill, but intelligence and culture.

If all teachers of country schools will labor, from this time forth, to create in the minds of their pupils a love for the several callings which they are likely to pursue in later life, the future homes of the American people will be brighter, neater, healthier, and happier.

LECTURE XXXIII.

NECESSITY FOR SCHOOL SUPERVISION.

The need of enlightened supervision in mechanical employments, in business, and in government is everywhere acknowledged to be absolutely essential. This is proven by the fact that every factory has its foreman, every railroad has its president, and every nation has its ruler. In systems of education, supervision is believed to be essential to success in every department except in the ungraded primary school. This is proven by the fact that every college has its president and every high school has its principal. The necessity for supervision in ungraded country schools has never been fully settled in the minds of the masses of the American people. This is proven by the fact that several States, after testing such supervision for a while, have virtually destroyed it.

In attempting to account for the fact that the masses are not fully satisfied of the necessity for supervision in ungraded country schools, some writers have simply declared that the people are blind to their own interests. But if the people are blind to their interests in matters pertaining to primary education, why, I ask, do they see in matters pertaining to mechanical employments and to higher education? Let us look at this question, and see if we can find out why some persons favor supervision everywhere else, but are not satisfied of its utility in ungraded schools.

In every work where large numbers of men and women are employed, except in ungraded schools, there is a definite work for the superintendent to do, — a work that all interested persons can see. The foreman of a factory is required not merely to keep his eye on the operatives, and to report at stated periods how busy they have been, but he is required to inform the stockholders how many kegs of nails have been made, how many tons of metal have been moulded, or how many yards of fabric have been woven, in a given time, and the amount and condition of unfinished material still on hand.

If we examine carefully the annual catalogue of any school of high order, we find, that in its make-up it is near akin to the annual report of the factory manager. It gives the names of graduates and the date of graduation. It presents, also, the names of all pupils who are still in school, and indicates the time in which each is expected to complete the course of study.

From the foregoing consideration of this subject, I believe it is safe to say that supervision is acknowledged to be essential wherever several persons are employed in any work which ought to be *completed* in a given time. As there is no method in ungraded country schools by which the superintendent can ascertain how many pupils have actually completed the common school course of study within the year, or what progress pupils have made, the necessity for his office is not so easily seen as that of the foreman of a factory or the president of a university. Adopt in any factory the loose methods of ungraded schools, and its stock would fall at least fifty per cent. Supervision in such a factory would still be essential, but it would be by many considered simply an expense without profit, just as it now is by many in ungraded schools.

The country school ought not to be an exception to well-established laws of industry and business. It ought to be in harmony with all higher schools. The same educational method should prevail everywhere from the primary school to the university. Every step taken in the direction of gradation and graduation in country schools gives the superintendent a more definite work to do, and shows the people, in a clearer light, the necessity for school supervision.

LECTURE XXXIV.

WOMEN AS TEACHERS AND SCHOOL OFFICERS.

"More human, more divine than we —
In truth, half human, half divine —
Is woman."

MORE than one half of the public schools of the States and Territories are taught by women, and fifteen States have enacted laws making women eligible to school offices. There is, however, in many places a degree of prejudice against women, even as teachers. The consideration of this subject is, therefore, a matter of no small importance.

In the selection of teachers and school officers, we ought not to close our eyes to the hints which Nature gives us; and as the father and mother are Nature's chosen agents for the management of the home, it would seem to be natural for both sexes to take part in the management of the school. And this is the method that is now finding favor in several States.

School boards may be easily made up of both men and women, and schools requiring more than one teacher may employ both male and female; but many of the offices require but one person, and most of the country schools employ but one teacher, so we are often called upon to choose between man's superior strength and woman's superior culture.

In order that we may see and study the preferences given to one or the other of the sexes, in the numbers employed and salaries paid, in each of the several States and Territories, I present the following table, taken from the last report of the Commissioner of Education at Washington: —

TABLE.

Summary of the number of teachers employed in the public schools, and the average salary of teachers per month, in the respective States and Territories.

States and Territories.	Number of teachers employed in public schools.		Average salary of teachers per month.	
	Male.	Female.	Male.	Female.
Alabama...............................	(4,145)		$22 65	$22 65
Arkansas.............................	689	157	50 00	40 00
California.............................	1,184	1,083	83 75	60 66
Colorado.............................	183	250	56 10	51 45
Connecticut.........................	753	2,354	64 65	36 20
Delaware............................	270	231	(30 75)	
Florida...............................	375	182	......	......
Georgia..............................	3,267	1,633	......	......
Illinois...............................	9,162	12,836	46 17	32 23
Indiana..............................	8,109	5,465	61 27	39 20
Iowa.................................	7,343	12,518	34 88	23 69
Kansas..............................	2,772	3,279	33 19	29 82
Kentucky...........................	1,600	2,700	40 01	35 00
Louisiana...........................	767	740	45 00	35 00
Maine...............................	2,253	4,543	41 84	25 64
Maryland...........................	1,343	1,668	41 95	41 95

WOMEN AS TEACHERS AND SCHOOL OFFICERS. 413

TABLE. — *Continued.*

States and Territories.	Number of teachers employed in public schools.		Average salary of teachers per month.	
	Male.	Female.	Male.	Female.
Massachusetts............................	1,118	7,390	$75 64	$33 04
Michigan................................	3,781	9,220	42 54	27 45
Minnesota...............................	1,711	3,031	36 75	28 31
Mississippi..............................	(4,125)		29 19¼	29 19¼
Missouri................................	5,904	3,747	(30 00)	
Nebraska...............................	1,571	2,158	35 46	31 80
Nevada.................................	36	77	112 63	85 20
New Hampshire	591	2,955	38 37	24 71
New Jersey.............................	954	2,356	63 78	37 04
New York...............................	7,850	22,311	......	......
North Carolina..........................	1,728	654	30 00	30 00
Ohio....................................	10,855	12,148	......	......
Oregon	720	502	50 00	35 00
Pennsylvania	9,096	11,556	37 38	32 30
Rhode Island	294	987	80 69	45 91
South Carolina..........................	1,639	1,035	28 32	26 87
Tennessee	3,741	1,260	28 53	23 53
Texas...................................	(3,100)		(53 00)	
Vermont	720	3,608	34 44	21 60
Virginia	2,967	1,773	33 10	27 37
West Virginia	2,797	896	34 89	32 09
Wisconsin...............................	(9,858)		40 48	26 35
Total number of teachers in States......	(257,454)		......	......
Arizona.................................	6	25	$100 00	$50 00
Dakota	100	154	......	......
District of Columbia	31	209	96 17	71 21
Idaho...................................	......	......	......	......

The foregoing table, when studied in connection with the diagram giving the attendance in the several States, seems to indicate that women, as teachers, are superior to men in securing a higher per cent of attendance. In order to make the matter more clear, I will give some illustrations of what I mean.

Let us take the diagram which I presented in my talk upon "Methods for Securing Attendance" (page 310). We find that the State of Massachusetts stands highest upon the diagram in the average per cent of attendance of its school population. From the figures which we find in the table just presented, it appears that Massachusetts also stands highest in the per cent of women it employs as teachers. That is to say, Massachusetts has an average attendance of seventy-four per cent of its entire school population, and eighty-seven per cent of its teachers are women. Next to Massachusetts, on the diagram, stands the State of New Hampshire, with an average attendance of sixty-five per cent; and it also stands next on the table, — eighty-five per cent of its teachers are women. If we reverse the order, and take the lowest State on the diagram, — Arkansas, with only sixteen per cent of its school popu'ation on the roll, and no mention made of its average attendance, — we find that only twenty-three per cent of its teachers are women.

A careful examination of this diagram and table will convince any one that, as a rule, to which there are some exceptions, States employing a large per cent of women as teachers, have a high per cent of attendance of pupils; and States employing a small per cent of women as teachers, have a low per cent of attendance of pupils.

If it could be proven that a high average attendance is owing altogether to other causes, and not to the teachers, the fact still remains that where there is a high average attendance, women, as teachers, are generally preferred to men.

The wide difference between the average salaries of men and of women, in some of the States, is owing to the fact that it has been customary in the country to pay men more than women, and in cities and towns to employ male principals. This custom, however, seems to be losing ground in some places. As proof of this, I quote from an editorial in a late number of the "National Journal of Education," Boston. It says:—

"In St. Louis no discrimination is made between the salaries of men and women teaching in the same grade of school; and in California the Legislature has prohibited the making of distinctions in the salaries of men and women teachers holding the same grade of certificate. In Chicago, curiously enough, there is a positive discrimination in favor of women; for though a man cannot enter the schools without passing what is called a 'principals' examination,' there are women occupying principals' positions who never passed any examination more difficult than that for teachers of the lowest primary grades. The women principals in the Chicago schools now outnumber the men principals two to one."

There is, perhaps, in some places, danger that the practice of employing women as teachers in preference to men may be overdone. I would no more place all the schools in the hands of women, than I would place the instruction of children in the home entirely in the hands of the mother.

I believe, however, that where woman's education is equal to man's, she is generally superior to him as an instructor. Indeed it seems to be a fact that a woman's teaching efficiency often is superior to her education, while a man's value as an instructor is frequently below his acquirements.

An excellent authority on education says: —

"Regarding female teachers, we wish to say that we believe it is especially fortunate that the younger classes in our schools are generally in charge of women. Women, as a class, or the real woman, is 'apt to teach.' She is patient, is in sympathy with the young, understands their needs, their little sorrows, their tender minds, and, by her affection, can influence, control, and guide. Women's refinement, clear perceptions, and pleasing address, admirably fit them for primary teachers; and in many cases it is believed that rude boys, verging on manhood in stature, will be better controlled and taught by a thoroughly competent and dignified woman, one of good sense and large experience, than by men."

I come, in conclusion, to speak of women as

school officers; and I shall aim simply to present the drift of public sentiment upon this subject.

An editorial in the New York "Tribune," of March 24, 1880, referring to a law which had just been enacted by the Legislature of that State, says : —

"The best feature of the bill is unequivocal in its application. Women are eligible to election or appointment as school officers of all grades, from the lowest to the highest. In this city they can serve as trustees, inspectors, or commissioners, and throughout the State they can direct the educational interests of town or country. That women are competent for such duties cannot be seriously questioned. For our part, we have never doubted that the efficiency of our schools would be promoted by the co operation of the sexes in their management in high as well as in low places. We hope that the first vacancies which occur in this department of our city government will be filled by the appointment of women, — as commissioners, as well as trustees and inspectors. The experiment has been tried with satisfactory results in fourteen States, and there is no reason to suppose that it will fail in New York, where so large and so intelligent a body of women are devoting their lives to education."

An editorial in a late number of the "Legal News," Chicago, says : —

"When Judge Bradwell, in 1873, introduced in the Legislature of this State the bill, which is now a law, making women eligible to all school offices, the opponents of the measure claimed, if passed, it would be a dead letter, as women would not consent to take office; and, if they did, they would only show that they were inefficient; and that if a woman was once elected to a responsible school office, she would never be re-elected. The bill became a law, and the very first year fourteen women were elected county superintendents of schools; and the Hon. Newton Bateman, State superintendent, gave it as his opinion that the average ability of the women that were elected was higher than that of the men. Every year since the passage of the bill, Illinois has had quite a number of women superintendents, all of whom have proved faithful, efficient officers, and not a defaulter has been found among them; and this is more than can be said of all their brother superintendents. A number of these women superintendents have, from time to time, been re-elected. Among them we will mention Mrs. West, of Galesburg, who is one of the most capable superintendents in the State; and Mrs. Mary L. Carpenter, who was elected at the first election under the law, and has been re elected at every election since. She has just entered upon her seventh year as superintendent of the public schools of Winnebago County, one of the best counties in the State."

The State convention, of the minority party in Kansas, in 1880, placed Miss Sarah E. Brown upon the ticket as a candidate for State superintendent of schools. In order to show the sentiment of the convention upon this subject, I quote from a correspondent of the New York "Times." Speaking of the convention, he says: "The nomination of Miss Sarah E Brown was the event of the day at the Democratic State Convention. She is at present school superintendent of Douglass County. Ex-Senator Ross (the nominee for governor) was loudly called for, and came upon the platform and said that he felt highly honored in being placed upon the same ticket with such a distinguished lady. He thought the nomination of Miss Brown eminently proper. Judge J. S. Emery, a member of the Lawrence delegation, which made a strong fight against the lady's nomination, was interviewed by a reporter. He said: 'The truth is, the opposition to her grew out of the fact that she has taken an active part in the temperance campaign in our county. She is strongly in favor of the proposed amendment to the Constitution, and this has excited the antipathy of the whiskey dealers. She is county superintendent of schools, beat the regular Republican candidate last time by a fine majority, and her nomination on our State ticket will give it great strength."

The experiment of electing women as school officers was tested in Great Britain before it was tried in the United States. The following editorial from the London "Modern Thought" shows how the plan works on the other side of the sea.

Speaking of women on school boards, it says: —

"London is not the only city which has gladly welcomed women candidates. Manchester elected Miss Becker three times. Brighton returned Miss Ricketts at the head of the poll; Bath, in 1870, elected two ladies; Birmingham, Huddersfield, Oxford, Exeter, all followed this example. In Scotland a very large number of ladies were elected, and in subsequent elections many other towns and small country districts have raised women to this position of trust. Nor has this confidence been misplaced. They have shown themselves fully the equals of men in their business capacity, and their superiors in philanthropic schemes."

LECTURE XXXV.

A GLANCE AT EDUCATION ABROAD.

My main purpose, at present, is to consider the comparative merits of the common schools of Europe and of the United States. Before I begin the discussion of this subject, however, I wish to give a glimpse of the light in which the higher educational institutions of the two countries are viewed by some of the leading Asiatic nations.

When China, in 1860, was compelled by Western powers to open her ports to the commerce of the world, she determined to educate her coming officers in schools of more modern thought than were to be found in the Chinese Empire. Glancing at the several systems of education upon the globe, she passed by the schools of Europe, and sent one hundred of her choicest young men to the United States to be educated. If it be maintained, as a reason for this, that China, at that time, was unfriendly to European nations, and regarded our people as her truest friends, I answer that notwithstanding the strong opposition to Chinese emigration which, for several years, has existed in some sections of this country, China still continues to send her young noblemen to the United States, in order that they may be trained for positions of trust.

The Empire of Japan, following the example of China, is sending some of her most promising sons to American schools, expecting that, when educated, they will carry back to their own country the progressive spirit of our civilization.

Perhaps I cannot better present this subject than by quoting the language of that celebrated lecturer, the Rev. Joseph Cook. In one of his late "Boston Monday Lectures," Mr. Cook said: —

"The presence of Chinese and Japanese students in our American schools in considerable numbers, studying after a careful method, and with a definite aim, is significant of something more than a spirit of curiosity, adventure, enterprise, the love of knowledge, or the greed of gain; of something more than better means of transit, the increase of traffic, the breaking down of exclusiveness, the victories of diplomacy. The Eastern civilizations are laying hold upon the Western, and not only our industries, our arts, our sciences, but also our history, our literature, our methods of inquiry, and our religious ideas, are going back to the Orient in the persons of educated young men, trained among us from boyhood under careful supervision, and quickened by the inspiration of a career waiting before them.

"The Chinese government has, in 1880, on the east coast, in our best American schools, a hundred or a hundred and twenty Chinese students from the upper classes in the 'Celestial Empire.' With respect to these, several points are worthy of special mention. They are selected with care, after a long probation. They are sent here to remain, on an average, fifteen years, and to pass through the successive stages of elementary, secondary, college, and professional or technical education. They are preparing for a great diversity of employments. They are not allowed to denationalize themselves, but all their studies are carried on with direct reference to their future career in their native land. Their conformity to our modes of dress, and our habits of society and living, is a matter of convenience and courtesy, not a surrender. They come to get the most and the best we can give, but only to take and use it for the benefit of their country. Far more than our boys at West Point and Annapolis, they regard themselves as already in the service of the state. On their return they are expected to devote their education to the service of the nation in its widest sense."

I might multiply proofs of preferences given to American colleges by disinterested nations; but I desire now to turn to my subject, — the common schools of Europe and of the United States.

Determined to present the most authoritative testimony upon this subject, I wrote to Hon. E. A. Apgar, State superintendent of public instruction of New Jersey, and late United States Commissioner to the Paris Exposition, requesting him to furnish me a brief but clear statement of the comparative merits of the common schools of this country and Europe. He very promptly sent me his official report of "Schools Abroad," and suggested that, so far as my space would permit, I might use such portions of the report as were suited to my subject. This report is dated Trenton, New Jersey, Nov. 7, 1878.

Prof. Apgar's reputation as an educator, extensive traveller, and close observer is sufficient guaranty that his opinions in matters of education are of the highest value; and, without offering any further opinions of my own upon this subject, I present the following from his official report: —

For many years I have had an earnest desire to visit Europe, and this desire has been gratified. Before starting, I was honored with a nomination by Gov. McClellan, and an appointment by President Hayes as United States Commissioner to the Paris Exposition. I was also favored by Gen. Eaton, Chief of the Bureau of Education at Washington, with letters of introduction to prominent educators and school officers in various countries. I thus enjoyed peculiar advantages in studying school systems abroad.

My tour extended through England, France, Belgium, Holland, the Rhine district, Switzerland, and Italy. I travelled in all about twelve thousand miles. I felt the same anxiety common to all travellers the first time they visit Europe, to see everything. Historical monuments, church architecture, picture galleries, sculpture, antiquities, museums, natural scenery, the Paris Exposition, etc., etc., all made demands upon my time. I, however, gave special attention to European systems and methods of instruction, and seldom left a city without either visiting some of the schools or ascertaining something of what was being done for the education of the children. In some respects their schools resemble ours, and in others the contrast is quite striking.

Buildings. — The buildings, as a rule, are not so good as those in this country. Most of them have either been rented or purchased, and awkwardly adapted to the uses of the school. Even in Paris the schools I visited were held in buildings which had not originally been erected for school purposes

Furniture. — Not in a single school, from London to Naples, did I find the school furniture equal to ours. The pupils usually sit on long benches capable of accommodating from four to six. Some of the forms are for two only; in their construction, however, no attention is paid to beauty, and but little to comfort. In general, I am justified in saying that the seats and desks for pupils and teachers in the schools of Europe are no better than those which were in use in ours twenty-five years ago. I saw many schools where there were evidences of as free a use of the jack-knife as the Yankee boy was ever guilty of in the days when his natural propensity in this direction was unrestrained. The blackboards I saw were quite inferior, and what seemed most remarkable was that only one, large enough for the teacher's use, was to be seen in each room. Only the teacher makes use of the blackboard. In this respect our mode of teaching, which requires much blackboard work by the pupils, is superior to foreign methods. The rooms are usually well supplied with maps and charts. Metric charts and apparatus are to be found in all the schools outside of England, and in all departments. Small natural-history collections are occasionally seen, but usually there is a large museum in the city, which the classes, accompanied by their teachers, visit, and thus some knowledge is gained of familiar objects in natural history. In this respect we, in this country, are sadly deficient

Salute. — The military spirit which prevails in Europe is manifest in the schools. On every occasion when I entered a room all the children rose and gave a military salute. This consists in gracefully raising the right arm, and placing the right hand, with the two forefingers extended, at the side of the forehead. It is a simultaneous and graceful movement, and constitutes a beautiful sight. It causes a serious interruption in the exercises of the school, however, and for this reason I should dislike to see the custom introduced into our schools. It is to be preferred, however, to the idle stare of a hundred eyes with which a visitor is too often greeted. Those pupils are best trained who continue their studying, and give no evidence of being conscious of the presence of a stranger. A visitor will, of course, be saluted by the teacher, but beyond that his entrance into the room should cause no interruption, either in the teacher's or the pupil's work.

Holidays. — The schools outside of England are closed on Thursday instead of Saturday, as with us. There are numerous other holidays, called festal days, which sadly interrupt the work of education. Some are prescribed by the church, others by the state. In Italy scarcely a week passes without one or two interruptions of this nature.

Studies. — The studies pursued are much the same as here. In all the girls' departments instruction is given in needle and crochet work, in embroidery, and in the making of lace. Usually one afternoon of each week is devoted to hand-work of this nature. Much attention is given to composition writing, far more than with us. The teachers all seem to take special pride in showing the compositions which the pupils have written. Drawing is more generally taught there than in our schools. It is begun in the lowest rooms, and continued throughout the course. Copy is used to some extent in the primary departments, but frequently in the lower grades, and generally in the higher, objects take the place of copy. In this branch I consider their method of teaching superior to ours, and better results are accomplished.

Coeducation. — In our schools, except in the higher departments, the girls and boys are generally taught together. In Europe this coeducation of the sexes is unknown. In all the departments, from the lowest to the highest, they are separated. In Paris I found a custom prevailing which I did not observe elsewhere; the boys are all taught by men, and the girls by women

In general, we have as good work done by the teachers of our country as can be seen in the schools of Europe, and in some particulars our methods of teaching are superior to theirs.

Tuition Fees. — Free schools for children of all classes, such as we have in this country, are unknown in Europe. The terms "public" and "free" are both applied to their schools, but with a meaning quite different from that which belongs to them as used here. A "public school" is one subject to governmental control, and a "free school" is one which, in a measure, is free from such restrictions and regulations as have been prescribed by the government Both classes receive assistance from the public treasury, but not sufficient to meet all the expenses. Tuition fees are charged in both. Those known as "public schools" receive more aid from the government than those called "free," and hence the latter are more expensive to the patrons than the former. The proportion of expense paid as tuition varies in different countries. In London and Paris about four fifths of the entire expense of maintaining the schools is paid by the government, and the balance is asssessed upon the parents of the children who attend. Last year the fees in London ranged from four to eighteen cents for each pupil per week. This is about the average in other countries; in some the percentage paid as tuition is lower, and in some it is higher. In several of the countries the governments have prescribed the maximum and the minimum for the charges that can be made, and the local authorities determine the varying amounts between these extremes that shall be paid by the school patrons, according to their varying financial conditions I found in some cases there was an ascending scale of fees charged, the expense being very slight in the lowest departments, and gradually increasing through the advancing grades. In the schools of Sweden a small tuition fee is charged for all children over ten years of age. The people of Sweden, generally, are educated. According to a peculiar law, no person is permitted to marry until he is confirmed, and he is not admitted to confirmation unless he can satisfy the curate that he is able to read. In all of the countries of Europe provision is made for the free education of those who are unable to pay. Such children, however, are looked upon as pauper pupils. Sometimes all such are gathered together, and the school is known as a pauper school. The rule is, those who can pay must. The distinction between the rich, or those in moderate circumstances, and the very poor, is thus made unpleasantly prominent.

Public schools, which, from the lowest to the highest grades, are free to all alike, both rich and poor, thus giving to all equal chances for success in life, can only be found in this country; and this fact, more than any other I learned abroad, impressed me with the superiority of our public educational systems over those in Europe.

Conclusion. — I am satisfied that we in this country have the best public-school system in the world. We furnish better facilities to the whole people for acquiring a fundamental education than any other country. There is no excuse for any of our children growing up in ignorance of the common or ordinary branches of knowledge. We have good colleges and professional schools also. Any one, after completing his public-school course, can avail himself of the advantages of these higher institutions of learning, and thus prepare himself for any of the learned professions.

In Europe the educational work had its beginning at the top, in the founding of the higher institutions of learning, and the progress has been downwards. The establishment of public schools in some of the countries of Europe is quite recent. In this country we began at the bottom, by first establishing the lower schools for the public, and our progress must be upwards.

LECTURE XXXVI.

UNIFORM MONEY, WEIGHTS, AND MEASURES FOR THE WORLD.

LIGHTNING and steam have brought the nations of the earth so near each other that a uniform system of money, weights, and measures seems to be almost absolutely essential. Such a system would bring the business of all nations into harmony, save millions annually in computations, and wonderfully lessen the labor of the school life of every child. The Metric System, now making rapid headway among all civilized nations, furnishes a uniform standard for everything susceptible of being weighed or measured; and of this system I propose to speak.

My object, in presenting this subject, is to aid in educating the American people in the belief of the fact that national legislation upon this subject is a matter in which every man, woman, and child is interested. It is a fact worthy of note, that under a monarchy the lawmakers are the leaders of the people, but in a republic the people lead the lawmakers. In this country, therefore, all laws looking to important changes must originate with the people.

By the courtesy of Hon. E. A. Apgar, of Trenton, N. J., late United States Commissioner of Education to Europe, I am permitted to present from his pen, as my concluding lecture, the following carefully prepared article on the subject of the

METRIC SYSTEM.

In the early history of the world, when civilization had made but little progress, tables of weights and measures were unknown. Trade was conducted in the form of barter. One article was exchanged for another, or a single one of a certain description for several of another. As civilization advanced and wealth increased, the necessity of a common understanding relative to weights, measures, and values became apparent. Out of this necessity arose the various systems that have prevailed among all nations and tribes. These systems were as numerous as were the centres of trade or traffic. Each tribe or clan had its own. They were in no sense related to each other; their units were incommensurable; and the ratios of increase and decrease were entirely the result of accident or caprice. In the commercial world confusion reigned supreme. As late as the year 1800, there were in Europe not less than eighty different lengths for the foot in use. Equal diversity existed in all measures for weight and capacity. In Italy, each province had its own system; in Germany, each state; in France, each district; in Switzerland, each canton; and so throughout Europe every local political organization traded, reckoned, and kept accounts according to its own arithmetic, which was like no other arithmetic in the world. Take two cantons of Switzerland, for instance. In Berne, the foot was 11.54 inches; in Zurich, it was 11.81 inches. In Berne, the unit of weight was 18.64 ounces avoirdupois; in Zurich, it was 18.35 ounces. In Berne, the measure of liquid capacity was 1.76 quarts; in Zurich, it was 1.92 quarts. Berne had four different bushels for different substances; that for wheat contained 1.55 pecks; in Zurich, the measure for the same substance contained 2.33 pecks. This only illustrates the confusion that prevailed throughout every country in Europe, only three fourths of a century ago. And what made the matter infinitely worse, these units for weight, measure, and capacity, which numbered at least five hundred in all, were incommensurable. There was, so far as is known, but a single exception to this. The *sagene* of Russia, which was their unit of length, was just seven times as long as the English foot. With this one exeption, there was not a single term used to designate quantity anywhere in Europe that could be expressed in exact numbers by any term used elsewhere. And even this does not illustrate the extent of the confusion that existed; the multiples and sub-multiples for the increase and decrease of these units were equally diverse. No other cause contributed so largely as this to embarrass business transactions among men. Commercial exchanges between different countries, or between different provinces, cities, or even individuals of the same country, were subject to continual misunderstanding, confusion, and fraud These embarrassments increased as commercial intercourse increased, until it became apparent that the only relief possible was that to be found in the general adoption, throughout the world, of one common system of weights and measures. Until nearly the close of the eighteenth century, however, nothing seems to have been done looking toward the accomplishment of this object. It was reserved for the Constituent Assembly of France, during the most critical period of that country's history, to devise, for the common use of all nations, a system of weights and measures that should be constructed strictly according to scientific method. The principles that the assembly had in view in this undertaking were: —

"That for everything susceptible of being measured or weighed, there should be only one measure of length, one of weight, and one of contents, with their multiples and subdivisions exclusively in decimal proportions, and that the three units used should be commensurable."

I will here briefly relate the history of this important undertaking: —

Prince de Talleyrand, in the year 1790, addressed to the Constituent Assembly of France a proposal, in which he urged the adoption of a new system of weights and measures that should be founded upon a single and unalterable standard. This proposal assumed the form of a decree, which was passed by the assembly, and received the sanction of Louis XVI. on the 22d of August, 1790. By the terms of this decree the king was requested to write to the king of Great Britain, inviting him to propose to the Parliament the formation of a joint commission of members of the "Royal Society" of England, and of the "Academy of Sciences" of France, to determine upon a unit for the proposed international system.

On account of the political animosities then existing between these two countries, the invitation for a conference extended by France failed to receive acceptance on the part of England. This, for many reasons, is greatly to be regretted. The matter was then referred, by a decree of the National Assembly, to a committee of the Academy of Sciences, consisting of five of the most eminent mathematicians of the country. Their report was made to the academy, and immediately transmitted to the assembly. This occurred March 19, 1791. The committee, in its report, proposed that the ten-millionth part of the quarter of a meridan be taken as the standard unit of linear measure, and that the weight of distilled water at the point of freezing, measured by a cubical vessel in decimal proportions to the linear standard, should determine the standard of weight and capacity.

This report received the sanction of the assembly, and a committee of the academy was appointed to determine the length of the standard unit for the new system. This was a laborious operation, and consisted in a trigonometrical measurement of an arc of the meridian extending through France, from Dunkirk to Barcelona, a work that occupied seven years. In the year 1799, an international commission assembled at Paris, on the invitation of the government to settle, from the results of the great meridian survey, the exact length of the *meter*. In this commission were represented the governments of France, Holland, Denmark, Sweden, Switzerland, Spain, and the Roman Republic. After the completion of its labors, the commission proceeded, on the 22d of June, 179., to deposit, at the Palace of the Archives, in Paris, the standard meter bar of platinum, and the standard kilogram weight. These standards have since become the units of weights and measures for nearly the entire civilized globe.

Although the length of the unit, the meter, had been determined with such extreme care, it was, nevertheless, clear that the measurement of the earth's meridian, or any other unvarying dimension, could never be made with absolute accuracy. It was, therefore, evident that if the standard meter at Paris should be destroyed at any time, its exact duplicate could never be found. Accordingly, on the twenty-fourth day of September, 1872, the International Metric Commission, composed of scientific men of all countries, including the United States, met at Paris, for the purpose of providing against this danger. They resolved to make a new bar to replace the prototype, and to make it out of better material, and with a better cross section; and also, that four others should be made and placed in charge of the International Bureau, to be kept in a comparatively uniform temperature, for the purpose of studying the effects of time, by comparison, at intervals. They also provided that another similar bar should be kept at invariable temperature in a vacuum. They even recommended that, for further security, samples be made of quartz and beryl. The convention also resolved that bars of the same form, cast from the same ingot of platinum and iridium, in order that the expansion, contraction, and other modifying influences should be the same for all the bars, should be constructed for all nations that applied for them. In accordance with the action of this commission, and in strict conformity with its directions, an ingot of metal, composed of ninety per cent of platinum and ten per cent of iridium, was cast large enough to make all the standards required. This casting was made in 1874, and all the bars were completed in 1875, and nearly every country of the globe has been supplied with one that has the same legal authenticity as the prototype standard itself. Thus nearly every nation has in its possession a standard for all weights and measures, as unalterable and indestructible as modern science and skill, exercising all possible care and caution, can make it. Every one of these copies of the prototype is accompanied with its certified equation, and the length of the *meter* is determined from these rods when encased in ice. From this standard is derived the units for capacity and weight, and each unit increases and diminishes by the ratio of ten. Thus all the tables agree with our system of notation and with our currency table. The *liter* is the unit for measures of capacity, and is equal in volume to one cubic decimeter. The *gram* is the unit for weight, and is equal to the weight of one cubic centimeter, or a millimeter of water at four degrees centigrade. The relation existing between the different tables is shown in the following tabulation, which represents at one view the entire metric system : —

METRIC TABLE.

Length.	Abbreviation.
Millimeter	mm.
Centimeter	cm.
Decimeter.	dm.
Meter	m.
Dekameter	Dm.
Hektometer	Hm.
Kilometer	Km.
Myriameter	Mm.

Capacity.	Abbreviation.
(cm.) cubed = Milliliter	ml.
Centiliter	cl.
Deciliter	dl.

UNIFORM MONEY, WEIGHTS, AND MEASURES.

CAPACITY. Abbreviation.
(dm.) cubed = LITER . . . . l.
Dekaliter. . . . . Dl.
HEKTOLITER . . . . . . Hl.
(m.) cubed = Kiloliter . . . . Kl.
Myrialiter . . . . Ml.

WEIGHT. Abbreviation.
Milligram . . . . mg.
Centigram . . . . . . cg.
Decigram . . . . dg.
1 ml. of water = GRAM . . . . g.
1 cl. " = Dekagram . . . . . . Dg.
1 dl. " = Hektogram . . . . . . Hg.
1 l. " = Kilogram . . . . Kg.
1 Dl. " = Myriagram . . . . . . Mg.
1 Hl. " = Quintal . . - . . . . . Q.
1 Kl. " = TON . . . . MT.

In the above table it will be understood that ten of any denomination make one of the next; thus, ten millimeters equal to one centimeter; ten milliliters equal to one centiliter; ten milligrams equal to one centigram, etc. The table of length is converted into a table of square measure by considering that ten of any denomination, squared, makes the square of the next denomination; thus, ten square millimeter equal to one square centimeter, etc. The same table is converted into cubic measure by considering that one hundred of any denomination, cubed, make the cube of the next denomination; thus, one hundred cubic millimeter are equal to one cubic centimeter, etc.

In the table of length the meter is the unit, and it is the term used in the measurement of dry goods, taking the place of the yard. Its length is about three feet three inches and three eighths. The millimeter is used in the measurement of small objects, such as the parts of insects. The kilometer is the term used for long distances, and becomes the substitute for the mile.

In the table of capacity the liter is the unit, and takes the place of the quart for ordinary use, from which it differs but slightly. The term centiliter is used in measuring small quantities. For the measurement of grain, etc., the hectoliter takes the place of the bushel.

In the table of weight the gram is the unit, and serves as a small weight. For very delicate weighing, such as is required in scientific experiments, the centigram is the term used. For ordinary use in a grocery store the kilogram takes the place of the pound. Its weight is about equal to 2.2 pounds. For heavy weighing, the metric ton becomes a substitute for our present ton.

The following table represents, in a condensed form, the progress that has been made in the adoption of the metric system by the various countries of the world.

Those countries where it may be said, with substantial accuracy, that the metric system is already in *exclusive use*, are printed in large capitals, and those where its use is *permissive*, in small capitals.

UNIFORM MONEY, WEIGHTS, AND MEASURES. 441

Date of Legislation.	Date of Adoption.	LIST OF COUNTRIES.	REMARKS.
1863	....	ARGENTINE CONFEDERATION.	Obligatory law incompletely enforced. Metric system used in customs.
1872	1876	AUSTRIA.......	German names allowed.
1836	....	BELGIUM.......	Used previously with different nomenclature.
1862	1873	BRAZIL.........	In some markets, commodities for exportation are quoted in the old measures.
1848	....	CHILI............	The metric system is legal.
1857	....	COSTA RICA......	Government was authorized to establish the metric system, but old measures are still used.
....	....	Denmark.........	Pound of 500 grams, decimally divided, adopted in 1852.
1856	....	ECUADOR	Metric system prescribed, but others still used.
1837	1840	FRANCE........	A modified metric system was previously used.
1868	1872	GERMANY......	In some special cases, till 1875 was allowed to complete the change. German names are permitted.
1864	....	GREAT BRITAIN..	In India special weights and measures may be authorized by the governor-general. The kilogram is called SER. The meter has been adopted in the construction of some of India state railways.
1836	....	GREECE..........	The metric system is used with modified nomenclature.
1817	1821	HOLLAND......	Dutch names are used.
....	1863	ITALY..........	Previously adopted in some parts of the present kingdom of Italy.
1857	1862	MEXICO.........	Law obligatory, but old measures still in use.
....	....	Norway..........	Likely to follow Sweden. The pound is taken to be equal to 500 grams.
....	....	PERU............	Government has adopted metric system. Citizens use a variety of measures.
1852	1864	PORTUGAL....	Other measures are probably used to some extent.
1864	1866	ROUMANIA....	....
....	....	Russia...........	An Imperial Commission has reported in favor of the introduction of the metric system. Its use in the custom-house was ordered in 1870.
1849	1859	SPAIN..........	....
1876	1889	SWEDEN.........	Compulsory law will take effect in 1889.
1851	1857	SWITZERLAND	The Swiss system is not completely metric, but has a foot equal to 30 centimetres; and, decimally divided, a pound equal to 500 grams, etc.
1870	....	TURKEY	It has been stated that the archive has been made equal to 75 centimeters; also, that the metric system was made obligatory in 1870.

Date of Legislation.	Date of Adoption.	List of Countries.	Remarks.
1866	....	U. S. of America,	The metric system is used in the mint, and on the coast survey.
1853	....	U.S. of Colombia,	Official system metric; various measures in private use.
1865	1867	Uruguay	Law obligatory, but old measures still in use.
1857	....	Venezuela......	Both systems used.

To sum this all up in twenty words, Russia, England, and the United States use the British foot; the rest of Christendom is committed to the metric system.

In the year 1871 a bill was introduced in the English Parliament to render the use of the metric system compulsory, and was lost by only five votes, the vote standing eighty-two against the bill and seventy-seven for it. From the closeness of this vote, it is evident that the time for the exclusive use of the system throughout England cannot be much longer postponed. Thus, in Europe, the countries, in rapid succession, have adopted these international standards. Can any one suppose that the progress already made is going to be arrested at the point it has now reached? No. The world must and will have a uniform system of weights and measures; and the only question that arises is, What system shall it be? And here it may be well to state that except the metric system, and that which we use, no other one existing can be advocated as having the least claim for the world's adoption. The choice must, therefore, be between our own and the metric. It would be exceedingly flattering to our Yankee pride if we could convert the whole world to our way of doing business.

Let us examine some of the advantages our system possesses, and perhaps we may convince the world that it is the best.

Our unit of measurement is the foot; three of these make a yard; five and a half yards constitute a rod; forty rods a furlong, and eight furlongs a mile. For surface measure, our square yard is nine square feet; our square rod is thirty and one quarter square yards, or two hundred and seventy-two and one quarter square feet; and one acre is one hundred and sixty square rods, or four thousand eight hundred and forty square yards, or forty-three thousand five hundred and sixty square feet. It is difficult to comprehend anything more ingenious than this.

For capacity our unit is the gallon, or our units, rather, for we have the advantage of having several of them. These are all related to the unit of length, and the relation is so simple that it can be remembered by at least one person in every ten thousand. The dry gallon contains two hundred and eighty-six and eight tenths cubic inches, more or less; the wine gallon contains two hundred and thirty-one cubic inches, and the beer gallon two hundred and eighty-two. Thirty-two of these gallons make a barrel of cider; thirty-one and a half a barrel of ale; thirty-six a barrel of milk; thirty a barrel of fish, etc. One has almost unlimited freedom of choice to take what he prefers. Our unit of weight is related to our measure of length; at least this is the presumption. It may be expressed approximately by a decimal two miles and a half in length. If the avoirdupois pound is too heavy, we can take the Troy pound, which is some lighter. These pounds have the advantage also of being divided differently, the one into sixteen ounces, and the other into twelve. These ounces differ, also, in weight; and, by a beautiful law of contrarieties, as the avoirdupois pound is heavier than the pound Troy, the avoirdupois ounce is lighter. These ounces are divided into drams, which differ also,—the one is about three times the weight of the other.

Our tables contain ratios or multipliers to suit the most particular. The beauty of our system in this respect must command the admiration of all.

We have, among these ratios, three 2's; nine 3's; two 4's; four 5's; one 7; five 8's; one 9; four 10's; two 12's; three 16's; three 20's; one 24; two 25's; one 27; six 30's; three 40's; one 50; three 60's; one 80; two 100's; one 128; one 144; one 360; one 640; one 1728; one $5\frac{1}{2}$; one $16\frac{1}{2}$; one $30\frac{1}{4}$; one $31\frac{1}{2}$; one $24\frac{7}{4}$; one $7\frac{9}{10}$; one 69_{δ}; and one $272\frac{1}{4}$.

If the superiority of our system over the metric from this exposition is not apparent, it probably

UNIFORM MONEY, WEIGHTS, AND MEASURES. 445

may be shown more clearly by a practical example, making use of the two systems.

I recently had occasion to purchase some pita wood to line insect drawers. The price for the wood was $1.80 per square yard, or $2.20 per square meter. There were twenty drawers in all; ten of them were $12\frac{7}{8}$ inches by $15\frac{3}{4}$ inches, and the remaining ten were $12\frac{7}{8}$ inches, by $14\frac{3}{4}$ inches. Or measured metrically, the first series were thirty-two centimeters by forty centimeters, and the second series were thirty-two centimeters by thirty-seven and one half centimeters.

In estimating the cost of the wood needed, from the measurements in inches, the operation is as follows: —

$12\frac{7}{8} \times 15\frac{3}{4} = \frac{103}{8} \times \frac{63}{4} = \frac{6489}{32}$

$12\frac{7}{8} \times 14\frac{3}{4} = \frac{103}{8} \times \frac{59}{4} = \frac{6077}{32}$

$\frac{6489}{32} \times 10 = \frac{64890}{32}$

$\frac{6077}{32} \times 10 = \frac{60770}{32}$

$\frac{64890}{32} + \frac{60770}{32} = \frac{125660}{32}$

$\frac{125660}{32} \div 1296$, the number of square inches in a square yard, is equal to $\frac{125660}{41472}$

$\frac{125660}{41472} \times \$1.80$, the price per square yard, is equal to $\frac{226188.00}{41472}$. This reduced equals $\$5.45\frac{18468}{41472}$, which is the answer sought.

The following operations are also required in the above calculation: —

103	103	144	1296	125660
63	59	9	32	1.80
309	927	1296	2592	100528.00
618	515		3888	125660
6489	6077		41472	226188.00

```
41472)2261880.00(5.45┼┼┼┼┼
      207360
      ──────
      188280
      165888
      ──────
       223920
       207360
       ──────
        16560
```

In estimating the cost from the metric measurements, the operation is as follows:—

```
     32                    37.5
     40                     32
     ──                    ────
1280 × 10 = 12800 sq. cm.   750
                           1125
                           ────
                       1200.0 × 10 = 12000 sq. cm.
12800 sq. cm. + 12000 sq. cm. = 24800 sq. cm., or 2.48 sq. m.
                    2.48 sq. m.
                    2.20
                    ────
                    4960
                    496
                    ────
                   $5.456    The answer sought.
```

In the first calculation there are eighteen operations and three hundred and three figures; in the second there are six operations and seventy-four figures.

If the value of mathematics depends upon the mental discipline it gives, we certainly should hold fast to our present system, for the discipline afforded by working a problem by it is at least tenfold greater than it would be if the operation were metric.

If the confusion existing in Continental Europe at the beginning of the present century was sufficient to induce the nations to accept the metric system, are not the absurdities we have pointed out, as existing in our country at the present day, sufficient to make it an object for us to do the same? By the use of the metric system we not only get rid of denominate numbers, but fractions will scarcely ever enter into our mathematical operations.

The whole world is a unit; the interests of all nations, by commerce and telegraphic communications, are so interlocked that neither can retain a system of commercial intercourse out of harmony with the rest We are out of harmony at present with all Continental Europe. This unnatural condition cannot continue, and as we cannot expect other nations to accept our system in preference to the metric, it must be considered as a foregone conclusion that ours must be supplanted by the metric. This change does not involve a question of possibilities or of probabilities, but is only one of time. Is anything gained by postponing the date of making this change? Nothing whatever. Every year's delay makes the change more difficult, but the change must be made whatever is the cost or trouble.

Thus far it can be said that we have not been indifferent spectators of the world's progress in this matter. We have made a beginning, at least.

In this country the system was legalized in 1866, and since then much has been done to prepare the way for its exclusive adoption. It is used by the United States Coast Survey, the greatest of our public works. The postage law authorizes its use by making fifteen grams equivalent to a half-ounce for all postal purposes. A knowledge of this fact will enable any one to save six per cent of his postage expenses, for fifteen grams exceed half an ounce by that percentage. The postal department is required to furnish metric postal balances to all post-offices that make requisitions for them, and many of the larger ones have already been supplied.

Besides this work done by the government to further the use of the system, many manufacturers and merchants are beginning to recognize the great advantages that are to be gained by the change. The American Watch Company, of Waltham, Mass., that employs one thousand hands, and turns out three hundred and fifty watches daily, has adopted the metric system in all its operations. All its computations, drawings, and tools are purely metric, and the superintendent says that nothing could induce them to return to the old system. Amherst College has taken an advanced position on the metric system, which will soon, in all probability, be followed by other leading educational institutions. They not only require a knowledge of the system for admission, but the professors of the several departments of mathematics, physics, astronomy, chemistry, geology, paleontology, botany, zoölogy, anatomy, and physiology use the metric denominations in their lectures and instructions.

The scientific publications issued by the Smithsonian Institute at Washington contain metric expressions only for all measurements. The American Library Association, recently organized, has adopted the centimeter as the unit for the measure of all books. The system is gaining ground very rapidly among physicians. Two societies composed of the most active advocates of the system have been formed for the purpose of hastening its exclusive use. The one is called the "Metrological Society," and has its headquarters in New York, and the other is known as the "American Metric Bureau," and is located in Boston.

Besides these home influences there are others of an international character tending to make the early adoption of the metric system by our country a necessity. Scientific men and associations, and scientific journals, are using the metric system almost exclusively in their experiments, calculations, and writings. The International Statistical Congress, composed of representatives from all nations, publish all their reports, containing information of vast importance to the world, in metric nomenclature. The International Social Science Association exerts a powerful influence in every country of the civilized globe. Its proceedings are given in metric terms.

The indications at present are that the last country to adopt the system will be either England or the United States, and neither will be long in following the other.

We led the world in decimal currency; why should we be so slow in reducing all our other tables to equal simplicity? When this country proclaimed itself independent of Great Britian, it is a matter of great regret that we did not declare ourselves forever free from all the absurdities found in their tables of weights and measures. Instead of doing this, we accepted them all, and added some others of our own. None of our standards agree precisely with those of England, except that for the measure of length, and until the year 1855 there was a variation in that also. The time is now at hand, in my judgment, for us to make our second declaration of independence. Congress should be petitioned to fix a time in the near future when this great and glorious change shall be accomplished, and we should all adapt ourselves to the new order of things as soon as possible. Teachers can do much to bring about this desirable result. The subject should be taught in every school. If the children now receiving their education become familiar with the metric units, they will find little trouble in their use in active life, and I have not the slightest doubt that the use of the system will be made compulsory before these children become men and women.

The desirableness of this change is beyond all conception. It brings all ordinary calculations within the arithmetic of every person who can add, subtract, multiply, and divide simple numbers. Two years, at least, can be saved of the time children now devote to arithmetic, and with this saving the pupils, when they leave school, will be far better prepared to perform the arithmetical operations business calls for, than now. Devote this time gained to the study of other important subjects, and the advantages derived will be multiplied manifold.

The teaching force of this country constitutes a tremendous power. Let it be found united in its efforts to secure, on the part of Congress, the adoption of the metric system, and the years will not be many before we are in possession of the greatest commercial blessing that can be secured.

THE END.

www.ingramcontent.com/pod-product-compliance
Lightning Source LLC
Chambersburg PA
CBHW022101300426
44117CB00007B/545